Dor Slinkard is an unstoppable storyteller. Be it through writing or voice, her stories will enthral. Inspired by life, especially as a jillaroo in outback Australia and later as a race horse trainer, her imagination thrives. In her lasting marriage to Wade, a jackaroo now horse trainer, they have produced two children and they, in turn, six grandchildren.

# Acknowledgements

Initially, I must give credence to the meaning of the words 'bugger' and 'kid.' Both are Australian slang words but take an official role in the dialect of someone who is a nuisance, re-the word bugger. And a kid is a child or a teenager.

So, I acknowledge both words to accurately describe me, as the child in us never dies.

My life was worth writing about because of the amazingly talented and loving people and the superb and spiritual horses who have filled my life thus far.

Amusingly, this is the only story of mine that my husband has not proofread. He said, "I know it all anyway."

I am a child of God, as we all are, and there is only one truth, LOVE. This is not a belief but a knowing. I have followed my passions and instincts, and I have come to know the true me.

By the same author

Henri-etta
Wrong Side of the Fence

***For the Love of* Trilogy**
Book 1 – For the Love of Patrick
Book 2 – For the Love of Freedom
Book 3 – For the Love of Justice

Dor Slinkard

# BUGGER OF A KID

# Introduction

I began writing my memoirs at age fifty-seven. Pre-dementia? I hope not. I've always loved telling stories, but an unexpected turn of events finally gave me time to start telling my own.

As horse trainers, my husband Wade and I, along with our horses, found ourselves in lockdown due to an outbreak of Equine Influenza. This highly contagious respiratory virus infiltrated Australia on August 24th, 2007.

The virus began at Eastern Creek Animal Quarantine Depot in New South Wales, where Veterinarians found four imported stallions to be the carriers. And it was 'human error' that had caused the outbreak. Within two weeks, all horses with symptoms and tested positive were identified. Those horses lived on properties in Centennial Park, Parkes, Moonbi, Wyong, Cattai, and Wilberforce, where we lived.

While we had no equine fatalities, it was upsetting and extremely time-consuming tending to our beloved horses. A thick mucus formed around their eyes and constantly ran from either nostril; they coughed and lacked energy. It was a frightful chore, batting eyes and noses with warm salted water twice daily and administering penicillin injections and cough medicine.

As I do, I try to make the best of a bad situation. My golf game improved markedly since I had time to practice, and twelve points disappeared off my handicap! I also wrote as much as I could, read books, and had the time to get the garden looking picture-perfect. Generally, Wade and I learned to take things a little easier; no visitors allowed! It was unheard of before the lockdown, and it triggered withdrawal symptoms because we loved to entertain family and friends.

Earning our living from training racehorses became impossible, but the government finally came to our rescue with a monetary package. The paperwork was endless, as it always is, but eventually, it paid off, and we survived.

The equine fatalities throughout Australia were fewer than

expected, though the number of horses contracting the highly contagious virus was massive. Some parts of Australia could still hold race meetings, although the competing horses had to be tested virus-free. It was a difficult and trying time for all concerned, but we, and the industry, survived. Horse people are tough and resolute.

So this enforced 'time off,' and having five beautiful grandchildren - Grace, Emma, Nicholas, Arianna, Izzy, and one adopted grandson, Jed - gave me a reason to continue writing about my life, which has been quite exciting and never boring! I hope my precious grandchildren and the generations yet to come enjoy reading about all the humour, wisdom, foolishness, and incredible love that has filled my life thus far.

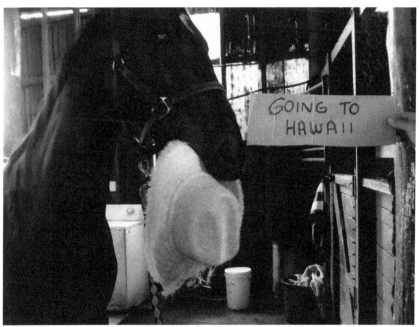

*One of my favourite horses, Freddy. He was a born actor.*
*And yes, that was his registered race name.*

# Chapter 1
# First Memories

March 6th, 1951, at Margaret Coles Maternity Hospital, Melbourne, Victoria, Betty Jean Forster, a four-foot and eleven-inch, red-headed dynamo, gave birth to me, Doreen Anne Forster. My father, Thomas Alfred Forster, was a handsome man of small stature and an absolute angel. I was also lucky enough to have a kind and thoughtful brother, Wayne, four years my senior, who watched over me in my childhood, so I always felt safe. Sounds perfect? Not always.

I still don't think I was a bad kid, and I can recall no major confrontations from my very early years. But, as I grew, I became the increasingly 'gung-ho' leader of my pack. I inherited my loving but volatile mother's fierce determination, guaranteeing that we would meet at loggerheads in the future - many times. I had an unbridled imagination and would try to shape what I'd conjured in my mind into reality. Like the lead girl in the 'Saint Trinians' movie, I would declare, 'I have a scathingly brilliant idea! I didn't know what 'scathingly' meant, but it sounded terrific.

Wayne, my dear brother, would take the blame on most occasions when things went wrong. He was concerned about Mum's temper and how she'd hit me around the legs, giving me a punishing whack with every word. "I-told-you-not-to-get-my-best-biscuits-out-and-give-them-to-stray-dogs!" I'd pray she would shorten her sentences instead of sixteen hard wacks. "I- told-you- never- to-do that!" See, only seven! Unfortunately, my prayers were rarely answered.

Oh, the pain I felt as a child, not because of the smacks, but for Mum and her only sibling, Aunty Dawn. They had lost their mother when Mum was five and Aunty seven. Their father, Charlie Norman, a spiffy professional gambler, was not the type to care for two small girls, even if they were his daughters. Fortunately, through a friend of the family, Charlie Norman, unlike today when adoptions and fostering are strictly Government business, 'found' the sisters a set of foster parents - a Mr. and Mrs. Frith. The only question back then was, 'Do you want them?'

I cannot remember when I first began reflecting on what Mum and Aunty's life must have been like after losing their mother at such a young age and having been dumped by their father. Perhaps it hit home when I was about four and sitting on Mum's lap, and she would tell me how much she loved me on those happy, cuddly occasions. 'I love you more than Kingdom Come,' she'd say. I didn't know what that meant, but I accepted it. Dad was not quite as affectionate; I suppose he couldn't get a look in when Mum was around. But his love went without saying. Dad was eternally there to oblige us, kids, by giving us his time, a precious commodity. I realised then, and even more now, how lucky were we to have loving parents. I only had to imagine not having them there, and I would shudder at the thought.

Nanna and Poppa Frith, of German descent, were childless before fostering Mum and Aunty. I have nothing personal against the Germans as a whole. However, in my mind, they gained a reputation for being extremely strict. Mum told us about floggings with a leather strap for the slightest misdemeanour, so Mum learned quickly. If she cried and told Nanna she loved her, the thrashing would cease. Nanna would then sit little Betty on her ample knee.

'Do you promise to be a good girl and never do that again?' Nanna would ask. Little Betty would say 'Yes, I promise,' and receive a warm cuddle. Of course, Mum promised to be 'good,' whatever *'good'* meant. The definition was solely up to Nanna.

Aunty Dawn, on the other hand, would suffer unfair beatings. She never gave in. Her bruises and sometimes broken bloody skin would bear witness to her resolution. It would break Mum's heart, so she'd plead with Dawn, 'Cry, and tell her you love her.' Under no circumstances would Dawn ever tell Nanna she loved her; she hated her. Their relationship became a battle of control in the extreme.

I truly felt sorry for the young sisters, and now, I know why Mum sometimes lashed out at us, or me, mainly. It was due to her abuse as a child; it carries on. After hitting me, Mum would often cry, hold me tight and say, 'I'm sorry, darling.' Nothing wrong with punishment, providing it ends with love! I reckon I still turned out okay -though some may argue. However, it taught me, to lead with my heart, not my temper.

Well, most times. Yes, I am a pacifist until you come into my corner fighting, or I see you being cruel to an animal or a child. Then you've asked for it.

Both Mum and Aunty told the same stories about Nanna Frith. But I also have my own memories of Nanna and Poppa Frith. Poppa suffered from one leg being shorter than the other. His looks and Nanna's were typically German; pronounced cheekbones, greying fair hair, and imposing height. He wore a built-up shoe attached to iron rods welded upon a flat piece of metal. What a huge task, having to walk around all day, lugging that heavy load. But despite her harsh treatment of my mother and Aunty, Nanna never laid a hand on any grandkids, not even me - the youngest and most vexing. With his fair-minded approach, I am sure my father, Tom, would have stopped Nanna in her tracks, no matter what.

Graham, Aunty's eldest son, came first in her favour, followed by his sister, Betty, then my brother, Wayne. Betty and Graham's younger brother, Brian, was fourth in line. And then, long last, was me. I never felt close to Nanna. Maybe knowing I was not her favourite. Hardly surprising, given my priorities.

The first time I'd been in Nanna's care, she promised to take me to the park and told me, 'If you're a good girl, I'll buy you an ice cream.' Everything was going to plan. We were about to cross the road to get my reward from the 'Milk Bar' (as we used to call the corner convenience shops in those days) when Nanna stepped down from the footpath and fell heavily to the ground. She struggled to get up but couldn't. I began to cry until a man came along and helped Nanna to her feet. I must say it took some doing! I will never forget his words of comfort, 'It's alright now, love. Nanna will be fine.'

'I want my ice cream!' I cried even louder. The ice cream never came because when the man let go of Nanna, she collapsed again, moaning in agony until the ambulance arrived. What a little shit I must have been! No wonder I was last on her list. Poor, old Nanna! In her defense, she did provide a home for Mum and Aunty, a warm bed, and plenty of food. Although cuddles were sparse and the sisters had to work hard for them.

Nanna had broken her hip when she fell, and I remember visiting her in the hospital. She had a reputation for being clairvoyant. That day, I listened to her incredible story imagining how it would feel to see your dead brother hovering above in a misty cloud, begging you to come with him to Heaven. Not long after, she acceded to his wishes.

Mum held Nanna's wake at our home. Laughter seemed definitely out of place, even to a four-year-old. When somebody dies, aren't you supposed to be sad? I'd see Mum or Aunty shed a tear and think, 'that's better.' But how did I feel? Numb. Sorry, Nanna.

The best part about Nanna 'floating up to heaven' (what a lovely thought) or dying, to put it more prosaically, was packing her things. I searched for Nanna's hidden lolly stash while Mum and Aunty were wrapping up her belongings. Including a vast china and crystal collection. After finding and eating more sweets than my stomach could hold, I began vomiting profusely. Half a lolly shop went down the toilet, but not before the other half had decorated Nanna's Persian rug. Ah, yes - Nanna's revenge!

I still own one of Nanna's crystal wine glasses. I can't remember how I came to have it, but occasionally I use it and think of her, accepting that the glass may have come into my possession as a 'message' from Nanna. After some ninety years, the glass has remained in one piece – not even a chip. I'm still working on that projection.

*Mary Elma, Mum and Aunty Dawn's Mum.*
*Love the hat!*

*Charlie Norman, Mum and Aunty Dawn's father. Charlie wanted to be a jockey, but his father, who was the Clerk of the course at Mooney Valley Race Course, would not allow it.*

Poppa Frith, Nanna's husband, remained in their home at Parham, a suburb of Melbourne, until Aunty and Uncle built him a bungalow in their back yard at Moorabbin. He then sold his house and moved in. Poppa kept to himself, though he'd join us for a family dinner whenever we visited Aunty and Uncle. I loved to watch him eat, and I'd listen to his jaw clicking as he chewed. It sounded musical, and I was tempted to play the spoons along with his 'click- click'. I'm sure it would have created a catchy tune.

Grandad Tom, Dad's father, and his second wife, Annie, were rarely seen in our home. However, I'm sure if my maternal Grandmother, Kitty, were still alive, we would have kept close company. Kitty was a petite, pretty lady with angelic qualities, just like Dad. I never met her as she died when Dad was a teenager. Sadly, Kitty left behind her four beloved children - baby Valda, six months old; Gloria, ten years; Tom, thirteen; and Albert, sixteen.

Grandad's brother and wife had tried but could not produce children, so baby Valda was given to them. Later, this caused a few problems when Valda turned sixteen and found out, purely by accident, who her birth parents were. A rebellious teenager and hearing news like that? It was asking for trouble. But Valda, with maturity, turned out to be a wonderful mother of two boys, Peter and Andy. Aunty Valda is a Good Samaritan and an excellent nurse.

In my eyes, Annie, Grandad's second wife, was a delightful lady with a perpetual smile and forever ready to please. She made the best afternoon teas, served with grace on delicate china. We would dress in our Sunday Best and drive a long way to their home at Baxter to enjoy a couple of hours drinking tea and eating cakes. Before we left, Annie would fill Wayne and my tiny palms with coins. Our family looked forward to those visits - well, I did.

Mum told stories about Annie's 'colourful' past. Not to put too fine a point on it, but in Mum's opinion, 'Annie had been the town bike!' I'm sure we were never supposed to hear or understand that. However, I'm sure Grandad must have kept her satisfied, as her 'town bike' exploits ended when they married.

Annie entered the marriage with her son, Jack. Jack eventually received the Forster family inheritance from Annie, Grandad's sole beneficiary. It caused a family uproar until Dad and Aunty Gloria decided to let it go, knowing that most of the money would be given to lawyers if they fought the case. However, one thing I will never forgive Annie for was when Grandad died, and before Dad or Aunty could claim it, Annie delivered his Treasure Chest to the tip. It held Grandad's memoirs, personal memorabilia, and a parchment copy of our family tree. It also contained many photos of our Forster family back in England and Grandad's medals from the First World War he'd fought in France. Pictures of Kitty, his first wife, and my grandmother. The chest held everything that would be cherished and passed down the Forster line. To this day, Aunty Gloria still cries about it. I can't blame her.

Kitty was a Salvation Army lass, 'an angel to the core,' they'd say. During the Depression, Kitty would offer a bowl or two of hearty soup and fresh damper from her woodfired oven whenever swagmen called to their property. The meal was given in exchange for chopping wood, fixing the garden fence, or maybe weeding the veggie patch - and so on. Kitty told Dad, 'I ask the travelling men to help with jobs because it adds to their self-esteem. Plus, I pay them to do the work, and they're welcome to stay in the barn until they've finished. Never will a swagman or a needy person be turned away from our door.'

Grandad Tom loved practical jokes. You could say he was the opposite of Kitty.

One Christmas, when little Tom had asked for a pony, Grandad left a headstall along with a bag of manure at the end of Dad's bed. When Dad woke, he went scrambling outside looking for the pony. Grandad called out, 'Where are you going, son?'

'I'm looking for the pony that got away!' Little Tom cried. And Grandad laughed. Kitty's sense of fairness came to the fore when she found Grandads hidden stash. She hurried out and bought a pony for Little Tom. Served Grandad right, the old bugger!

Little Tom didn't like school, so most days, Grandad dragged him there by the ear and threw him into the classroom, only to watch Little Tom fly through the window on the opposite side of the room. It took Grandad and the teacher a while to wake up. Eventually, the teacher locked the window. Now, who was the smartest cookie in that lot?
I asked, 'What did you do when you escaped, Dad?'

'I'd go rabbiting and bring home plenty. So, I'd rarely get into trouble for skipping school,' Dad would say with a smile.

Dad was an all-around good sportsman. He could out-swim, out-run, and out-play anyone in either tennis or golf. Plus, he'd dive like an Olympian. Let me not forget boxing. However, Mum said she'd refuse to marry Tom if he became a professional boxer. This offer had been on the cards when Dad left the Army; he had scouts chasing him all over Victoria. The word had passed around - 'There's a young Private in the Army by the name of Tom Forster who could be a world champion.' Dad had one hundred official boxing matches in the Army, and his knockout blows had won most of them. No wonder managers sought him out.

I must add that Dad was an avid reader of books and newspapers. The lack of an early education did not suppress his eagerness to learn. He could discuss politics and world events intelligently with the best of them. His views were Liberal, but we assumed Mum swayed him to vote Labor. Most times.

"I'm a swinger." He would say. "I vote for who I think should be leading the country at the time."

When writing this, Auntie Gloria, Dad's sister, is still alive in

15

her nineties, and Aunty Valda is in her early eighties. I keep in touch with both; God bless them, which gives you a clue as to how long I have been back and forth writing my memoirs. Sadly, Aunty Valda died before having had a chance to read them.

*Primary School. I'm second row, fourth in from the left.*
*Our teacher, Mr Hallingbone, was one of the best.*

# Chapter 2
# Childhood

I'm going back to my gorgeous, fun-loving Mummy. She still is one of the funniest ladies I've ever met—what a waste to the entertainment industry. 'Born to be on the stage,' they'd say after she'd entertain everyone with her different characters and quick wit. She'd have her audience lying on the floor in stitches. Yes, her quips always came to the fore, especially if someone seemed to be taking themselves too seriously. She'd stop the maudlin or the egotistical with her satirical humour.

When only five, Mum asked Poppa to nail his tobacco tins to the bottom of her shoes. Little Betty would then tap dance on the concrete footpath in the park that adjoined the back garden of their home in Prahran, Victoria. People would inevitably stop to watch this imitation, Shirley Temple. Mum basked in the accolades until Nanna would spoil her fun by yelling, 'Come inside, Betty, and stop making a spectacle of yourself!' Consequently, Betty performed in the park whenever Nanna was not at home.

Little Betty became quite famous for her performances. We can only imagine where she would have gone with her talent if only she had had the right parents. Nanna never had it in her to be a stage mother – definitely not the type! So, Mum's talents were put on hold until much later when she married her adoring Tom and was able to do as she wished. Unconditional love is rarely found.

Mum never learned how to play the guitar, but she managed to fool everyone by simply strumming while they sang along so loudly it drowned out her slapdash playing. However, the mouth organ was her forte; boy, could she play that thing! Her ear for music and sweet voice assured Betty received high praise and admiration from her audiences. No matter which way Betty chose to entertain, she excelled. She could even stand on her head and spell 'Lux' with her legs. Just thinking about it makes me smile! (Always wearing trousers, of course)

Before Television, our family dressed in costumes and entertained each other. They were the good old days. It's a shame that life's simplicity has changed so dramatically. I sometimes wonder if it is for the betterment of humanity. It depends, I suppose, on which way you look at things through the lens of a digital camera or a Box Brownie. Handwriting versus Computer, or fix your problems your own way – often the physical way! However, I shouldn't knock computers; I'm writing on one, making my job more manageable.

Anyway, Mum progressed to entertaining professionally. She ventured out later in life with my eldest cousin Graham, an extremely handsome young man. They became a comedy team when the 'The Bobby Limb Show' was popular on TV. It featured Dawn Lake's over-the-fence, 'you tell 'em, love' skit. Graham dressed up as Dawn Lake's next-door neighbour, a mute, unattractive female - difficult for him because he was so handsome - while Mum portrayed the Dawn Lake character, attired in a daggy cotton frock and Orlon cardigan and hair rollers tucked neatly under a scarf, which was typical for Mum. The rollers, I mean.

*Mum dressed as Dawn Lake from the Bobby Limb TV show,*
*and my cousin Graham dressed as her mute over-the-fence friend.*

Off they'd go to Men's Clubs and Golf Nights. The money was quite good, but the constant jibes directed at my cousin for possibly looking too good as a sheila led to Graham's early retirement. Maybe he received unwanted advances? He would never tell.

Mum and Aunty's luck changed for the better when they met their lifemates. I'm sure matching the two sisters with their husbands was planned from above. Maybe their mum? Aunty married Ernest Turner, a handsome, intelligent, quiet man with a wicked sense of humour. I think we owned decent looks as a family, including my first cousins. I know you can't help how you turn out in the looks department, but I believe we control how we turn out as a person.

I had to write about appearance because Mum would forever comment if she saw someone not looking their best. 'Look at her. She must've taken ugly pills!' or 'You'd think she could comb her hair. It looks like a rat's nest!' I'd cringe when she'd say such things because it's not in me to put people down. Instead, I do the opposite. I love seeing beauty in everything, and yes, I'm a bloody angel! I help others look their best or help with gardening or beautifying their homes. Mum's denunciations were her only fault in my eyes, but they usually made others laugh.

All of us may as well lived in the same house. We spent every free moment with Aunty, Uncle, and our three cousins. Although our home was in Ashburton and theirs in Moorabbin, the distance between them seemed nothing while driving in our Erskine or Uncle Ernie's Wolseley.

*Left to right. Auntie Dawn, Uncle Ernie, Dad Tom and Mum Betty.*

I think it's an appropriate time to share my poem about Mum after she departed for Heaven.

### MY MUM BETTY
*Call her what you will,*
*she'd answer to you still.*
*Betty Boil.*
*Flippy the Flash.*
*The Rich Aunt.*
*She seemed to have loads of cash.*
*Her generosity had no match.*
*Born a pocket dynamo.*
*Straight red hair and freckles to spare.*
*'She should be on stage,' they'd say*
*and look in dismay*
*as she'd stand on her head*
*and spell 'Lux' with her legs.*
*She overcame the loss of her Mum.*
*At the tender age of five.*
*But God knows, she was glad to be alive*
*Accepting what Fate had to give her.*
*Blessed with an abundance of love and good humour*
*those gifts remained throughout her future.*
*A flashy temper in times of despair,*
*but no one seemed to care*
*for the love would flow through.*
*And she felt sorry for YOU,*
*For whatever it was, YOU did.*
*I learned to run as a kid*
*because Mum's temper wouldn't last long.*
*And by then, I was long gone.*
*Picasso met his match*
*when little Betty was hatched.*
*She'd paint anything.*
*Rocks in the garden.*
*Her next of kin.*
*Even the garbage bin.*
*Immaculately groomed,*

20

*her hair rollers became heirlooms.*
*She loved her family above all.*
*Including her poodle.*
*We'd hear her call,*
*'Mimi, come here!'*
*'Mimi, come here, darling!'*
*'Mimi! Come!'*
*'Mimi! Come here, ya bitch!'*
*We later found Mimi was deaf.*
*But only to Mum's pitch!*
*A loving Mum and a wonderful wife,*
*a friend to anyone in strife.*
*A true-blue Aussie who loved footy and beer.*
*Though she only drank in good cheer.*
*God bless you, Mum, to your equal – there is none!*
*I don't know a person you haven't made laugh.*
*And whatever you did, it was never by half.*
*You gave your all so we can stand tall*
*and say, 'That's our Mum.'*
*So watch out, Heaven, here she comes!*

\*

I would have changed homes anytime with Aunty and Uncle, as their home in Moorabbin was within walking distance to the beach. Our house in Ashburton was neither here nor there as far as attractions were concerned. I suppose it was a short train trip to the city, but cities have never appealed to me. Give me the ocean or the bush, and I'm happy. Our winter weekends were mostly spent with our cousins, 'Goin' rabbiting' as Uncle used to say. He had four ferrets, Percy, Peter, Paul, and Devil; the latter was named for the apparent reason. The men would take the ferrets to hunt rabbits while we '*women-folk*' gathered mushrooms and picked blackberries. We had no trouble receiving permission to enter properties. We were doing the farmers a favour by ridding them of vermin rabbits, and Aunty would always give the farmers' a generous supply of blackberry jam. That helped.

At day's end and upon returning to Aunty's home, we'd divvy up the rabbits while Aunty Dawn cooked the mushrooms and served them on thick buttered toast. It would happen while the blackberries simmered in copious amounts of sugar. If we were lucky, Aunty would have vanilla ice cream. Before the jam began to form and the blackberries were still in a delicious, syrupy stage, Aunty drizzled the mixture over the ice cream. Yummo!!

We'd go fishing during summer, always on a boat that Uncle Ernie built. He made four boats and named them after Aunty Dawn, beginning with Dawn One. These were not your ordinary dinghies; they had cabins and mod-cons. The cabins were roomy enough to hold two single beds, which could be used as storage boxes. The reason for so many boats? Uncle was always offered a price too good to refuse. But he'd make the buyers wait until he'd nearly finished the next, as his fishing wouldn't suffer for the lack of a boat.

Each bed was covered with a soft mattress and plenty wide enough for the average man to sleep on; thcy sat on either side of the cabin. Surrounding the inside of the outside deck, Uncle built seats utilized for storage. One had a waterproof lining that held ice, keeping Uncle's catch fresh. On the middle deck sat an enormous engine, surrounded by a wooden frame with a cover used as another place to sit. The side panels were unhooked when Uncle needed to check the engine. The boats had deep hulls, and I remember Ernie standing at the steering wheel as we walked around and under him to enter the cabin. Uncle was a painter for the Victorian Railways; therefore, he painted the boats to perfection. Ernie strategically placed a kitchen sink at the back of the boat to wash the fish. He also made a chopping board fitted with a clamp to hold the fish while he scaled them.

If we weren't rabbiting or boating, we spent our weekends at each other's homes. Aunty was predictable. She'd bring her heavenly passionfruit sponges filled with fresh cream or melt-in-the-mouth lemon meringue pie, accompanied by homemade sausage rolls. Mum would cook a chook and a leg of lamb, or sometimes meatloaf, all of which we served with various salads and fresh bread.

At day's end, when we were leaving Aunty's, Dad would be backing out of the driveway, and they'd all be standing waving us goodbye. It became a ritual to hear Aunty call, 'Watch the shrubs, Tom!' And he'd say, 'Bugger the shrubs, Dawn!'

"Don't say that, Tom!" Mum would scold, and he'd laugh in that funny way, like a hiccup. It happened every time!

# Chapter 3
## Neighbours

How lucky we were, never to go hungry. My heart ached when I heard about kids at school who weren't as fortunate, so I made sure no kid went hungry or cold when I was around. There's my 'angel quality' again! Only joking.

I'd ask Mum for an extra sandwich in my lunch box. She'd scratch her head and say, 'You can't be that hungry, and you can't have worms. I just wormed you last week, but you're eating more and getting thinner.' The truth was, I'd given most of my food away. (Should do that now, an excellent way to lose weight.) The odd piece of clothing, especially warm jumpers, mysteriously went missing. One day, my (literally)poor little friend, Laurel, was accused by Mum of being a thief because she'd seen Laurel wearing one of my jumpers. I then had to tell Mum the truth, and she cried. We were not rich in a monetary sense but rich in more essential values. Even the starving neighbourhood dogs got my blessings with Mum's homemade biscuits or a half-finished leg of lamb. And didn't I get a few whacks for that!

Living in a Court, I'm sure, encouraged friendliness toward our neighbours. Maybe our houses sitting in a circle connected us to that old saying, 'form a circle, a circle of friendship, perhaps? Anyway, this happened; we were all friends who helped each other. Maybe I shouldn't say 'all.' Some neighbours came and went and were not the type you'd mix with; I remember Mum saying that after she discovered the woman who'd recently moved next door left her children unattended while she went to work. This upset Mum terribly, so she called the Department of Child Welfare after she'd marched into their home and rescued the four children, the youngest being only two. They were wallowing in filth and seemed to be starving. I remember Mum bathing them in a bath smelling like Dettol, dressing them in clean clothes, then feeding the four little darlings until they could eat no more.

I could only imagine how those children felt when deserted by their mother, unloved, unfed, and left alone in filth. It haunted me to the point where I needed to write them into a fairy tale so they would find a happy ending. Yes, in my story, a loving family came along and cared for them, and they all lived happily ever after. Sadly, we couldn't look after the children, as there was no room in our small house. It was a miserable day when those four little urchins left to go to an orphanage. Though I prayed for them every day, I don't know what became of them. I think it confirmed in me, once again, just how lucky my brother and I were.

Mum seemed pleased with the couple who later moved in next door. They worked tirelessly on the garden and eventually returned it to its former glory. They painted the house white and the window frames and front door dark grey. It looked brilliant. Although they were a childless couple, they were always kind to us kids. Sometimes when we'd fetch our ball that had landed in their backyard, they'd smile and say, 'That's okay, love,' after we apologized for disturbing them, of course. Their friendliness towards us kids led me to suspect that they couldn't have children, rather than not wanting them. The thought often occurred of how wonderful it would be if they could have cared for those poor little children who had become orphans.

The neighbourhood homes were built of solid brick; some appeared rendered, like ours. The Government had them specially built for Returned Soldiers, including my dad and most men who lived in the community. Their children were around the same age as us. You can imagine us Baby Boomers playing together and making fun, building billy carts, cubby houses, bonfires, resurrecting rusty bikes and toys from the tip, and selling them for pocket money. Let me not forget us collecting used soft drink bottles. You'd get tuppence for any glass bottle. This money came in handy for the odd block of Cadbury Dairy Milk Chocolate to which I was addicted.

My best friend in the court was Patricia Album, or 'Lumpy,' as we called her then though I don't know why. Trish, we call her now. She had an elder sister, Sandra, a brother Robert, and twin brothers who came much later. Mum said the twins were 'change of life' babies, aka a mistake, because back in the late fifties, having a baby around the age of forty was considered just that. Now it's the standard practice, as most women want a career before starting a family. I won't comment on either decision, as everything is relevant, depending on time and situation. But

I'm pleased I had my kids at a young age. I still have lots of energy for the grandkids!

*My dear friend Trish with her son Luke. Daniel laughing at the dog.*
*One of our many trips home from Sydney.*

Trish's dad, Fred, was a great bloke. He drove a motorbike with a sidecar, and when Mum was in labour with me, he took her to the hospital! Any wonder I loved riding motorbikes as a teenager? Not now – oh no, no, no! Too many scars to remind me of the danger. Robert, Fred's eldest son -Trish's elder brother, stuttered quite severely. Mum did an excellent job of almost curing Robert by telling him to take a deep breath before speaking. 'Just think clearly about what you want to say, Robert, and then speak slowly,' Mum would tell him, and it worked well, most of the time. However, her theory went out the window when Robert became overly excited. It was tough for us kids not to laugh - but we tried hard not to.

Wayne and Robert shared a motor car in their teenage years, and they'd drive around most Saturday nights, checking out the dance scene. A drive to the beach on Sundays would see them admiring bikini-clad beauties. One weekend, while Robert was in control of his stutter, which was ninety percent of the time, they were involved in a minor car accident. Although the accident was not bad enough to call the police, it soon became so due to the reaction of the young and furious drivers. The young Policeman approached Robert and asked, 'T-t-tell me, w-w-where d-d-do you l-l-live?' when the Police arrived, Robert was still shaken and in a stuttering dispute about whose fault it was.

Robert replied, 'I l-l-live n-n-not t-t-too f-f-far f-f-from hh-here.'

The policeman immediately worked out that the accident was Robert's fault. When Robert later reported the story to us, he said, 'It t-t-took m-m-me all my bloody t-t-time not to kn-kn-knock the b-b-bastard out w-w-when he c-c-copied my stutter!' We heard later that the young policeman *also* had a stutter. Now that was funny.

With help from Fred, Robert and Wayne built the most amazing treehouse in Fred's backyard. ( It was many years before the boys owned cars.) The giant red gum tree sat along the fence adjoining the next-door neighbour's property. Mrs. Elderly, I'll call her. When finished, a sign read, 'NO GIRLS ALLOWED.'

Trish and I tried bribery, begged, and did everything we could to be allowed to enter the boys' mysterious and unique cubby house. To no avail. We fumed when we heard the boys were allowed to sleep in the cubby during school holidays. They were four years older than us, but still, it seemed unfair. My envy turned to rage, but I honestly don't think we deliberately set fire to it. On the unforgettable day of the treehouse fire, the boys were at a footy match. It was getting late when Trish and I finally broke the latch off the door. The skull and crossbones painted on the front made our break-and-enter even spookier. Together, we examined every treasure the boys had accumulated. It was getting dark, so we lit the kerosene lantern, and just as we did, we heard a car drive up, and doors slammed shut. 'Quick!' I said, 'Let's go!' We jumped over the back fence into Mrs. Elderly's.

Nobody noticed Trish and me walking calmly from her backyard. And no one seemed to notice the cubby was on fire until it was too late.

Garden hoses became a poor excuse for putting out the flames engulfing the cubby, the fence, and the gum tree. Further excitement reached our neighbourhood when a red fire engine roared up with bells and whistles! By the time the firefighters took control of the blaze, half the wooden fence (no Colourbond in those days), the entire cubby house, and most of the gum tree had turned into ashes.

Of course, the boys received the blame; hence, NO replication. A small part of me felt sorry for them, but mostly I thought, 'Serve them bloody right for excluding us girls!' A faithful Women's Libber right from the start!

Not long after that episode, Mrs. Elderly died. I hoped it wasn't from shock at the fire which almost engulfed her home. At least I prayed it wasn't!

Fred's mother, who often stayed with Fred and his family, later purchased Mrs. Elderly's house. It was a popular move, as she seemed to have nothing else to do but bake scones, cakes, and biscuits all day. And most days, we kids shared afternoon tea with her. Such a sweet lady – no pun intended! I remember her calling, 'Come inside, children! I've baked scones!'

The scones came hot from the oven, and we'd sit on pink Laminex chairs around a matching table, breathing in the tantalizing aroma. We'd watch intently as Grandma Album loaded butter on steaming hot scones, observing the butter melting as she spooned her blackberry jam on top. It was a juggling act to get the scones into our mouths without the jam and the butter dripping down our chins. We devoured them and washed our faces later. Did I mention the blackberry bushes which surrounded Mrs. Elderly's fence? They sprung to life again after the fire. So the jam-making continued. If the blackberries were there today, the council would have ordered their extermination, declaring the plant a noxious weed. Pure sacrilege!

On the left-hand side of the Album family, the Delany family lived. They were not as close to us as the Albums or the Carols who lived on the right side of Fred's mum. Karen was the oldest Delany daughter, then my friend Judith, and the youngest, Paul, who was a right pain in the arse, a bully, and a cheat. While growing up, I was not proud of how I treated Judith - or 'Judas' I called her. She could annoy me like no other person. I make no excuses other than it's the way I am. And I still find it hard to suffer fools gladly. Sorry, Judith - maybe I'm the fool?

It's hard to remember what it was about some people who annoyed me. However, I remember wanting to go to school so badly that I pretended I was there. I'd ask Mum to play the teacher. 'You are a very bright student, and you will do extremely well at school,' Mum would say. Mum's compliment excited me even more. Yes, I was keen from age four, and after I'd blown out my four birthday candles, I made a wish - 'I want to go to school tomorrow.' Sadly, my wish did not come true.

Judith Delaney was a year older than me and the day arrived when she proudly and smugly announced, 'I'm going to school tomorrow! Na-na-na-na-na!' I exploded and grabbed Judith's cheeks, pulling them out until she screamed through a contorted mouth. I was enraged and envious at the same time - a lethal combination. Poor Judith. She still contacts me after all these years. I've asked God to forgive me, but I haven't asked her yet. I will now, 'I'm sorry, Judith. Please forgive me?'

I remember my first day at school and Mum later collecting me - too early. I refused to go until the bell rang, and even then, I wouldn't budge. 'You must go home, Doreen. Please. It's time to go home,' the teacher said with a weary smile.

I think teachers profoundly affect our enjoyment of school. I was lucky. I remember only one awful teacher, Mr. Dando, the judo expert. He taught judo to the boys after school. It was becoming trendy around 1958 in Australia, but no girls were allowed. It gives you an idea of how misogynistic he was.

I was a good kid in class, quiet and attentive. It may have been why the teachers placed me at the back of the room. I know it's hard to believe now, but it's true!

I was born with myopia; in other words, short-sighted. Nobody noticed until I was in Dando's class and found it hard to read his minuscule handwriting on the blackboard, especially from the back row. My guess at what he'd written was more often wrong than right. Dando became frustrated with the bizarre remarks from this usually quiet little girl, who, the previous teacher, had claimed to be a bright student.' I copped it with all sorts of sarcastic comments from Dando, which made the entire class erupt with laughter.

I can't remember whether Mum took me to the optometrist first or she inflicted upon Dando her temper and unyielding stance on bullying. I think she got her facts straight with the optometrist first, so she had a bullet to fire at Dando.

After Mum gave Dando a mouthful, his attitude changed. I'd love to have known what Mum said, but whatever it was - it worked! He sat me in the front row in case my glasses were ineffective. The petite dynamo strikes again!

My brother, Wayne, looked after the rest; he warned the kids in my class that if he caught them sniggering or calling me names for wearing glasses, they'd get a hiding from him. It was always nice to know I had a family I could rely on; however, I soon learned to save myself, thanks to Dad and his boxing lessons.

Now, back to the Delany family. As I mentioned, Judith's brother, Paul, was a bully of the first degree. I was nine years old when I'd had enough of his tyrannizing behaviour. It happened the day Paul, unprovoked, broke the head off a doll that we girls were playing with, and then he walloped Trisha with the headless body before he ran off sniggering.

I marched home fuming and told Dad about what that mongrel Paul had just done. Dad looked up calmly from his newspaper and explained how to give Paul his own back.

'Call Paul over," Dad said. "Tell him you have a secret. When he's up close, punch him as hard as you can in the belly, and when he bends over - give him an uppercut!'

Dad then showed me how to close my fist correctly. I visualized Paul's humiliation. Yes, my anger had built up over the years and merged into incandescent fury. I needed to do what Dad had just told me. After all, he'd been a champion boxer in the Army.

Paul's comeuppance went as planned; I knocked him out and strutted home the hero explaining what I'd done to Dad. He seemed shocked at first, then suddenly sprang from his chair and walked outside to see Paul conscious and walking across the road, nursing his chin. I noticed the wry smile on Dad's face. He said nothing.

It would have been five minutes later when we heard a knock on the front door disturbing Dad from reading his paper. As usual. He opened the door to an angry Mr. Delaney. I stood behind Dad as Delaney hurled abuse about my aggressive behaviour. Dad replied through gritted teeth, 'Your son's a bully, and he got what he deserved. And if you don't get off my porch, you'll get the bloody same.'

Delaney left before Dad had time to close the door. Dad was renowned for his boxing prowess in the neighbourhood, not that he ever went looking for a fight. He was a pacifist, but he'd never evade the task when needed.

Guardian Angel Tom.

Those were the good old days when you fought your own battles, and the bullies were dealt with face to face - if not by you, then by another family member.

Bullies certainly existed then and still do. But it was an upfront, in-your-face kind of bullying when the perpetrator could be identified and punished. Unlike today, when the anonymous trolls hide behind social media platforms, leaving the gentle, sensitive kids to deal with the abuser. It is a sad situation. Today, far too many kids take their own lives when being bullied. When I was young, I cannot remember hearing about teenagers taking their own lives due to being bullied.

However, I did hear about returned soldiers committing suicide. Dad later explained to me. 'Those men had suffered badly in the war, mentally and physically. Not all people are the same; it's just that some don't have the ammunition to fight the war within.' I thought then and still do now that Dad's explanation was profound. However, I also tend to stick to Dad's other philosophy.

'There's too much political bull-shit happening these days. Why don't they just get straight to the point!"

I know there were exceptions to the rule back then, but most kids were less likely to run and hide or tell tales in those days. Remember - we were the children of the Anzacs! We were empowered, not aggressive. I've taught my kids and grandkids the difference between aggression and empowerment. I say to them often, 'You should never judge anyone, but you don't have to put up with bad behaviour.'

By this, I don't mean knocking someone's block off when they misbehave (like I did to Paul, but I still refuse to say sorry). You should try to ignore insults and walk away, or turn the other cheek, knowing you are above acknowledging that sort of behaviour. It is the best way, of course. However, sometimes Guardian Angels are needed, as my dad proved on the odd occasion. Not only for our benefit but for others who, like Dad said, 'Don't have the ammo to fight the war within.'

Paul the Bully hadn't quite finished his reign of terror. Two days later, I played concerts with my friends in our neighbours' backyard, the Foots family. Their dad, Neville, was a plumber and had a long, wide wooden bench attached to our adjoining fence to hold his plumbing supplies. With a bit of shifting, we could make room to dance and sing.

At the time, I'd been attending gymnastic classes and owned a pair of wooden dumbbells; those dumbbells were my props for the show I was performing. My audience - my gang - saw Paul's head and what looked like a giant stick appear just above the fence on the other side - he was in our backyard! They pointed in Paul's direction, and without a word, I took the cue and turned to see Paul, who was about to whack me with a whopping great stick. Instinct *may* save your life - never forget it - but I nearly *ended* Paul's life with my dumbbell. I gave him a hard whack on the head.

I must say, I was a little concerned as I watched him stagger away, hands-on head and blood oozing between fingers. 'Oh, shit,' I thought. 'I'm going to get it this time.' However, when my friends told the truth to our parents, I was let off with a firm warning. All I can say is that whack must have instilled some sense and sensibility in Paul. I'd won the war! Paul and his amended attitude joined our gang. You could say he then knew who the boss was! Although I was not bossy, I was just a leader with a kind heart and a strong sense of fairness. And I've never met anyone who has disagreed with me- I wonder why?

United, we stand divided, we fall. That's my motto!

*Our first home in Ashburton.*

I've jumped over the fence again into the Foots backyard.

It wasn't until Neville (the dad) suffered from terminal cancer that Mum became a much closer friend to Gwenn, his wife.

Mum helped Gwen with anything and everything, including

feeding and minding the kids, Neville Jr, Lorraine, and Shane, while Gwen spent most of her time in Hospital caring for Neville. I should also mention that Mum cleaned and tidied Gwen's home daily.

Eventually, Neville came home to die. Maybe it was his wish, or palliative care was not available, I don't know. Though I do know it was a horrific time for everyone. Neville became skeletal after being fed only fluid filtered through a tube into his stomach. And whenever needed, Mum and Dad helped with this arduous task.

During Neville's last days on earth, he suffered the hottest summer. Day after day, it reached over 100 degrees, we couldn't afford air conditioners, only electric fans, so Gwen, along with Mum, would sponge him down with cold water while the fan blew directly on him. My heart went out to Neville, and to add to my sadness, other people, especially children, were noticeably repulsed when seeing him. This seemingly un-rewarding situation showed me true humanitarianism, and I will never forget my parents' sacrifices while helping the Foots family in this sad time.

When Neville finally died, it seemed not long before Gwen returned to the fun-loving, sexy woman she'd been before, and Mum would have a go at her for being a flirt—plus having more than one boyfriend at a time. I think Gwen introduced my mother to enjoy more than her usual quota of shandies. ( Beer and lemonade). And on occasions, the pair would become happily drunk. It ended with Gwen standing on our kitchen table singing, 'Two Cigarettes in the Ashtray' or 'Cry me a River. I'll never know why she had to stand on the tabletop to sing.

As I've mentioned before, Neville's workbench adjoined our back fence. It supported Gwen when she'd climbed over to visit us. When intoxicated and trying to find her way home and into bed, Mum insisted on Gwen phoning three times to let her know she was home safe.

It wouldn't be easy to climb over a tall timber fence when inebriated.

One night the phone didn't ring, and Mum thought *Gwen's just forgotten.* The following day, Lorraine (her daughter) found Gwen sleeping soundly under the workbench. She wasn't so lucky two weeks later when she slipped and broke her leg after too many shandies.

So, the boys dismantled the workbench and built a gate. Much safer!

We were fortunate to have loving, non-violent parents, except for Mum's whacks around the leg and occasionally yelling at Dad, albeit for something she said he'd done wrong. I don't think Dad was ever aware of what he'd done wrong. Nor were Wayne and I come to think of it. Poor Dad, he'd always cop it sweet. Then he'd annoy Mum by singing.

'Don't be angry with me, dear, don't turn me from your door. I know that I've been wayward, but I won't be anymore!"

"Oh, shut up, ya silly bugger." Mum would say.

And we'd all laugh.

# Chapter 4
# Character Forming

I was a born performer! Amateur, of course. Same as Mum. We loved to sing and dance and entertained friends and family throughout the years, though neither wanted to become professional. Maybe we realised we weren't good enough, so we'd only perform for those who loved us. I suppose we'll never know.

Anyway, there was a time when I was delusional about my talent, so I advertised far and wide! (Locally.) Yes, we were going to put on a concert. I must have had reservations, as I'd told my gang if the audience didn't like our show and wanted their money back. One of them (the fastest runner) had to jump the two back fences that led to the local shops and spend the money on chocolate. "You have to do it before the audience has a chance to demand their money back," I ordered.

To tempt an audience, I told a (white lie.) I painted a sign.

'JUDY GARLAND TO SING AT OUR CONCERT!'

That drew a crowd. The kids came in droves, and we were delighted, thinking; *we'll be able to buy enough Cadbury chocolate to last a year!*

Unfortunately, my rendition of 'Somewhere over the Rainbow did little to enthuse the audience. Just as well, plan B was successful. Well, sort of; later, we had to share our chocolate between about sixteen kids!

In my performing days, Mum's wardrobe became a Pandora's Box.

We kids, on many occasions, were left alone while Mum and Dad went shopping, and they were never away too long. And remember, when living in a court, everyone looked out for everyone else.

Shopping days were the best time to raid Mum's wardrobe.

Our large wooden garden shed became my cubby house. I think Mum decided it would keep me from messing up her house.

*Always the performer. I surprised Ross Daisley on his fiftieth birthday.
I met and spoke to Barry Humphries once and told him about my
Dame Edna skits, and he said, 'you're far too attractive to play her!'
And I said, 'I also do Les Patterson.' He said, 'Now I am shocked!"*

One Saturday morning, when Mum and Dad had gone shopping, I decided that we (my gang) would dress up and pretend to be ladies at the races. Mum's most delicate cocktail dresses and fashionable suits were handed around by yours truly, along with high-heeled shoes and hats to match. We had a wonderful time imagining our Racehorse had just won, and we'd been invited to afternoon tea by the Chairman of the Race Club. A couple of hours later, my instincts warned me. Danger!

'Mum and Dad will be home soon; I can feel it.' I said in earnest.

My friends undressed in a hurry and handed me Mum's clothes and accessories. I was so busy hanging the clothes in the cupboard that I forgot to take off the mauve lace cocktail frock. OHP's too late. I heard the car coming up the driveway, so I ran to my cubby house and promptly threw the cocktail dress behind a pile of stuff. Yes, the cubby house certainly needed a tidy-up. Mum thought so too.

The same afternoon she ordered Dad, unbeknown to me.

'After lunch, Tom, will you tidy up Doreen's cubby house, love. And put all burnable items in the incinerator?'

'Of course, doll face.' His standard reply.

Can you guess what happened? That's right; the mauve dress was thrown into the fire by an unassuming Tom. And my bags were packed by a furious Betty.

"You're going to the girl's home this time!" She yelled LOUDLY. She had to yell. I was across the road playing with the gang.

I guessed what had happened, I could see the smoke from the incinerator, so I quickly escaped running to Gardeners creek.

Out of breath and crouched in our hideaway, I began thinking. *Mum'll be over her temper soon. Yep, she'll just warn me again, or maybe she'll take me to the Girl's Home this time. Oh shit.* Not only was I frightened, but angry because, in my opinion, Dad should have taken some of the blame. Why didn't he recognise it was one of Mum's good frocks before he burnt it! Bloody dill! (God, I sound like Mum.)

It was then that I had another scathingly brilliant idea. I needed to escape, yes! I could build a raft and float down Gardner's creek into the ocean, I assumed? Then my life would be filled with adventure, just like Huckleberry Finn. I would use the 44-gallon drums that someone had dumped and tie logs and branches on them. It would be authentic. It kept me busy, especially after Trish came and told me that Mum was about to call the Police! Trish had failed to say it was because Mum and Dad were worried about me.

I thought the worst. I thought I'd be thrown into jail for what I'd done.

So I worked hard and fast, trying to build a raft that would float me away from trouble. It was dark when my bravery and vision of sailing out to the ocean failed. I had two choices, trust the unsteady raft I had just built or go home and face the consequences.

By the time I walked home - heart in hand, I found Mum sitting in the kitchen, sobbing. Everyone else was still looking for me. Mum's greeting, I assumed, was the same as the prodigal daughter's return. Why hadn't I thought of it before - go missing for a while?

*

Mum took great delight in telling this story.

'One day, when we went to the Royal Melbourne Show.' She began with the same sentence every time, "and after hours of walking, we rested on a seat outside the boxing tent.' (Unintentionally, I'm sure.) "I said it would be nice if we could afford to give the kids more than one ride on the merry–go–round Tom. 'And wouldn't it be nice if we could afford a Chinese meal on the way home?'

(I think show bags were Sample Bags back then and were free until they ran out.)

After Mum's plea, Dad had a scathingly brilliant idea.

"I need to go to the toilet Betty." He said, patting her shoulder affectionately.

"Well," Continued Mum. "It seemed a long time before your father returned, but when he did, he came waving a fist full of pound notes. And the manager of the boxing tent, begging your father to join his boxing team. You'll be the next champion, he said. Your father had just fought the never defeated champion and knocked him out in the second round! I'm his manager, I said. And we don't need you!"

It seemed Mum had more fight in her than Dad, as the manager walked away, cursing.

For the rest of the day, we bought whatever we liked, including our Chinese dinner. Dad's win apparently, paid our mortgage for two months. The next day Mum bought a new dress, Dad, a suit, and us kids some fancy clothes. Mum always smiled with the memory. But still, she would never agree to Dad having a boxing career. Tom remained an amateur and only used his fist when need be.

*Dad, at age sixteen, joined the Army to fight in the Second World War.*

I have enclosed the poem I wrote about Dad after he died. I hope I've explained what a gentle soul Dad was and how long it took before his patience ran out and he considered his foe needed a knock-out blow. Now that rhymes.

### MY DAD TOM

*Of all the memories I hold of my dad.*
*One springs to mind at the start.*
*It was only the crucial things,*
*That he ever took to heart.*
*Never did he fuss or hurry,*
*With things that made others worry.*
*Instead, he'd make light of events.*
*It made me think he was Heaven sent.*
*Born away in the Malley scrub.*
*And still not old enough for a beer at the Pub.*
*He took to War at age sixteen.*
*Never one for tales of horrific scenes.*
*Only good times with mates since passed.*
*When he returned, it was peace at last.*
*A gentle man with little to say.*
*Though fists of a giant came into play.*
*When things got tough.*
*And words weren't enough.*
*Only evil fools would meet his blow.*
*I'm sure God was pleased to know.*
*Arc Angels are hard to find, but my dad was one of a kind.*
*He met and married the love of his life.*
*Betty, his darling doll face wife.*
*Their life would never again be the same.*
*When I arrived and my brother Wayne.*
*No matter how good or bad things went.*
*Dad's patience would never end.*
*Mum would get cross and try to be boss.*
*To calm her down, he would toss.*
*Don't be angry with me, dear.*
*Don't turn me from your door.*
*I know that I've been wayward.*
*But I won't be anymore!*
*That met with loads of laughter.*

*And we were happy after.*
*Dad gave me confidence and inner strength.*
*And I grieve that he went.*
*But he gave me faith in God above.*
*And to Dad, my heart is filled with love.*

*

I should now convey a couple of Dad's 'good time' War stories.

On Tom's behalf.

When on leave in Cairo, Tom fought with an Arabian man who bit his ear lobe off before a local doctor sewed it back on. However, Tom chose to tell Wayne and me that a close bullet had taken his ear lobe. "My mate searched through the sand for hours and eventually found the piece of ear lobe missing. Then he sewed it back with a hair taken from a donkey's tail."

I would proudly tell that story on most Anzac days until Mum said.

"Tell the bloody truth, Tom."

I would have rather he didn't. Far more exciting telling friends about a close bullet! Any wonder *I* can tell a story.

During the Middle East desert campaign, gifts arrived for the soldiers every Christmas. They'd receive fruit cake, Anzac biscuits, knitted socks, photos from home, etc. "All gifts should be kept in Tom's trench. After all, he's the lucky one." Said one of Tom's mates, so it was unanimous.

After completing the task, no room appeared in Tom's trench. It was filled to the top with gifts. When the battle began, Tom jumped into a mate's dugout. The gunfire eventually ceased, and the dust settled before the Soldiers took a store of the carnage. Luckily, Tom had escaped again! His trench had been blown to bits! Dad's recollections continued.

"We all went scavenging around picking up pieces of fruit cake and Anzac biscuits." Then he'd laugh in that funny way, like a hiccup. Tom also told the story about his return home onboard a ship.

The most popular game played was two-up; it helped pass the time.

And Tom had a great instinct, which he always followed.

"Near home, exactly two hours before docking in Melbourne, I'd won enough money to buy a three-bedroom home, a Pub, and a holiday house." So Tom told us.

Alas, peer pressure, it seemed, got the better of Tom's intuitive nature and perhaps his greed, though he was never greedy. Tom stayed in the game for double or nothing and lost the lot. Whether this story is true or not, he told us kids to teach us the old lesson. 'A bird in the hand is better than two in the bush.'

Mum used secret language whenever she sent Dad shopping for her menstrual pads. The names varied, saddles, comforts, or cream puffs. Dad thought Mum had invited people for afternoon tea when one Sunday morning, she asked.

'Go to the shops, please,' Tom, and buy me a packet of cream puffs, will you love.'

And so, he did!

Later I heard Mum screaming.

"I didn't want cream puffs, you silly bugger! You know what I meant, Tom!"

I thought if she didn't want six chocolate éclairs, I wasn't going to waste them! I'd scoffed two down before I felt a hard clip over the ear, but it was worth it. Why didn't she just call them menstrual pads?

The Carol family, who lived two doors up, became good friends. The eldest sister Dianne appeared subdued and kept to herself. Maybe because she was a dedicated scholar, studying all the time. Jilly, the younger sister, was a little older than me, a kind, happy kid I admired. John was my age, and he annoyed my brother Wayne. Maybe John being younger and trying hard to be part of the older boys' club irritated Wayne. I think.

We remember little things that keep a particular person in our memory bank for good or bad.

Being the eldest and most responsible, Dianne was permitted to make (all by herself) a unique, delicious, bubbly honeycomb. It still reminds me of that fabulous fifty's song— "honeycomb won't you be my baby, honeycomb be my own...." The anticipation when watching the mixture froth away in the saucepan to produce perfection or disaster was nerve-racking. However, I cannot remember a failure. Not once did it turn out chewy. It forever held that magical crunch and delivered many sensations to our palate.

The Carol family were Catholics, and we, the Church of England. Every Friday night, we'd share fish and chips at our house. It came about because Dad worked for General Motors Holden and always drove the latest Holden car. So, he'd bring fish and chips home after work. This fact alone had most neighbours thinking we were Catholics.

It didn't matter to us, as those Friday nights were always fun-before TV arrived. We entertained ourselves, especially when playing

'Eye Spy.'

Little John Carol took his turn. "It's something that starts with JC."

Well, do you think we could guess what it was?  After about ten minutes and asking little John for a final clue. "It's everywhere," he said.

We gave up.

His answer? "Jesus Christ!"

# Chapter 5
# Love and Loss

So many people have contributed to my story by weaving their magic into my life. Some now come to mind. No exception is Dad's sister, Aunty Gloria – possum, they called her. The saying stemmed from her childhood when she was a perpetual tree climber.

Gloria's husband, Max, was quick-witted, kind, well-groomed, and smelt of expensive aftershave. He was a favourite with me, although his satirical humour could be controversial with adults.

I had my last dance with Max while he suffered from Alzheimer's and was cared for in a nursing home. I flew to Melbourne, stayed with Aunt, and made a point of cheering Uncle Max up on the days I was there. I told him what a great dancer he used to be.

"I still am!" He said proudly.

We had no music to play, so we sang and danced together. That memory has now brought tears to my eyes. But I take solace in the thought that to leave a person smiling is to give a precious gift. Uncle Max died only a week later.

*Uncle Max at the nursing home. In front, Auntie Gloria with Uncle Max.*
*Back row, Maxine's dearest friend Glennis and me.*

I should stick to my childhood memories, but recent memories seem relevant because the child in us never dies.

Aunty and Uncle had one child, my beautiful cousin Maxine: born two days before me. 4/3/1951. Being born under the same star sign - Pisces, meant we understood each other. Maybe. Though Maxine was probably a little more complicated than me. No, I'll say intriguing. It's more apt. I wouldn't say she was spoilt, but she was catered to by Max's mum, her Granny, and of course, Gloria and Max, her parents.

Uncle Max worked as a NEW car salesman and became a well-respected sales manager for various manufacturers, including Mazda. Uncle Max also purchased a delicatessen in Burwood, and on weekdays, Mum would help Aunty with the school lunch orders. I'm sure Mum earned a wage because I remember Aunty saying she should pay Mum double as she cheered her up. Always the clown, my mummy.
Maxine and I would play happily in the backyard before we began our school years, usually riding pretend ponies.

I attended Alamain state school and Maxine Burwood Ladies College.

I can't remember any snobbery attached; maybe it came later when Maxine went to MLC. Though I don't think she joined the girls who thought they were superior to Swinburne Tech girls. Maxine never acted superior; we were always close. However, life leads us down different paths, and attending other schools and living so far apart meant we inevitably found new friends. However, Maxine and I would often get together, especially when riding horses in our teenage years. And as teenage girls do, we'd diet all the time. I'm sure the famous model, Twiggy, set the example. Thin, thin, and then thinner!

I shall now enter the story I wrote in honour of my beloved cousin after she died from cancer at age 44

## ENCORE
Nearing my destination, a melancholy mood landed as the sun beamed its last rays through the windscreen. Soon, it would disappear beyond the horizon into the encroaching night. Sheep grazed peacefully in roadside paddocks, unaware of their mortality. Cattle gathered under the gum trees, flicking their tails against the flies, unwittingly in time to the passing seconds of their lives.

The thought of my existence felt surreal as I drove the last stretch of the country road leading to my cousin Maxine. It occurred with sudden clarity that every moment in time is unique; it is never the same as the next, nor the one before it. My long journey signaled admission that at age forty-four, Maxine, two days older than me, had been bravely but unsuccessfully fighting cancer for the past two years. Now she had peacefully accepted her approaching finale.

I finally arrived to see Maxine sitting by the window waiting for me. She was perfectly still and haloed by the golden glow of the day's fading sunlight, her alabaster skin angelic in its translucence, and her blue eyes glistening with unshed tears. I stood momentarily speechless, shocked by her appearance, and filled with the sorrow of this, our last goodbye. Suddenly, I knew what to say.

"You bitch!"

"Why?" She said, stunned.

"You're thinner than me!"

Arms around each other, we laughed and cried, sharing the memory of our youth. Maxine had finally captured her breath enough to say, "Oh God, you knew how I needed to laugh. Everyone is well-intentioned, I'm sure, but they're so *mushy*. They all ask the same question. 'How do you feel, Maxine?' I see their *terrified* expressions. They think I might tell the truth!" She gave me a measured look.

I thought, what *does* a person dying of cancer say to the question, 'How do you feel?'

"How the fuck do you think I feel - I'm dying! That's what you should say, Maxine." I provided the words, and we laughed.

It appeared my down-to-earth sense of humour was long overdue as Maxine counted her final days on earth.

We sat close in the twilight and reminisced about our childhood when we'd entertain our friends and relatives, singing songs that later became our anthems. Maxine was from the school of drama, and I, comedy. Therefore, the individual pieces we chose were reflections of our inner beings. "When the red-red-robin comes bob-bob-bobbin' along," I would sing brightly, smiling. Maxine would then change direction with her sincere rendition of "Look, look, my heart is an open book - I love nobody but you!" Complete with sentimental expressions and animated gestures explaining every word.

She was hilarious, but our laughter was not the appropriate response as far as Maxine was concerned. We were supposed to cry, then applaud, calling, "Encore! Encore!"

Her histrionics at having her audience laugh completely outdid the drama of her performance. It took some time to console Maxine and assure her that her voice was sweet, and yes, she sang in tune. And secondly, the sincere words of the song alone would be enough to convey the message of true love. However, this did little to persuade her to temper her melodramatics, which stayed throughout her future performances. So we, on most occasions, tried hard not to laugh.

Many more happy memories came to mind over the next hour or so.

One reason for my first comment was, "you're skinnier than me!"

As teenagers, we needed desperately to look as much like 'Twiggy,' the fashion model, as possible. We'd weigh ourselves every weekend and hold our breath until the other exclaimed, "I've lost more than you!" It was war! Don't worry. It never turned to anorexia.

Maxine's mum, my Aunty Gloria, had been busying herself in the kitchen as we talked. Occasionally, Aunty offered more detail to our stories, which we had missed in the telling, and then she'd laugh along with us. Before long, it was time for Maxine to take her medicine.

This Aunty took care of while I unpacked. When I returned to the lounge room, Maxine lay asleep in her recliner with a shadow of a smile. Aunty hugged me. "You're a breath of fresh air! Bless you!" She then told me she hadn't heard Maxine laugh like that for months. Hearing this, I cried.

Uncle Max arrived home from his business, and we three melded into cocktail hour, enjoying our gin and tonics while Maxine slept. It allowed us to speak about how her teenage children and her husband were coping. A deep sadness overcame us, contemplating Maxine's passing. Though we carried on, determined to bring happiness to the evening.

Later, Maxine bravely sought to enjoy her evening meal as we sat around the dining table. Her husband, Michael, and her two children, Danielle and Dean, had joined us but would return to their home soon after dinner - a situation in place for the past month. Maxine had explained to the children and Michael that they needed to keep their daily routine in their home. She had insisted on it, firmly stating that at no stage of her decline did she want or need a fuss to be made. Maxine assured them that her thoughts and conversations would focus only on their fun activities and their plans for the future. To this end, she remained adamant.

After a pleasant evening and a good night's sleep, Maxine decided she and I should drive to her family home and say hello to her beloved horse, Starlight, so named because of his fine silver coat. It was a perfect sunfilled morning for a drive. A brisk nor 'easterly breeze blew through Maxine's window, and I turned to ask, "are you warm enough?"

Maxine nodded; her eyes closed she breathed in the fresh morning air. I knew she needed to feel the wind on her face and a slight chill in her bones, reminding her she was still alive.

Soon, I was in awe of two magnificent white gums standing as monuments to time, their roots firmly planted on either side of the driveway leading to her weatherboard home. I slowed the car to a crawl and took in the beauty of these giants set against the paddocks of ryegrass swaying in the breeze. My attention then changed to the horse now trotting towards us.

"Is Starlight the only horse on your twenty acres?" I asked.

"Oh, no, he has a pony for company." Maxine opened her eyes and gazed across the undulating grass.

"And a few snakes, I suspect. You should have it slashed, Maxine."

"Thank you, Dor," she responded with a wry smile.

"What for?" I asked

"Forgetting that I'm running out of time."

"Well, I'm sure you'll have enough time to organize the slashing before your funeral!"

Maxine laughed, then stopped when Starlight whinnied. His trotting switched to a gallop, and he slid to a halt beside the car.

"Drive closer to the fence so that I can pat him!" Maxine demanded.

She spent many minutes speaking softly to Starlight. He snorted his replies while nodding against her hand, consciously saving Maxine the energy of stroking him. I sat relaxed, observing and considering my years of experience with these spiritual animals. I was certain Starlight knew his days left to see Maxine would soon end.

I drove up the driveway at a snail's pace, admiring this beautiful horse's loyalty as he walked beside the car. He wasn't going to let Maxine out of his sight. This unforgettable and touching moment confirmed the reason for my love and understanding of horses.

Maxine's family could discuss her situation and console her with their love; Starlight had no words to speak but showed love in his eyes and compassion with every movement he made towards her. Maxine told me stories of her time riding Starlight around the bush tracks and how she'd won him over to be one of her best friends and confidantes after being a skittish young horse. I believed it.

Maxine began to weaken, so I returned her home. Uncle Max and I helped her from the car and into bed, where she slept soundly until the nurse came some four hours later.

"Do you need a morphine shot?" the nurse asked.

"As long as it doesn't spoil my cocktail hour," Maxine replied with a giggle.

"You shouldn't be drinking alcohol," the nurse admonished her.

Maxine gave the nurse a challenging look and retorted, "And I shouldn't be dying this young, either!"

And so, the bar was open. I'm sure to Uncle; it became the highlight of my visit. To celebrate what life we had left rather than mourn the inevitable. It was a special time we shared, in close company, with both life and death.

The ten precious days I spent saying goodbye to Maxine brought many valuable lessons. One was reading an interesting and helpful book on dealing with death. In the end, I asked Maxine if she could guess the one idea that I thought stood out above all else written in the book. She considered for a moment before answering.

"I think so. Was it the part where the author, Petria King, refers to having all the people in the world stop for two minutes at four o'clock every day while they visualize rainbows of peace being sent all around the earth?"

I smiled. "Yes. Isn't it a lovely idea? And do you know what I'm going to do, Maxine, at four o'clock every day? I will send you a rainbow full of peace and happiness."

Maxine wiped away a tear, smudging the mascara I'd brushed on only minutes before in readiness for our cocktail hour. She managed a smile, "I'll be waiting."

To quell my own emotions, I called Uncle. "Drink waiter. May we have two vodkas with orange juice and a barrel full of laughs? Thank you!"

"Right away, ladies, I'm at your service," Uncle replied.

I left my beautiful cousin with trepidation and deep sadness, knowing it would be the last time I would see her alive. Maxine lay resting on her bed, her blue eyes trying vainly to express hope. They searched mine for an answer. "Is it alright to feel scared?" she asked weakly.

With my overconfidence and belief in the power above, I asked. "Do you remember ever since we were little, I would forever tell you I was right?"

She chuckled, "Yes, I do."

"Well, my question is - did you believe me?"

She laughed a little before saying, "Yes, most times."

"Then my answer is this - you must believe in love, happiness, and Heaven. Forget about fear. And to prove I'm right. Once again! Send me a sign from Heaven when you've made it. And every day, I'll send you a rainbow at four o'clock. Is that a deal?"

Her delicate, cold hand shook mine to seal the deal. I kissed it and then allowed my lips to linger on her forehead for the last time.

Aunty told me each day after I'd left, Maxine had the maximum allowable dose of morphine. Every time she woke, she'd ask Aunty, "What time is it, Mum?"

Aunty would tell her, no matter what the time. "It's four o'clock, darling. Here comes your rainbow," and Maxine would drift off to sleep with a smile.

*Maxine and her husband Michael, with their children*
*Daniele (yawning) and Dean at his Christening.*

Within the first week after Maxine died, I was touched when seeing rainbows appear from nowhere and for no apparent reason. But I knew why. On her seventh day of departure, I was driving my car and began to think of Maxine when Bob Rogers, the famous radio announcer, played her song - 'Look, my heart is an open book, I love nobody but you.'

After playing his selected songs, he announced the information and added, "What on earth made me play 'look, my heart is an open book'? I'll never know. I haven't heard that song in years!"

But I knew.

I regret I didn't contact Bob and explain why he felt compelled to play Maxine's song. I would have told him that some say it takes seven days after death for a spirit to leave our earthly realm. And on this seventh day, Maxine played her song for me, and I applauded. "ENCORE, ENCORE."

# Chapter 6
## My Love of Horses

From a baby, Mum, with one hand, would push me in a pram, and with the other, she'd pull the shopping jeep. It was about two miles to the nearest shops, and we'd pass a large paddock full of ponies. I began recognizing horses from age one. So Mum said.

"The first word you ever spoke was horse." Mum thought it particularly strange, as she'd say ponies, while she fed them stale bread and wilted carrots. Then she'd lift me to touch their soft, warm noses.

"Where on earth did she come up with the word horse?" Mum would ask everyone.

I assume it came from my past life?

My passion for horses grew more prominent, as did I. When I could put a sentence together, I was demanding.

'Mum, please buy me a horse. PLEASE.'

Why did I always demand my needs from Mum and not Dad? Because she was the boss and had the last say no matter what Dad said. "Anything for peace," Dad would say. I suppose peace was what he'd fought for, for seven long, bloody years in the hot Arabian Desert, firing artillery, which rendered him almost deaf. An excellent way to be when Mum was yelling!

My continuous plea for a horse went unanswered. Mum never understood how much horses meant to me. Horses were my life, love, and passion; how could she deny me the only thing I had ever wanted! That may be an exaggeration?

I remember the races blearing through our fancy cream Formica Radio, sitting on the kitchen bench. It had a red velvet lining under a criss-cross pattern on the front. Even at a young age, I thought how brilliant it looked. I suppose I could at least listen to the exciting call of horses racing—a small compensation.

The races in the fifties, I think, were run only on a Saturday, or at least it was on those days when Mum would place bets with an SP Bookie. The kitchen table became her ironing board, and every Saturday, she'd do the weekly ironing, hopefully after the weekly wash had dried. The enthusiastic voice calling the races intrigued me, as did Mum's quickening of the iron when her horse was in the lead.

"Go! Go, you beauty!" She'd yell.

The iron, I'm sure, took the place of the whip. I've never seen clothes ironed so fast.

Mum laughed when I pulled the radio away from the wall and looked behind.

'Why did you do that, darling?' She asked.

'I'm looking for the horses.' Was I stupid?

'You can't see the horses behind the radio. But if you're a good girl, daddy and I will take you to the races one day soon.'

Isn't it always; 'if you're a good girl?

In Mum's words, I wonder why I continued to be *a bugger of a kid.* So many rewards I'd been promised for being '*a good girl.*' But it didn't matter how GOOD I was; Mum wouldn't buy me a pony.
Well, not for a long time.

I must have been a GOOD girl,' because not long after that day, we all went to Flemington Races. As children often do, I picked every winner and became the most popular and celebrated child.

My racing fascination began when admiring the Jockeys wearing colourful silks. The mysterious men in suits with hats pulled down, covering their nervous expressions while giving instructions to the jockeys. The scenario sent a shiver of excitement through my tiny veins. The crowd's roar almost drowned out the sound of thundering hooves as the field of thoroughbreds went galloping past, guaranteeing that this was the world in which I would live. When I grew up, that was. How amazing! Yes, I knew it then, at the tender age of four.

Mum was a football maniac, and Dad merely enjoyed the game. The secret truth was that Dad preferred to go to the races. So, between Dad and me, we came up with a plan. Dad would say after we'd arrived at a football game (Carlton, of course), and here we go again.

'If you're *a good girl* today, I'll take you to the races next Saturday.'

I was then THE angel child, but if Dad's offer was not forthcoming. I was the devil child. I'm not sure if Mum ever clued to our conspiracy. I think she was so enthralled with the footy, which I hated and still do, that she let everything else slip.

What kept our race plan intact, I'm sure, was that Dad and I inevitably came home with more money than we went with; we were a great team. Dad had a good eye for a horse, and what's more important, he followed his instincts. If Dad liked a horse, he'd back it, no matter the odds.

We had limited money to gamble with, as he was the only breadwinner. Dad was a Forman at General Motors Holden. But we managed with our small bets to do very well, which paid for our Chinese dinner most Saturday nights. It was more expensive to sit in the restaurant, so we took our saucepans and Billy cans to be filled, usually Chop Suey, sweet and sour pork, and fried rice. I think it's a great idea to bring your own pots. EG-too much packaging and waste, just for the sake of lazy convenience! Bringing your own pots should happen today, as the meaning of convenience sometimes has an inconvenient ending.

*

I must take a break and bring you into the present. Ironically, Wade (my husband) trains 'Footy Fan' by the Stallion Aussie Rules. On 2/11/2013, she won six out of eight starts and earned her place in the Field of Grey Stars on Oaks day in Melbourne on 7/11/2013. It will be more than a coincidence if she wins! If my spiritual beliefs are correct, I'm sure Footy Fan will have the Aussie Rules footy fans in Heaven, giving her a helping hand!

*

After viewing Footy Fan on our arrival in Melbourne, Wade took one look and said, 'she's gone off the boil.' He was right, and she didn't win. But thanks to her generous owner Tom Sewell we all had a good time anyway. Thank you, Tom.

*

Dad and my love of racing remained strong throughout the years. One of my most memorable days was when he took me to Flemington, Melbourne Cup day 1960. I was nine years old. Dad was not a member, so the hustle and bustle of weaving through crowds of what seemed to be giants was terrifying. Finally, we reached our destination - the saddling enclosure fence. I clung to the wire while Dad fought his way back and forth to the betting ring. He'd not leave without giving me the same warning.

'Don't talk to strangers and don't go with anyone, no matter what! If anyone tries to take you away - scream for the Police.'

While not being harassed, I was almost squashed to death by the crowd when they merged, so determined they were to view the horses that, *little me*, became invisible.

My Melbourne Cup experience remains indelible. I thought on that day; that it was the reason I was born. *One day, I will look like one of those glamorous ladies and own one of those magnificent racehorses.*

The experience of surviving a jam-packed racecourse, feeling like an ant - almost squashed to death by giants; was not pleasant. But the dream derived from watching Thoroughbreds paraded at their best and feeling the thrill and passion of the winning owners; was enough to instil in me the racing dream. I left, determined not to return to the Melbourne Cup until my vision had come true. On our way home, Dad asked. 'Did you enjoy the day, darling? Do you want to go again next year?

'Yes, I loved it, Dad. But I'm not going back until I look like one of those ladies and own a horse in the Cup.'

I've kept my promise. I've never returned to a Melbourne Cup, although I have attended Derby Day and Oaks Day, but not the Cup.

*Chris Lawlor, friend and client, to the right of the picture.*

*A fabulous sketch of Ray Selkrig on Shamrock King.*

Wade and I have nominated a few horses over the years but never had the good fortune to participate in that fantastic race. Still, our life is not yet over.

I did manage to choose the winner back in 1960. New Zealand bred and trained 'Hi-Jinks.' He paid 50/1. He was the horse our dear friend Ray Selkrig told me many years later; he just missed out on riding. He was the first jockey offered the ride on Hi Jinx, but Ray chose to ride another horse. When that horse was scratched, Ray phoned the trainer of Hi Jinx, Trevor Knowles, and asked if he could have the ride back.

'Sorry, Ray, I asked Billy Smith to ride him one minute ago. Sorry mate.'

One year later, Ray had his first and only win in a Melbourne Cup on 'Lord Fury.' This and the next MC would have been nice; lousy luck, Ray!

*

My perpetual longing for a pony was fed even more after that special day Dad and I had spent at the Cup. No matter what, Mum said I'd own a pony, and soon! I was older then and more determined.

I became the gang leader and, by this time, a young entrepreneur.

The knackery was not too far from home, within walking distance, and I'd been there on many occasions to inspect numerous horses who, in my opinion, still had life in them. So came another scathingly brilliant idea! Because I knew Mum would perpetually cry poor!

"We can't afford to feed a horse. Let alone buy the saddle and the bridle!" She'd say.

So I decided my friends could help me earn enough money to buy our own horse. Of course, they would! Syndication, they call it now. I wrote a chapter about my childhood not so long ago that I entered in a short story competition - named 'Looking Back, Looking Forward.'

My Non- Fiction story didn't win, though it reached the top twenty of around a hundred. Please don't quote me on numbers.

*

'Looking back—looking forward.'

My condition could be described as a passion, a disease, or an addiction. All I know is I was born that way, and I'm sure I'll end the same way, absolutely spellbound by the noblest of beasts—the horse.

My childhood dream was to spend my life with horses. Every night, after being tucked into bed, I'd pray.

"Please, God, help me own as many horses as possible. And please, God, find me a husband who loves horses as much as I do. Amen."

Well, what do you know! All my prayers were answered. In retrospect, I should have also stipulated that my husband had a million or so in the bank. That I didn't, I now put down to the naivety and idealism of youth!

I literally drove Mum mad when asking her to buy me a horse. I say this because she would go mad every time I'd ask.
So, being a determined and formidable entrepreneur at a noticeably young age, I talked the neighbourhood kids into earning money so they, along with me, would own a share in a champion horse.

"From the knackery?" They asked.

Of course, they quizzed me about buying a champion from a herd doomed for the glue pot. "This horse," I promised, "will be no ordinary horse. And, we'll only have to earn two quid to pay the knackery man." I finished my spiel with, "Sometimes they make mistakes, haven't you read the story - 'Black Beauty?" That worked.

We set about collecting empty soft drink bottles to cash them in. We arranged street stalls and sold anything we could. We washed cars (not many in those days) and mowed lawns with rotary blade mowers. We ran errands for the old lady who lived independently and whose legs had almost failed her. Yes, we did it all! Our blood, sweat, and tears went into the communal money jar, along with the bobs, zacks, and pennies. I remember the day well when finally, I counted out the two pounds we'd saved.

Off to the knackery, we ran with our money rattling a happy tune. Against his better judgment, the boss man relented and cupped his weather-beaten hands to accept the coins. He then handed me what I thought to be *the* most magnificent horse I'd ever seen. When in fact, he was a twenty-year-old, sway back, chestnut gelding.

A dull rainy suburban day in Melbourne had suddenly become remarkably splendid. My delight at riding (almost) my own horse home was indescribable, as was my mother's reaction when I led the gelding up the home straight and into our backyard. I could see the bedsheets flapping wet on the clothesline and thinking, *Mum won't be in the best of moods; this is her weekly wash day*. No dryers in those days. Dad wrung all the clothes out by hand. My knowledge of Mum's temper on such days made me a little nervous, but surely, she'd be proud of my friends and me, saving enough money to buy our own horse? Yes, I'd done it! Almost by myself! And yes, she would be happy for us. No doubt she would!

Beneath the flapping sheets, I saw Mum's exposed 'Betty Grable pins,' as she called her short fat legs. My mother was four feet eleven and was most of the time loving and very funny, but she had a temper to rival hell.

I was either brave or bloody stupid to think she'd welcome six snotty-nosed kids and an old swayback horse into the backyard.

Yes, I was bloody stupid.

"Mum," I called, "come and see what we've saved up to buy!"

One look from Mum said it all. The kids bolted, and the horse would have - if he'd had the energy. I stood my ground with Neddy, trying hard to state my case. However, the straw broom supported by Mum's fiery temper won the argument. *Poor Neddy and I* were swept out of the backyard with the broom and Mum's words. "Get that bloody thing out of here, do you hear me? Take him back where you got him!" Her words kept ringing in my ears as I returned Neddy to the knackery. But it was closed. There I stood, a heartbroken ten-year-old holding onto her dream horse.

Was I going to give up that easily? 'No!'

I'd already arranged a paddock where I could keep Neddy, so I rode him there and let him go. I then walked home to talk some sense into Mum (or get my way). Unsurprisingly, this did not happen. Old Neddy, I assume, met his maker. When under Mum's insistence, I sadly, on Monday after school, returned him to the knackery. I was reimbursed the money by *a not-surprised* knackery man.

*

I think the above story confirms my determination and my passion. I need not repeat myself. Although I must say, soon after, it was hard for me to sleep due to excitement. Yes, there was talk of buying me a pony. I'm sure Dad had a lot to do with persuading Mum, and just hearing the whispers of how they *may* be able to afford a pony sent beams of hope. I left them alone to work it out. I was wise enough to know that pleading my case for the thousandth time would only turn Mum against the idea.

For my parents to make up their minds about buying a pony seemed to take forever. I continued to ride other kids' ponies kept in the communal paddock during that time. We called it the Cutting because the train line was supposed to keep going, but it ended at Alamain. The Government had built a long mound of dirt, or narrow hill, to support the railway line. They'd initially planned two more stations. However, a bridge needed to be built to span Gardeners Creek. Perhaps that was why the train line ended. Not enough money in the kitty.

The nearby homes sat a reasonable distance from the train line. Common sense? It meant sufficient land stood available to graze the local ponies. We tied the ponies on tethers for some time until one industrious parent went to the council and asked permission to fence the five acres.

Try and get the same permission now. The answer would be NO! Plus, it would take more than two years to get a response. BUT back then, Councillors had a heart and common sense. And of course, with no threat of litigation, in the late 1950s, they said. "Yes, if the council doesn't have to pay for the fencing."

Together the parents built the fence within a week.

I fell in love with a piebald pony who lived at the cutting. His owner was a shit of a kid who mistreated the pony. Watching the boy whip it up and down the hill broke my heart. He'd push the poor pony until his sides were white with foam and his lungs heaved for air. When the pony almost collapsed with exhaustion, the boy would leave without giving him a drink or washing him down. I said nothing, knowing I needed backup to deal with this degenerate. I waited until he was out of sight, and then I'd tend to the pony's well-being. Eventually, the pony got wise and began raring up and flipping himself over to get rid of the kid. Or he'd lay his hind hoof into the kid whenever he walked behind. They labelled the pony dangerous, especially after the kid suffered a fall and broke his collarbone.

I decided to ride the piebald and show the boy's parents their son was the trouble. Not the pony. Before this happened, I heard he was to be put down, and the boy's parents would buy him a better pony. A BETTER PONY! He had a bloody good pony until he destroyed it.

I had more guts than brains. I believed the Piebald loved me, especially when I'd taken care of him after the boy had left him for dead. NOT SO. It took two broken bones to convince me otherwise. I must say, I did pretty well, considering I rode bareback and used only a halter, not a bridle, to steer him! Later, with my arm in plaster, yes, I fell off. I went to see the pony to tell him I didn't blame him. But he was gone. I don't know what happened to him, and I never asked for fear of the truth.

The local kids who owned ponies and kept them at the cutting were friendly and would let me have a ride. Yet another consolation to my yearning, I suppose.

Finally, the talk of finances needed to buy me a pony concluded. Unfortunately, Dad announced calmly. "There are not enough funds." (I still don't believe it). Then Dad told me about the offer from Aunty Gweny Baker (she was married to Dad's first cousin.) Now, I'll try and explain. Granddad's sister Rita married Johny Baker. He owned a road-building company and became quite 'well off,' as Mum used to say.

They were real characters. Anyway, their son John Jr married Gweny, and they lived in a magnificent Blue Stone house, sitting on twenty-five acres at Ferntree Gully. Their daughters both had ponies. (Sorry, I went off on a tangent.) Well, anyway, they had an old pony which they said I could have. The only problem was that he had to live with them; I was not allowed to bring the pony to the cutting, probably because he was too old and may fret for his home.

I remember Mum reporting happily, 'We don't even have to buy a saddle or a bridle; they have plenty. Isn't that wonderful?'

In the truest sense, I finally owned my pony. All be it a long–

distance pony. I couldn't help but wonder, *would Dad drag himself away from the races or the footy on weekends to take me to Ferntree Gully so that I could ride my old pony around the paddock for an hour? And would Mum let him?*

Ferntree Gully was an hour's drive from home, and you've guessed, it became too much trouble on most occasions. Either the Bakers had something on, or we did. However, I did get to ride Billy every so often. Which was good because I could tell my friends I owned a pony.

Lucky for me, I became close friends with most kids at the cutting. I'd ride my pushbike there, which took two minutes, then I'd help care for their ponies, and they let me ride—a good bargain.

Another outlet for my passion was the local milk run. I'd sit in the cart pulled by eight Clydesdales that lived not far from our home, and when possible, I'd muck out their boxes and pick-up yards in exchange for riding them bareback around the park adjoining the stables. A bob or two would be thrown my way for the effort. But that was not important; I just wanted to ride.

Horses also pulled the breadman's cart. Breadman wasn't as friendly as the milky, but he allowed me to sit on the horse's backs while they strolled around the streets. All went well until Breadman caught me feeding fresh bread to one of his horses.

'I'll pay for it,' I said, but it made no difference. I was in trouble.

When I was young, I read nearly every book about caring for horses, their conformation, plus riding techniques. I became a walking encyclopedia and used my knowledge to pretend I was a vet. I'm sure my pony-owning friends got sick of me telling them all I knew. But now and then, they'd ask for my advice, making me feel important.

My love of horses never wavered, eventually leading me to Jillarooing. What a romantic adventure, riding horses around the bush, living the life I'd fantasized about; however, before I enter my young adult years, I must write about our fantastic Holidays on the beach, including horse riding.

# Chapter 7
## Rosebud Holidays

The only distraction to draw me away from horses was our beach holidays at Rosebud. Even the name Rosebud sways in my mind like a summer breeze. Plus, another upside, when I was old enough, we could hire horses to take on trail rides, yippee!

Mum would say. "Your holidays began at Rosebud before you were born." That's right. Mum was pregnant with me when they first ventured there.

Rosebud is a part of the Mornington Peninsula Victoria. The coastline, from Frankston to Sorrento, is to this day unchanged. No significant buildings, besides toilets and shower amenities, plus the occasional community hall, have graced the ocean side of the road. Therefore, the natural tea tree jungle leading to the beach remains only manicured, allowing clear access for campers.

We, from memory, stayed each year in Camp Site 'Seven.' This ritual began the day before Christmas and lasted three weeks. We'd return every Easter, and Dad and Uncle would take a few extra days off work to make it a week away. It all began in 1950 and continued until 1966.

Uncle Ernie, in my opinion, was a genius. He had an inventive mind, which allowed him to build anything from scratch. Uncle loved to fish and therefore built his boats, which included cabins. No one would ever guess they were homemade, so professional was his detailing. ( As I have explained before.) A good fisherman, Like Uncle, knew where the fish went to feed and spawn. He had excellent instinct and knowledge about such things and always fished in familiar spots per the tides. Uncle would line the boat up to a tree or a boathouse and use his compass when further out from shore. I remember when a sudden storm whipped up from the southwest. So my uncle left anchor and headed home quickly. He returned the next day and lined up exactly where he thought the anchor was. Ernie threw a large iron hook overboard, and with one attempt, he brought the anchor to the surface. Astounding!

Most times, only the men would go out early morning fishing. Meaning 2 or 3 am. And I cannot remember them ever returning without a huge catch. You wouldn't believe it if I told you how big the flathead or snapper was, so I have added a photo of Uncle and the boys holding the regular size catch of the day (enormous).

*Left to right, my brother Wayne, cousin Brian, Uncle Ernie and cousin Graham, holding up the usual schnapper catch of the day!*

They caught so many fish that fellow campers would wait for the anglers' return and stare in awe at our men carrying huge buckets full of fish to shore. One morning a man asked Uncle.

'How much would you sell the fish for Ernie?'

Uncle replied. "Well, I usually sell them to the fish shop. But if you'd like one or two fish, no worries, mate."

And so began the weighing up and the cash exchange on the beach. It became highly lucrative. I remember Dad and Uncle claiming the money they'd received paid for our entire holiday.

And then it ensued. One morning the camp Ranger witnessed

the exchange; he'd caught wind of what was happening. (It was against the law to sell fish without a license) Uncle dealt with the Ranger, whom he knew, with decorum and bribery. He offered the Ranger as many fish as he and his family could eat for FREE. Therefore the threat of closing Uncle's fishing trade was quickly squashed.

We ate fish every day on our Rosebud holidays. And my mouth waters with memories of the sweet, succulent flathead tails and tasty snapper steaks. The steaks were so huge that Uncle needed a small hand saw to cut them. Aunty would then toss the fish in seasoned flour and cook it in butter and olive oil. (We knew a lot of Italians). We'd squeezed an ample supply of lemon juice over the crusty outside, and then we'd eat with gusto, only because we knew there would be second and third helpings. The following serve we savoured slowly, as it should be. I never tire of eating fish or anything that comes from the Ocean. But nothing has ever tasted as good as the fish I ate straight from the sea as a child.

It must have been some years later before Uncle, by accident, invented beer batter, and I'm sure he did because I'm a foodie. I can't remember anyone else cooking or telling me about fish cooked in beer batter - back in the fifties. I was in Auntie's tent on the day she was preparing to cook the fish in batter, 'just for a change,' she said. She'd run out of water to mix the flour, so she asked Uncle to go and fetch a bucket of water from the communal tap (as we did). Ernie was drinking a glass of beer at the time. And I reckon he'd downed a few before that. He said to Aunty, 'let's try something different, love,' and before she could say no, he'd tipped his beer into the flour.

Aunty was not like my Mum, who would have yelled at Dad for doing such a silly thing. Auntie said, 'I don't see how that's going to taste any good, Ernie.' and walked away.

Uncle proceeded to mix more beer into the flour until it became the right consistency. He covered the fish in dry flour, then dipped it in the beer batter before cooking it until golden brown. I was the first to try this amazing discovery, as I was the only kid there on that occasion.
Now I try to explain how delicious the sensation was when biting into a bubbly light crispy batter that had trapped every drop of fresh, perfectly cooked fish within. Heavenly. Now that was profound!

Now I'm laughing at what Wade said after I'd asked him how he would like to die. He couldn't think of a way.

"Well, I'd like to die eating oysters," I said. And Wade said.

"You probably will, you'll eat a crook one, and it'll kill you."

Most nights' we kids, if we were not too tired after swimming and running on the beach all day, would light tilly lamps and go floundering with the adults. The process was not enjoyable for me, as we had to spear the flounder when they came close enough to the light. But I'd never refuse to go because Uncle, later, would cook the Flounder on a large piece of metal that sat above red-hot coals, all set up under a makeshift lean-to. The only problem was that our dinner plates were not big enough to hold the flounder.

*

I will bring you into the present as I've done before when something unique happens. Last Saturday night, the 8th of November 2014, the Conargo Pub burnt down. The pub sat opposite the crossroads to Hay and Jerilderie, leading from the Deniliquin Road. It was at this Pub that I first met Wade. Going further with stories about the pub would become another book. All I can say is that you will read about the shenanigans later. It's sad to think about iconic places burning to ashes. But then I suppose we all do. That's why in my opinion, it's essential to keep our stories alive, as life is all about storytelling.

*

*The iconic Conargo Pub, where Wade and I first met.*

Back to Uncle. Not to be outwitted, Uncle proceeded to carve from timber large flounder-shaped plates that were duly sandpapered and sealed. Nothing could outsmart Uncle's intuitive and fantastic mind. He had remedies and alternate ways to solve most problems. It was a tragedy when he suffered a rare skin allergy later in life, which led him to become a virtual Guinea Pig for the new wonder drug, Cortisone.

It eventually killed him. Uncle's legacy was that he helped determine what doses of cortisone were beneficial and what were lethal.

I will explain another of Uncle Ernie's inventions, which are widely used and most popular today. Ernie figured that his sturdy homemade trailer, which he used to carry camping gear and equipment, could become a base for a caravan with some ingenuity. The trailer was wide and long enough so Uncle could attach long boxes with sturdy lids on either side, used as seats with room inside to hold whatever. At the rear, he'd built a cupboard that contained a kitchen sink. He placed an iron rod on every outside corner of the trailer, which could be removed and packed away. The rods fitted into metal pipes that sat in an iron holder. The poles held masses of canvas covering the entire trailer, and he attached spring beds to either side. They, too, could be folded away. A timber-pitched roof ran down the middle of the trailer. The top sat as a cover over all things when packed away. Under the double beds hung clothes and stuff, and the other side allowed room for camp stretchers. We were also lucky Uncle developed a space ample enough for the entire family to eat and cook. Uncle's caravan looked the same as the ones today. The type extends a bed out on either side and then folds back into a neat trailer.

We camped in a basic tent next to Uncle's caravan. Mum and Dad slept on one side and Wayne and me on the other. The only addition to our tent was a wooden rod that ran across the middle and down the center of what was 'our bedrooms.' The rod between us held our clothes, serving as a curtain. We ate breakfast in our tent, but all other meals we took under the caravan annex with Uncle, Auntie, and cousins.

Uncle Ernie built many fabulous things for me, mainly as birthday presents. One was a large kitchen dresser that I kept in my cubby house. Come holiday time; Mum used it to hold our plates and cutlery. 'Ernie spent a long time,' Aunty said, building me a doll's house. It was nearly as tall as me - at five, painted white, with a red roof. Two stories high with doors between every room with battery-run lights. Lino on the kitchen floor and carpet in the bedrooms. The bathroom had a small hand pump to pump water into the bath. The water came from a little tank with pipes attached, sitting at the back of the house. It was miraculous. I could have charged admission to see it! I wonder why I didn't keep it for my children. I *think* Mum gave it to one of our distant relatives. What a bloody shame.

The campers, we called ourselves, inevitably made friends with the families who'd come to campsite seven every year. Our nearest and dearest friends arising from our annual pilgrimage were the Cartwrights. Father -Sir Geoffrey (a pun), Mum Suzie, son Leslie, and younger daughter Lee, or Lee-Lee, we called her.

Leslie and I enjoyed a special friendship. He loved anything to do with the theatre. And he still does. Therefore, the idea of producing a live show came to Leslie after spending many years entertaining our parents on our camping holidays.  When teenagers or bordering on, Leslie decided it was time! So, with a clipboard in hand and me tagging along around the campsites, Leslie approached every tent within a mile radius, asking.

'Do you have children who can sing, dance, or recite poetry?
We're producing a charity concert over two nights to be held in the park. All proceeds go to the Spastic Centre or the Deaf and Dumb charities.' Would you mind bringing a chair and two shillings for admission? This speech, I reckon, Leslie gave one hundred times over.
Our Concerts became a great success, and the biggest highlight was when Mum, Aunty Suzie, Aunty Dawn, and older Cousin, Betty, dressed up as the Beatles - miming, 'she loves you yeh – yeh -yeh.'

The crowd went wild; encores numbered six. Later, the entire audience crossed the road to the 'Silver Bell' milk bar for refreshments. The poor owner found it hard to cope. So Mum and the girls, still dressed in Beatles costumes, hopped over the counter and gave him a hand. The next day he donated two pounds to our chosen charity. He said he'd never made so much money in such a short time, and he'd never had so much fun.

Our charity concerts continued for many years.  And when thirteen and growing boobs, although self-conscious, I donned a sarong, pulling my hair up into a tight bun. With frangipani behind one ear, I sang Bali-High to the best of my ability. I received a standing ovation and many woof whistles. I wasn't ready for that.

The next day on the beach, a group of teenage boys approached me. 'How ya going? Boobies high!' They chanted.

That was the last time I sang Bali-High. Except in the shower.

So many good times we shared on those beach holidays. Be it playing cards around a bug-infested tilly lamp or pretending to be Pirates holding water fights between boats. We had fun and excitement at the carnivals. We Caught the Ferry to Queens Cliff, wandered around historic buildings, and bought doubleheader ice-creams to savour on our return trip. Or we'd just swim and play water games in Port Phillip Bay from morning until twilight.

Sometimes, Dad would enjoy too many beers and sing, *'Ned Kelly was born in a ramshackle hut; he battled since he was a kid....'* All night, until he'd finally doze off, or Mum's yelling "shut up, Tom" put a stop to his tone-deaf singing.

One Easter, during the night, a horrific storm hit the campsite. Of course, Aunty and Uncle were high and dry in their caravan while our tent collapsed under a deluge of rain. Have you ever tried to climb out from under a ton of wet canvas to save your family from suffocating? Well, Dad did, to the tune of Mum yelling.

'Tom, Tom, fix the tent. What's wrong with you Tom! Stop swearing Tom! Quickly! Fix it! I'm bloody freezing! What's wrong with you Tom? Stop swearing!'

'You'd bloody swear too, Betty, if you stood in a fuckin bull ants' nest! Frigin hell!"

I could see how the scene resembled a comedy skit.

Aunty and Uncle laughed while struggling unsuccessfully to remove us from under a ton of wet canvas. Eventually, we managed to crawl out, cold and damp but uninjured. We then spent the rest of the night warm and dry under the extended annex of their caravan.

Poor little red-headed Mummy didn't like sand or saltwater. And her pale freckly skin refused to endure the scorching sun. Therefore she spent most of her time sitting in our tent with her feet in a bucket of iced water - fanning her face. The Ice Man would come around the campsites daily selling huge blocks, which we'd promptly put in our ice chests. He'd call, "Iceo, iceo! Iceo for Betty!" Aunty would laugh every time, but Mum would tell him to 'shut up.' It seemed there was always someone laughing at little Mummy.

Aunty convinced Mum to join us on Uncle's boat one scorching day.

'It's a lot cooler half a mile out, Bet. The sea breeze is lovely, and there's plenty of shade on the boat.' Aunty said in a caring manner.

Auntie's skin was the opposite of Mum's; Aunty tanned easily and loved the water. Anyway, Mum didn't own a pair of bathers, so Aunty lent her an ancient pair she'd kept for emergencies. Keep in mind the bathers hadn't been worn for ten years. Little chubby Mummy slithered and pulled her way into the old woollen bathers. She then eased a cotton shift over the top, flopped on a sun hat, and was ready. It was a lot cooler, half a mile out on the water as Aunty had promised, and Mum lay back under the shade of the cabin, caressed by a sea breeze. She was happy.

Aunty, Uncle, Dad, and us kids, dived overboard, playing like dolphins.

'Come in, Bet!'

'Come in, Mum!'

'Come in love!' The water is lovely.' We called.

'I don't want to get my hair wet, though.'

"Alright, Bet, hold my hand and throw your leg over the side, then just slip slowly into the water," Uncle said.

Uncle Ernie was in the water and underneath Mum, so he copped a bird's eye view of where the moths had eaten the crutch out of Mum's bathers.

'I hate to tell you, Bet," he said, with a broad smile, "but you have a big hole in the crutch of your bathers!'

'Oh, my God!' Mum said. 'If that were Archie, he wouldn't say a thing. He'd just keep looking!'

We nearly drowned laughing. Archie was a bit of a lady's man.

The summer carnivals situated along the beach were a great attraction. A mini-Royal show with every ride imaginable. Chocolate wheels, fortune tellers, wood chopping competitions. Unfortunately, no boxing tents. So, we'd save our pocket money to have one good bash at the carnival each year. I became a guru at psyching up the numbers on the chocolate wheel, which invariably stopped on my numbers, and voila, I'd win!

My list of prizes? A white budgie in a yellow cage. A sizeable blow-up boat. A surfboard, not top quality, but good enough to ride small waves. A red pushbike. The list then becomes incidental. But I can't remember a year when I didn't win something good. I wish I could still do that now - like psych up the lotto numbers?

Could we *really* Hire horses to ride at Rosebud? Yes!

And what can I say? Poor neddies – poor us. We kicked and pushed our ponies tirelessly for miles through the bush. Didn't the horses know we'd paid good money to ride them? No! Was it fun? Yes! But only when we turned their head for home. I soon learned to grip with the knees and hang on; anything else was a waste of energy. We'd eventually get back safe if we didn't get wiped out under a low-lying branch! Amazing how the business owners got away with the lack of care and safety. From memory, at least one ambulance arrived every second day, and I'm sure the undertaker waited in anticipation.

*

I halt my memoirs once again as, on 6/3/2016, a recent tragedy occurred. Our dear young friend, Olivia Inglis, aged only seventeen, died when riding cross country on her horse 'Togah.'

Togah was one of our ex-racehorses. He took one step too short before an enormous jump which led to the fatal accident. I have written a poem for Olivia. Hoping it will inspire memories of her beautiful soul.

### Olivia's Equestrian Heaven.

*Do you think the Olympic games are only held on earth?*
*Well, let me tell you, in heaven, clouds are turf.*
*The jumps are made of liquorice sticks.*
*So, if you fall, you can take a pic.*
*Olivia has lined up in the 2016 cross-country course.*
*Ready to win on Togah – her trusty horse.*
*Oh! And there they go over the first, what a burst!*
*The power of their wings is beyond belief.*
*I look to see if they have impressed the Chief.*
*The next is over the water jump.*
*Or lemonade pump – if the truth is known.*
*Yes, over that, they have flown!*
*Now onto the four-foot log - made from chocolate frogs.*
*They're going great guns.*
*Oops, don't get stuck in the puddle of gums.*
*No, they're riding free and riding fast over a pancake stack.*
*There's no looking back!*
*And now the barrel of snakes – lolly ones, of course!*

*It seems they're relishing this jumping course!*
*Around the rainbow bend, they ride.*
*Taking it all in their stride.*
*With a huge smile on her face,*
*Olivia takes the next sugarplum jump with grace.*
*They keep up a cracking pace!*
*Olivia sees the gold medal plain and clear.*
*Her family and friends are there to cheer.*
*One last jump to take -it's her favourite chocolate cake!*
*Yes! They've cleared it with not a smear of cream to be seen.*
*Olivia now stands on the marshmallow podium, Togah in hand.*
*She is presented with a bag of gold dust that she sprinkles down on us.*
*We know you will keep winning in heaven, our dearest Olivia.*

\*

Writing about my long and fortunate life after losing someone so dear and young is now challenging.

*A treasured memory. Driving a young Olivia and her beautiful mum,*
*Charlotte, for a leisurely ride around Windermere Farm*
*with Snoopy doing the honours.*

\*

It seemed our Rosebud holidays came around quickly, perhaps due to the many parties we campers held in between. The families who'd formed a friendship at site seven organized the parties in their homes every month. They were great fun for adults and kids alike, and Mum would entertain with her self-taught guitar playing. While the oldies sang, we kids played games, mainly bull under the rug, or hide and seek.

Wayne and I would count the parties beginning in March after Wayne and my birthdays. They were great affairs held in our backyard, sheltered under the tent, and having fun in our Clark above-ground pool. "Only ten months to go!" We'd say, or "eight parties, and we'll be back at Rosebud. Yippee!"

I can honestly say our Rosebud holidays held some of the happiest memories in my life thus far. We must be honest when writing memoirs, and I think the fact that they were such carefree days spent with family and friends, living happily and close together, made it so special. We need challenges; we need to learn. We need to share our time and support each other. We need to find happiness and love more than anything. And these were rolled into one parcel when we shared those magic days.

\*

After mentioning our Clark above-ground pool, I must respect the memory.

When Dad erected the pool, I complained, 'It's not deep enough to swim in, Dad.' Not a problem for the ever-obliging Tom. With help from neighbours, he dug a two-foot-deep hole slightly smaller than the circumference. Clark Rubber back then supplied an ample pool liner. It, therefore, covered the extra depth. Yes - it worked! We could swim! Not far, maybe three strokes. Bless Tom.

At the back of us in Gonna Court and across the road from the Foot's family lived Donald, a delightful Down Syndrome boy who would perpetually climb fences into our backyard, mainly when we were all in the pool. He'd stand on the outside and wee on us, and we'd have to duck dive to escape. Then he'd jump in the pool and play until he heard his mum calling him, but he'd never leave unless she came and dragged him home.

"I'm sorry." She'd say with a worried look.

Mum soon squashed her apology. "Don't be silly. Donald's welcome if he doesn't urinate in the pool."

One day Donald came sporting a massive jar of lollies.

"I share," He said with a huge smile.

The only trouble was that his right hand was loaded with lollies firmly entrenched in the jar. Donald wasn't going to let go of his lollies, not for love or money! Two hours later, and still trying to persuade Donald to let go of the lollies, we realised his hand had swelled twice its size. Dad then rushed him to our local doctor. The nearest Hospital was near thirty miles away. I don't know how the Doctor did it, but finally, he freed Donald's hand. Did any of us kids want his lollies, then? NO, thank you.

\*

Dad was such a bushy with his Mr. Fixit attempts. One day, Mum asked him to fix the rod in their solid oak clothes cupboard, which Mum had purchased on a part payment plan from the local family-owned furniture store. The owner trusted Mum never to miss a payment, and Mum wasn't going without, so all our furniture was top quality. If it weren't so, I'm sure she could have afforded to buy me a pony!

"Tom! The rod in the clothes cupboard has collapsed. Come on, love. You'll have to put the newspaper down and fix it." Mum called. (Another hint at being able to afford a pony. More clothes than she needed).

"In a minute, Bet, I won't be long."

"Tom! She yelled. "Put the bloody paper down and come fix this thing; I've got clothes everywhere!"

"Okay, Bet, I'll be there in a minute. I'm just finishing this article."

"I'll finish you if you don't come and fix the bloody cupboard!"

Tom reluctantly found a hammer and a four-inch nail. He asked me to hold the rod from inside the cupboard. I was the only one who'd fit. He stood on the outside and hammered the enormous nail through the solid oak wood straight into the holding rod. Not pretty, but it functioned. Mum was outside hanging clothes on the line. When she returned, she was not impressed.

"Oh no, Tom! You've ruined my beautiful cupboard. If Ernie fixed it, you wouldn't see it. You fool!"

"Well, all I can say, Bet. Next time ask Ernie to fix it."

And with that, Dad sat back in his favourite armchair and continued reading the paper.

Funny how we usually follow the ways of our parents, primarily how we treat our marriage partners. I'm like Mum with her 'get off your bum and do it' approach, and Wade is laid back and a bit slack when fixing anything properly. Just like Dad. Though Wade, I must say, is a little more enthusiastic if I ask him to cook something special. He loves to cook!

# Chapter 8
## Teenage Years

I commenced secondary school on February 2 – 1963. I was twelve, turning thirteen on March 6. It was a life-changing experience in many ways. I didn't have to ride my pushbike to primary school anymore, then traveling a long way by train to Secondary College gave me a jolt into young adulthood. How important did I feel when wearing a smart School uniform, including a hat and gloves, waiting ladylike for the train to take me all the way to Glenferrie station? VERY IMPORTANT!

On arrival, other girls dressed in the same uniform walked in groups half a mile down a lane, bringing us to Swinburne Technical College's gates.

I loved it.

*Swinburne Tech years. I'm top right-hand side. Love the hairdo?*

The camaraderie throughout our teenage years changed us subtly and slowly, as did our interests, especially in boys, well, not physically, just looking and giggling. Swinburne Boys' College sat across the road from the girls' school. However, we took selected lessons within their grounds. This caused a stir, as the boys could see us from their classrooms while we studied Art and English. They were the only subjects held on the boys' side. Horses still held my passion back then; boys ran a poor second. Therefore, I was not distracted from Art or English and did well in both subjects.

My inspiration to write came in two unforgettable moments. First, when I was in primary school and wrote my 'Fairy Story,' it caught the imagination of all who read it, including the principal. And I was duly complimented by him.

The other was Mrs. Atwell, our English teacher at Swinburne, who said - and I quote.

'When you write your first novel, Doreen, ensure you have a good editor. Your stories are wonderful, but your spelling and punctuation are terrible.'

I laughed, though Mrs. Atwell was sincere.

'I'm telling you, Doreen, you will write novels someday, and I guess they will be best sellers!'

That hasn't happened- yet.

However, it was the greatest compliment and encouragement anyone could have given me, especially at an impressionable age. I'm still trying to prove Mrs. Atwell right. She was a great teacher, perfect in fact, and I first impressed her when she asked her pupils to write a poem about chimneys in year seven. Immediately, a chorus of deflated sighs filled the classroom.

'How can anyone write a poem about chimneys?' Most said.

No problem for yours truly – smarty pants.

In less than one minute, I wrote.

\*

*Chimney's - chimney's look at em all,*
*Some are short, and some are tall,*
*Nevertheless, we'll have to sweep em all.*
*All right, says he, let's get to work and don't stand around like a*
little twerp!
*I've searched the country for another job, you see,*

74

*But chimneys is me life to be!*

Mrs. Atwell found it difficult to believe I could write that poem in one minute, so she gave me another test.

"Write a poem about a Clown." She said. "I'll give you five minutes."

*THE CLOWN.*
*Does the painted smile on my face make you laugh?*
*Do my silly tricks have you doubled in half?*
*Do you think I'm silly?*
*Do you think I'm not chilly?*
*Well, I am sad and cold as can be.*
*But even sadder if you don't laugh at me.*

*

I wrote 'The Clown' in twenty seconds. Mrs. Atwell believed me then.

Art. Now that was fun. We had a dithery bohemian teacher who just loved my colourful, naive approach. So much so that I received the highest points allowed, 99. I couldn't believe it. Other girls in class could copy Rembrandt to the point where we could not see the difference. But our teacher would say. 'Art is all about expressing what is in your soul!' Mum, the Queen of satirical humour, couldn't believe my mark and asked whether the teacher was a lesbian. Maybe she was, I didn't know, but I knew what Mum meant.

*This is the first painting I did for my grandkids.*
*It seems I have a colourful soul; I'll give the teacher that.*

With my outgoing personality, sense of humour, and adventure, I was popular at school and therefore voted Form Captain every year. Never was I elected School Prefect. NO. You had to '*be a good girl* and be voted by the teachers. Our headteacher became frustrated after the girls had voted me Form Captain for the fourth time.

Her rebuff was hilarious.

'You can't keep voting for Doreen just because she has lovely eyes and nice hair!' I'm sure the girls hadn't even considered those two qualities- even if they were true - or not? We laughed ourselves silly, nearly as silly as our headteacher was. (Sorry, I shouldn't be cynical) Now, what was her name? Oh, well, she was our math teacher, and didn't we give her curry, tongue in cheek, of course. I'm now feeling sorry for our gentler teachers, who just didn't get it, therefore, had little or no control over a bunch of mischievous teenage girls. Though there were some teachers, we genuinely feared. We would never cross their path. No matter what. They were the vultures, always waiting for us to make a mistake so they could swoop down with their sharp beaks. I'm sure I learned much more under our genteel teachers. The meek shall inherit the earth! I hope so with the help of a few Arc Angels, maybe.

In my second year of Tech, we had permission to attend our school dances. How exciting, especially when the Swinburne boys joined us. However, those Vultures scrutinized our every move with sharp beaks. Still, we made secret dates with the boys, be it a movie, a walk in the park, or the footy! Not me, I don't like football, but I like soccer; it's such a clever game.

I was lucky to meet and dance with Russell Morris, Australian musical icon and writer of the song, 'The real Thing.' He was a Swinburne boy.

Normie Rowe also performed for us once. What a fantastic night that was, and to this day, I can remember the light grey suit Normie Rowe wore, along with a slim black tie, white shirt, and black shoes. He sang many great songs, but I think his number one hit at the time was, 'It aint necessarily so.' how lucky were we?

The girls screamed the place down. Not me; I was more interested in hearing Normie sing than silly girls screaming. Which reminds me, my cousin, Graham, took me to see the Beatles in Melbourne in June 1964.

That concert also turned into a screaming match. I was infuriated by those stupid girls who'd paid good money to see the Beatles but never heard or saw anything. Crazy!

*The Beatles*
*Thought I'd throw this picture in. Fabulous, weren't they?*

I did okay academically at Swinburne. However, academia fought my passion. I wanted to work with horses—no genius skill required, just simple common sense. I quit school after passing 'Intermediate' (tenth year). However, I kept writing poems and short stories with the encouraging words of Mrs. Atwell echoing in my mind. God bless her.

There were several options I could have followed, Art and Writing. Maybe a Cadet Journalist?' But I didn't like the thought of reporting murders, or anything dark, especially if I had to investigate the grim details. And the who's who of the social column bored me.

I soon found a job at 'Milnes Chemist'- Bourke Street, Melbourne.

'This is only for the time being.' I told everyone, 'it's until I get a job in the country with horses – Jillarooing maybe? Yes, that would be perfect, riding horses around the bush all day.'

Milnes Chemist was also a supplier of stage makeup and wigs for its theatrical clientele. Celebrities, actresses, and entertainers would literally swan into the shop, floating their egos about, spraying perfume, and trying on wigs while waiting for their headache draft. I loved the drama. 'Oh dear, I have such a headache,' they'd say, with hand on their brow for effect. It was fabulous meeting the actors; I had visions of joining their ranks and becoming a star.

Most teenagers do - don't they?

I had many friends who lived within walking distance of home. One was Anthea Braiding, now Anthea Crawford. Yes, the famous fashion designer. Ant, I called her as did all her friends - and still do. Ant and I were friends in Primary school. Later, Ant went to 'The Methodist Ladies College,' the same year I went to 'Swinburne Technical College.' However, the weekends we spent together. Ant's mum was a beautiful, elegant lady. And probably because Ant was her only child, Ant's friends were invited to their home every Sunday. We listened to records, danced, sang, and played silly games. I taught them how to play bull under the rug. Now I shall explain. One person leaves the room, and the chosen few hide under the blanket; the rest hide elsewhere. The guesser comes back after we call, 'ready!' Then they predict who's under the blanket. The first time we played the game at Ants, someone farted. We threw the blanket off, laughing ourselves senseless.

Mrs. Braiding, in those days, would cook the most fabulous food, including spaghetti Bolognaise, which was almost unheard of back then. Thai chicken, fried rice, sweet and sour pork! The list goes on. It was like going to a restaurant, as Mum would only cook chops with three vegs, plus the odd meatloaf and roast, which tasted good but always the same.

Ant was my main buddy when we were old enough to go to the discos or dances. Every week we'd sew something unique and stylish to wear. Ant would design the garments; her mum would cut out the pattern, and my job was to hand sew, which I was not good at, so I was told to do it again and again after being reprimanded. Any wonder 'Anthea Crawford's garments are perfection to the extreme.

The fabric we used came mainly from Op shops. Toorak was our favourite, with many high fashion labels and stunning materials. Sometimes, Ant only needed to slightly alter a skirt, a jacket, or a blouse, and we'd wear the latest fashion. What a genius she was - and still is.

We had great fun in the summer holidays while staying at Wilsons Prom. Ant and I would go with a group of young friends -safety in numbers? We all camped in a vast boat shed, and not once was there an argument or anything untoward happening. We just partied. Innocently.

My most memorable journey away with Ant was when she and I were sixteen and travelled to Sydney by train. We stayed at Kings Cross in a hotel owned by a friend of Mr. Braiding. 'My friend will look after you,' said a confidant Mr, Braiding.

At *the safe* Hotel, Ant and I had the pleasure of meeting the 'boy girls' from 'Les Girls.' Being late September and a lot warmer than Melbourne, the hotel roof presented the best place to get a quick tan; the boy-girls told us this. And it was there we got to know the stars from 'Les Girls.' What an eye-opener for innocent sixteen-year-olds! They were amazing to look at and so much fun to talk to, just gorgeous! I fell in love with Sydney and its gregarious people.

When cruising on the Manly Ferry, we met two genuinely lovely young men from the northern beaches. From then on, we kept their company, and they showed us around Sydney by day and took us to all the best discos by night. We were sad to leave them - and Sydney, though we did keep in touch with the boys for a while, but distance eventually drew us apart.

On the train back to Melbourne, I confessed to Ant that I'd had a premonition, showing a glimpse of me living in Sydney. NSW, to be exact, and I would be married with two children.

Home safe and sound. Mum hugged me and then laughed.

"I bet you haven't got a penny left." She said.

"I would have if I'd taken up all the offers I had when I stood on the street corners of Kings Cross!" The smile left her face.

We were naive about drugs; I suppose we never mixed with the type of kids who delved into the forbidden. However, we were not angels, mainly when the discos like 'The Thumpin Tom' in Melbourne stayed open all night. We worked out a plan. I would tell Mum I was staying at Ant's or another friend's, and they would say the same to their mum, leaving us free to dance all night. Long inviting couches lined the inside perimeter of the building, which resembled an old storehouse. If we were lucky, we'd find a spot to nap for an hour or so, and then we'd be up dancing again. Very innocent, really.

When I arrived home Sunday morning, tired and bedraggled, Mum would say, 'you look like you haven't slept?' And she was right.

Mum would forever warn me. 'If you miss the last train home, hop in a cab. It doesn't matter what time, wake me up, and I'll pay for it.'

Ant and I seemed to attract all *the nice boys*. One night at the

Thumpin Tom, two well-dressed, well-spoken young men offered to drive us home.

They said. "We live in Mount Waverley, and your home is on the way. We'll drive you.' 'Don't worry about catching the train with your friends."

Ant and I discussed the offer, which we thought was innocent, as were the boys. And that was another thing Mum warned. 'Never accept a lift from strangers. It doesn't matter how nice *you think* they are!' Good advice, Mum.

Unfortunately, we ignored Mum's advice and accepted their offer. I thought it strange that the other boy sat in the front. Usually, boys pair up with their preferred girl. Right? Well, the reason was the boy in the passenger seat had a gun hidden in the glove box, and not too far into our journey, he took the gun out and pointed it at our heads. At first, I thought it was a joke. However, when he explained what they would do to us before they killed us. Ant froze, and I raged.

I don't think it's necessary to repeat what they said; you can imagine the abuse and the threats.

'You'll have to kill us first,' I said. 'you won't get any pleasure out of us alive!' I opened the door and was about to throw myself from a fast-moving car. Ant screamed, 'don't, Dor, please don't jump. You'll hurt yourself.' God love her. But how absurd when they were going to rape and then kill us. Not me or Ant - if I could help it!

I remained until the perfect opportunity arrived. The driver slowed down to cross St Kilda road. I was in the middle of disembarking when the passenger boy yelled, 'I'll shoot you!'

'Well, shoot me! Jump now, Ant! Jump!' I yelled.

I threw myself from the car and hit the road hard! Shit, that hurt! I rolled continuously, grazing my arms and knees while my dress ripped to pieces. I fought to stand, and when I did, I realised I was in the middle of St Kilda road. Horns honked as cars swerved, trying to miss me. I stood stock-still, shaking with anger, thinking those bastards had Ant. *'I have to hail a car; someone will help!'* A car eventually stopped. It was filled with young men. I prayed as I'd never prayed before. I had to trust them. I explained what had just happened quickly and clearly.

'They still have my friend in the car!' I screamed at last.

'Jump in! We'll catch the bastards.'

I was overwhelmed with joy and relief when I spotted Ant sitting in the gutter a little way up the road. She was alive!

Ant and I became good friends with the young men who saved us that night. They kept our secret. As teenagers, I think we hold narcissistic tendencies – left over from childhood? Yes, Ant and I had only thought of ourselves and how much trouble we'd be in if our parents knew. I often wondered if my act of bravery had curtailed those degenerates from trying the same trick again. I hoped they'd lay awake every night, wondering if I dobbed them into the police.

I trust karma got them in the end.

*

Back to the discos, Ant and I loved dancing and creating fashion. I could sing okay, and the young and un-famous Max Merritt was playing at the Thumpin Tom. I was lucky to share a jam session with his band that night. My performance impressed a talent scout, so he approached and talked me into joining a band he was putting together.

'Why not? I'll give it a go.' I said - full of confidence. As usual!

More excited about the expectation than I, Mum took me to Reg Grey, a notable singing coach. His daughter Samantha Sang had an incredible voice, and her songs topped the Pop Charts on many occasions. I never reached her heights, probably because Reg said, "you're tone deaf!"

Or maybe he dismissed me because I was a better singer than his daughter? I'm only joking.

However, I did have fun for a while as the lead singer in 'Georgie Babies Blues Band.' Twelve-bar blues or jazz is relatively easy to sing; you just need to feel the blues. We performed at several dances, entered a radio competition, and ran second - not bad? Though the night scene was not for me, I loved horses and the bush. This disappointed Ant, as she had visions of me becoming a famous pop star and herself a renowned fashion designer. Well. HELLO!

I think that's when our friendship faded. We had different roads to travel.

# Chapter 9
## Taking Risks

While working in Melbourne but still trying to find a job in the country, I acquired a Kawasaki motorbike! They say nothing comes easy. And having Mum and Dad agree that I should own a motorbike was as problematic as buying me a horse.'

'Now you want a bloody motorbike. What are you trying to do? Kill yourself!' Good question, Mum.

It appeared later when riding my motorbike; it was precisely what I was trying to do. However, I was SO tired of traveling by train to work every day. Including the four previous years, I'd trudged to Swinburne by train. It was torture.

'I need a motorbike to get to work!'

That was my main argument. Eventually, Tom and Bet gave in. However, their worries manifested the day after I'd bought the motorbike home. A perfect Sunday presented a cloudless blue sky and the warmth of summer. "What a picture-perfect day to ride along the Mornington peninsular," I said to Trish, who stood admiring my new motorbike.

I only had P plates, so no pillion passengers were allowed.

'So, do you want a ride down the beach, Trish?'

'You're not allowed to carry me on the back, Dor.'

'Oh, don't worry, I'll take the P Plate off.'

'Do you have a spare helmet?'

'Mmm. That's a problem. I know! You can stick a Tupperware bowl on your head and wrap a scarf over the top. You won't see the difference!'

'Okay, sounds like fun!' Said a naïve, trusting Trish.

And it was fun until a young Motor Bike Cop spotted something that was not kosher about Trisha's helmet. He proceeded to chase me down the Nepean highway. I suppose that's when the real excitement began. I weaved around every car on the road, ducked into side streets with the precision of Tom Phillis, 1961 Australian Motorcycle Champ, and was delighted to see the cop in the rear vision mirror having trouble catching me. Ducking up another side street, I took a sharp left turn into a lane.

'You lost him, Dor!' Trish yelled with glee.

'No, I haven't.'

The cop knew his way around. He'd ridden past the lane and come up from the opposite direction. He sat on his bike, arms crossed, facing me.

Bugger!

I could have turned around and made another dash, but I gave in. I took my helmet off slowly, shook my long red hair (I'd died it strawberry blond), and smiled sweetly. That worked. No, not quite.

He confiscated my bike, called for back-up, then sent us home in a police van, along with the Tupperware bowl. He'd let me off with a warning. And he delivered my motorbike the next day - personally. Can you believe that? Well, it's true!

'I need to speak with your father.' He said to me with a wink and a smile.

He didn't know Mum was the boss.

"Please don't tell your daughter, Mr. Forster," he said privately. "But she handled that bike like a professional. She almost lost me. It was a real shock when she took her helmet off, and I realised she was a girl."

Of course, Dad told me what he'd said. I think Dad was proud. Mum wasn't! 'You're grounded for a month! Except,' she said, 'if you go out with that nice young policeman.'

That nice young policeman had also asked Dad for permission to take me out on a date. I said 'NO,' until he phoned the next day, then I said 'yes,' but only once. He thought I owed him something. I probably did, but he wasn't going to get his reward!

I can't help myself when challenged. Always a competitor! Shortly after that fateful trip down the Nepean Highway, I rode to the local shops, where I sat on my Kawasaki eating ice cream. Two young boys stood close by, admiring the bike.

'I bet ya can't make a wheel stand.' One said.

'I bet I can!'

I revved up the engine then let the accelerator go full bore. The front wheels went straight up before coming down a little crooked, making contact with an old bomb car. Its jagged bumper bar had sliced through my knee. I felt something but didn't worry. When I got home, I noticed my jeans were ripped. My brother, Wayne, was close by, 'have a look at my leg Wayne.' I said. He looked - then vomited.

After Wayne recovered, he drove me to the doctor, who sewed three layers of stitches to the wound. It had reached the bone. Back in the sixties, we could phone our family doctor in an emergency, and they would accommodate our need – anytime, night or day, unlike today. We wait for hours in a crowded hospital emergency room. Probably due to the population explosion? Though shouldn't we have an equivalent amount of Doctors?

Not too long after, when riding my motorbike during the night on unfamiliar roads, looking for a home in which a friend was throwing a party, I crashed into a curving gutter. Probably a mixture of poor eyesight and lack of concentration. I'd conveniently lost every pair of glasses Mum had ever bought me. I hated wearing glasses. Although not riding fast at the time, I'd managed to topple the bike on my 'not healed wound.' It burst open. Thankfully, I soon found my friend's home. She bandaged my wound in the view of many horrified faces. She then offered to drive me home. No. Not me.

'I'll ride home later but not before I party.'

'Independent Annie' was another of Mum's labels for me.

The next day I went back to my not-so-happy doctor to be stitched up again. Did I mention he was the doctor who brought me into the world? I'm sure he thought one day he'd write my death certificate.

I'd befriended a young man who also rode his motorbike to work. We had some fun dodging each other and weaving through peak hour traffic. One hot summer morning, we took a different route to work, around Commo Park on the banks of the Yarra River. What a great place for a race! I sent him a challenge and was in front until I skidded through a wet, greasy patch. It was the most dangerous bend around Commo House, precisely when the flower beds were watered. The water streamed onto the road. Lethal! Hot bitumen and cool water! I'd chosen on that day to wear open leather sandals and fashionable, oversized goggles – not the real deal. However, the goggles did save my eyes when I went headfirst into a road spin. My left foot took a pounding. Every layer of skin on the top side was gone. My top lip sliced open while the inside of my bottom lip gathered bitumen. It's still there today. Oh, yes, the tip of my nose lost a load of skin, though it eventually healed perfectly. I ended up unconscious in a flower bed. When I awoke, three men wearing white uniforms were leaning over me.

'Am I in heaven?'

'No love, you might think you're a 'Hells Angel,' but you didn't make the grade.'

To this day, even with plastic surgery, the scar remains on my top lip. Though my left foot gave me the worst pain, it had to be doused with acidic fluid twice a day. It stung like hell. This was to prepare the area for a skin graft. I don't need a reminder of that accident. However, three remain—the prominent scar on my left foot. The botched plastic surgery attempt on my top lip and the bitumen still showing on the inside of my bottom lip.

# Chapter 10
## Jillaroo

My friends all chose a safer option to travel. Cars!

One friend, Leah, had saved enough money to purchase a brand-new vehicle. She wanted to run it in. 'Let's do some miles,' she said. It was when cousins Brian and Graham, plus Mum, Dad, Aunty, and Uncle, journeyed to Deniliquin for the occasional relaxing weekend. The boys mainly went duck shooting and wild pig hunting while staying at the Conargo pub. The oldies stayed at the Motel in Deniliquin. They loved it there, throwing a line into the Edward River, hoping to catch a Murray Cod.

The Edward River runs alongside the town and is a branch of the Murray River. Twin River city, they call Deniliquin. Anyway, we all thought it a good idea to do some miles in Leah's car and meet the legendary Nevil Lodge, proprietor of the Conargo pub and dear friend of our family. Little did I know that I would meet my future husband on this trip and secure a long-wished-for position as a Jillaroo!

We headed off after work on a Friday night and arrived safely at the Conargo pub around nine o'clock. Lodgy, as we called him, had rooms set up for us, his young lady visitors. We threw our bags in the basic timber rooms, which stood in a row out back of the pub. We then walked a few steps to the door leading into the Historic Bar filled with laughing jackaroos, plus an assortment of storytelling country folk. The scene embraced me.

I took a sweeping look around and spotted Wade sitting at the end of the bar, deep in conversation. He wore a cream cable knit jumper, his blue collared shirt showing above the high neck, moleskin trousers, and riding boots, the uniform of the graziers. He was probably the only bloke who didn't turn to look at the new attractive females who'd just walked in.

I had a premonition. AGAIN?

'See that fellow at the end of the bar,' I said to Trish. 'Well, I'm going to marry him, and we'll have two children.'

Trish laughed. 'Oh God, there you go again with your spooky stuff!'

Cousin Brian, and Graham, happened to be at the pub that weekend. It was duck shooting season - of course, they were.

The conversation was all about shooting ducks, poor little things. So, I changed the tact.

'Do you think we girls could find a horse or two and have a ride tomorrow, Brian?'

'I reckon your best bet would be Wade. I'll ask him.' He's in charge of the horses on 'Boonoke Station.'

To my surprise, Brian walked up to my future husband. They spoke for a minute before Wade got off his stool and came to meet us. My heart fluttered.

'Hello, ladies." Wade said. 'It won't be a problem; I'll bring the horses in tomorrow morning, say around ten o'clock. You can ride all day if you want.' Wade finished with a charming smile.

*Wade received a trophy for the best wool judge at the*
*Deniliquin Agricultural Show. Handsome, wasn't he?*

The trouble was Brian then talked us into going duck shooting. At daylight!

'You'll have time for a kip before you go riding.' Brian said.

'Duck shooting then horse riding. No worries!' I said.

It was still dark when we heard a loud bang on the door.

'Wake up, girls. We're ready to go!' Brian called.

As Brian did with everything, he explained and showed us with precision all safety measures to do with the gun, how to hold it, aim, re-load, etc. We went prepared!

Little Leah was short, and the gun she held outsized her dramatically.

'Are you sure you can handle that thing, Leah?' I said, a little concerned at her stance. She didn't look comfortable.

'I'm all right, just shut up and let me concentrate, Dor.'

'Okay, if you're sure you're alright.' I was worried.

The ducks were set in flight by the blast of a shotgun. We were in the perfect position to plug one. I pulled the trigger and shot purposely away from the ducks. I probably hit a tree or something. I was a good pretender. But not little Leah. She had a determined look on her face. She went down like a shot duck! I was just about to say, 'you don't hold the gun like that, Leah,' when she pulled the trigger, the butt came back and hit her jaw.

'Oh shit! Is she dead?' I said to Trish.

'Nup, she's just knocked herself out.' Trish said calmly while feeling Leah's pulse.

'Get some water Dor.'

I threw a bucket of muddy river water over Leah's face, which duly woke her.

'What happened?' A dazed Leah asked.

'Don't worry. You copped a duck on both counts.' I said, tongue in cheek.

Later I said to Brian. 'Make sure you give her a dead duck. She'll think she shot it and have it stuffed, then hang it on the wall as a trophy.'

After Leah had fully recovered, we went back to the pub and slept until 3 pm. Poor Wade, I thought when I woke. He's gone to so much trouble bringing in the horses. What will he say? I was dreading seeing him again. Well, not really. I'd fallen in love at first sight.

There were no mobile phones in the late sixties - early seventies, and I didn't want to drive to Boonoke and face him. Maybe I would never see Wade again? But I knew in my heart; that the premonition would come true. I now laugh because Trish, many years later, said, 'you only married Wade to prove you were right!'

I did see Wade that night at the Conargo pub, and he said.

'What happened to you girls? I was so worried.'

That was the best thing he could have said. He was concerned about us. What a nice bloke I was going to marry. However, I later found out it wasn't Wade who went to the trouble of rounding up the horses. No way. He was the overseer and chief delegator, and he still is if you let him. Bluey, the roustabout, had rounded up the horses, saddled them, and waited hours for us *not* to come. Sorry, Bluey.

After that inspiring weekend, I went home to Melbourne and answered an ad in the paper. 'Riding instructor needed for 'The Healesville Riding Camp.'

Mr. Milne, the chemist I worked for at the time and whose shop was right next door to Pellegrini's Restaurant, Bourke street Melbourne, was a lovely man, as were his senior staff who called me 'littly.' They did so because I weighed only seven and a half stone!! I don't know. I weigh. No, I'm not telling. They were sad to see me leave, and I was too, though horses will always win!

*

The best part about teaching little upstarts to ride push-button ponies was meeting a great girl named Clare? I can't remember her surname. However, she came from 'Clare' in South Australia. Interesting? Clare from Clare. We had loads of fun together, but still, we did our job well. I stayed for about six months until Clare said she wanted to go home. I thought about staying, but I didn't think much of the boss, who was even more stuck up than the rich kids whose parents had paid inflated prices to have them starved by the miserly cook. I was paid a pittance and went hungry, plus I received only one riding lesson. The job included that I have one lesson weekly from the boss, who, in his advertisements, stated he had been (many years before) on the shortlist for the Olympics. *Yes, that's right, he was short.*

I left.

I learned from him never to treat your staff as if they are below you. Wade and I certainly did not, and we ensured our staff never went hungry. I think it's rare in the racing game for trainers to serve their staff bacon and eggs every morning. It was a reward, as riding fractious thoroughbreds in all types of weather is not easy. They deserved a good breakfast plus our respect.

*

After that episode, Mum phoned Lodgy about finding me a live-in position as a jillaroo. I think she felt sorry for me, knowing how much I wanted to go bush. Lodgy told Mum I could live at the pub and help him in the bar. At the same time, he would ask around if anyone was looking for a jillaroo. It sounded good to me.

I'm sorry I missed telling you. On that first trip to Conargo, I made friends with Leonie Morris, whose parents owned the general store. It sat across the road from the Conargo Pub. Leonie took a short break from studying for Victoria's HSC, or Matriculation.

The plan was for Leonie to come to Melbourne and stay with us for a week. We would then go back to Conargo on the bus. I'd stay with Lodgy until I found a Jillaroo job.

*The Conargo Junction Store, owned by Leonie's parents, Mr. and Mrs. Morris.*

Leonie and I had a great time in the 'Big Smoke,' I showed her many sights of interest because she'd never been to Melbourne. My favourite was the Museum where Pharlap stood, looking as he did in real life. I'd spent many a lunch hour when I worked at Milne's Chemist, sitting, eating my sandwich, and admiring Pharlap. He was my hero horse.

We celebrated at a disco on our final night before busing it to Conargo. That night I bade a sad farewell to my friends, including Ant, who was not pleased with me spending the rest of my life in the bush.

Before this night, I persuaded Ant to enter the Norma Tullo competition for budding fashion designers. Norma Tullo was on the lookout for a young talented designer to mentor. Ant was nervous about entering the competition, and I am not taking any credit, but I remember coaxing Ant to submit her drawings.

'What have you got to lose, Ant. Nobody knows you. But they will when you win!'

Ant's unique fashion sketches won! The rest, they say, is history!

\*

Working at Nevil Lodge's pub was an unforgettable experience. And the characters I met there are etched into my psychic and will be born again as characters in my novels. Not that they would recognize themselves. Hopefully not.

As I've said before, I am as game as Ned Kelly, a competitor and sometimes a smart arse. After admitting that. While helping Lodgy pull beers in the Conargo pub, a notable trickster asked me.

'Hey love, heard yer lookin for a horse?"

'Yes, I am.'

'Well, I got one for ya. Ya can have him. If ya can stick on him!' His words brought laughter from the motley crew, who sat slumped around the bar.

'Good! Bring him here. I'll have a go.' I said, excited at the chance.

The next day I was pelted off my gift horse in the middle of the Conargo - Deniliquin road. I wrote a poem long after the fall, as my recovery was slow.

### THE GIFT HORSE

*There he stood about to be mine.*
*A flighty gelding, you know the kind.*
*I slipped the bridle over his head.*
*Not knowing the trouble that lay ahead.*
*To the general store, I led him.*
*To buy some apples that I fed him.*
*My beach towel was a problem too.*
*I threw it on his back,*
*jumped on board, and made a blue.*
*The hot north wind was the trouble.*
*It caught the towel and flicked it double.*
*Off like a Bondi tram he flew and left me laying all askew.*
*Right outside the Billabong lu.*
*Well my friends, that's the end.*
*There'll never be a flightier gelding I'll ride again.*

\*

I was ambulanced to Deniliquin hospital, where Wade later visited me; not that I recall. I couldn't remember a thing for nearly two weeks until Mum and Dad arrived to drive me home in their new Monaro sports car - the latest Holden. They made a bed for me on the back seat, and I vomited nearly all the way home. The car reeked, but Dad didn't worry, and neither did Mum. I was so sick!

*Mum and Dad waving goodbye at Windermere Farm, years later.*
*Yes they still had the Monaro. It would be worth a fortune today.*

It seemed an eternity before I had my appetite back. However, when Kentucky Fried Chicken was advertised on TV, Mum and I were in the lounge room, where I preferred to sleep and heal.

'Would you like some of that chicken love?' Mum asked sweetly.

'Yes, please, Mum.'

Dad drove an hour to the nearest Kentucky fried. They were such good parents. KFC has never tasted as good as it did that day.

It wasn't long after that I was ready for another attempt at finding a jillaroo job, and my parents knew there was nothing they could do to stop me. I was a bugger of a kid!

Leonie, my friend from Conargo, came for another stay. And when done with the city lights, we caught the bus back to Deniliquin. I was fortunate as a young and handsome David Clarke sat behind us. We lined up for coffee when the bus stopped at a cafe, and David approached.

'I'm sorry, ladies, I didn't mean to eavesdrop.' He said. 'It's just that I heard one of you say that you were looking for work as a jillaroo?'

'Yes, I am.' I said excitedly.

'Good." David said with a charming smile. "Though I must admit, we can't afford to pay you much. But we'll treat you like family, and you'll learn about racehorses in the bargain.'

'Suits me. When do I start?'

After hearing our story, Leonie's mum, Mrs. Morris, said she knew the Clarke family, so she phoned Mum.

'I can vouch for the Clarke family Betty. I've known them since I was a young woman. Doreen will be fine with David and John Clarke; they're lovely young men, and John's wife Maggie is charming."
Deal done!

I hitched a ride on the mail truck to Hay Post Office. We arrived after a long, arduous three-hour trip delivering mail to every homestead within cooee. I was left outside this charming, historical building, which I'm sure could tell many a tale. I stood with a suitcase in hand, looking like orphan Annie, and waited until David eventually arrived in his Ute. We chatted as we drove the miles needed to reach 'Merriola.' It adjoined the Murrumbidgee River. The Clarke's raised fat lambs. Irrigation was easy.

Hay Hell and Booligal! I was there.

David asked what I was good at, so I told him about my horse experience, "and I love to cook."

"Great, why don't you whip something up for dinner. When you've unpacked, of course. We won't need you outside this afternoon. Settle in. Make yourself at home."

I inspected my comfortable bedroom, unpacked, and then scanned the kitchen, planning to show David who was the best cook in the bush. I made a lamb casserole and an apple pie using tinned apples I'd found in the pantry. Homemade custard that I made with powdered milk. And just to top it off, I cooked Anzac biscuits for smoko, or whatever they called it, in the bush. I was alone in the house, so I kept cooking. Ah yes, a large tin of sultanas, bloody hell, the lid was hard to get off. I'd noticed all perishables were kept well sealed and high up in the pantry, except tinned food. I also noticed tiny black dots in the cupboards. What were they? Currants?

The men were still out mustering - where I wanted to be. Oh, well, I'm sure they'll need me tomorrow. I felt weary, so I read the Land newspaper and dozed off before something woke me. Was it hunger? No, I heard laughter coming from the kitchen.

I investigated and saw David with his brother John, laughing, looking at the crumbs left from my cooking spree. Nobody told me they had a bloody mouse plague! Only the casserole survived because I'd put it in the oven with a tight lid.

It's hard to explain how incredible that mouse plague was. Even the cat got tired of chasing mice, so he'd turn it into a game. He'd catch one or two and then place them in the middle of a puddle. His huge paw smacked them when they were about to reach safety. Eventually, the mice ran out of energy and drowned. He'd then stalk off to find more victims. We set similar water traps. One was a small spring-loaded plank of wood sitting over a large bucket of water, and we'd place molasses or something just as sticky at the end and over the water's edge. It wasn't long before the bucket filled with drowned mice.

The owners of Boonooke, 'the Falkner's,' permitted Wade to break in a horse of his choice and prepare it for the picnic races. Wade took the opportunity and named the horse Vanglow. When Wade fed 'Vanglow' during the mice plague, he'd sit beside the feed bin and brush hundreds of mice away so the horse could eat his oats. An arduous task.

The mice suddenly disappeared about a month after I arrived, thank God.

*Wade holding Vanglow after training him to win the Deniliquin Cup!*

I loved my time at Merriola, especially riding my pony around the sheep. Though John warned me, 'never take the pony in the Murrumbidgee River, the current is so powerful; it will carry you away!'

No! Not me! I'm a great swimmer; I'd been in the school swimming squad, plus the local swim club. Besides, how could *I not* go into the river? It was so damn hot when out mustering!

The first week in February, temptation won. I took my overheated pony for a swim. We were okay until we edged out into the middle of the river. The current caught us, and down we went like hopeless baggage. Thankfully, the river hit a bend, and I took hold of a large overhanging branch. I had a tight grip on the pony's reigns, so I pulled her along, waiting for my strength to return before I heaved us both to safety. That was close. Bloody hell!

I didn't tell John or David, even when they interrogated me.

'Where the hell have you been?' John asked.

Head lowered; I stuttered a lie about getting lost for an hour or so.

I never did that again.

The Merriola homestead sat high above the riverbank. When down by the river, I'd often look admiringly at the home with its wide gauzed veranda, running the entire width. On hot afternoons breezes cooled by the river drifted through the gauze and waved our weariness away, especially if accompanied by an ice-cold beer! It was heavenly.

David was right. They treated me like one of the family. I attended the B&S Balls and the Bur Cutters Ball and joined gatherings with their family friends. Maggie, John's wife, was a sweetie and cared for me like an elder sister. Thank you, Maggie.

While I was there, John had three racehorses in training, and my job was to feed, groom and lead one horse at a time to John's work track, where he'd ride them, then I'd take that horse away and get the next one ready. It was my first time going to the races to strap racehorses, and I loved it! On the odd occasion when they'd win, it was even better.

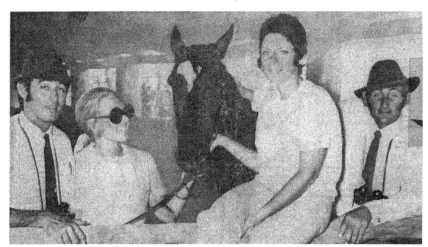

*Not a good photo, sorry. But a memory to cherish.*
*Left to right, David Clarke, Sally Vear, 'Oxley Comfort' the winning horse,*
*me and Graham McFarland, at Hay Races. Around 1969.*

I felt good about the easy way their racehorses lived. After doing their work, we ate breakfast while the horses grazed in the homestead garden. *Mrs. Clarke would not be happy having her garden trimmed by four Thoroughbreds each morning.* I'd think. Luckily she was not there, and the horses had free reign while we ate our chops and eggs. Later, I'd tip the horses' feeds into their feed bins and leave the gates open into their day yards. I'd then walk back, open the garden gate to let them out, and they'd all walk, or jog, back to their respective yards. I'd follow and shut them in. Easy peasy and the horses were happy.

My time with the Clarkes ended when Mr. and Mrs. Clarke returned to live at Merriola. They'd been living at Brighton - Victoria for many years, though they decided they wanted to come home.

I remember Mr. Clarke senior wasn't too well and died shortly after returning to Merriola. Mrs. Clarke stayed until years later when David sold his share of the property to John. David then moved to Queensland, taking Mrs. Clarke with him. I later heard David established a successful property development business on the Gold Coast.

# Chapter 11
## Love of Country

I think it's the right time to fast forward due to an amazing revelation. After twenty years of knowing our friend and fellow horse trainer Ethne Potowski, she asked me over a cup of coffee, or was it champagne?

"Where did you come from, Dor. And what did you do before you married Wade?"

I told her my story from wo to go, trying to make it as short as possible. However, when I got to the part about being a jillaroo for the Clarke family at Hay. "I don't believe it.' Ethne said. "Maggie's my sister, and John's my brother-in-law!"

Well, you could have knocked me over with fairy floss! Of course, the conversation lasted a very long time. We promised to return to Hay and attend their only race meeting where John Clarke was President. We did, and what a hoot!

Approximately 350 patrons and a few cattle dogs attended, and the race fields averaged five. Nevertheless, we had a great time and more than a few drinks, especially later reminiscing about my jillaroo days with John and Maggie. The next day, John sadly admitted it would be their last race meeting, as the committee members needed to sell Livestock just to put the race meeting on. How sad; it knocked me back. Then I began thinking about how we could save the day! Another scathingly brilliant idea, or two, came to mind.

"We'll introduce Fashions on the Field. And I'll gather all the prizes." I said. "First-prize, I'll get a flight for two with Hazelton Airlines to Sydney. A two-night stay at the Hilton, dinner for two at Doyle's. The second prize is easy! My friend Anthea Crawford will give us a $500 gift voucher. The local Hay Jeweller, I'm sure, will donate $250. And to top it off, I'll ask Yalumba Wines to give me 4 cases of champagne. One bottle for each entrant. Hopefully. And the B&S Ball held in the Race Club utility shed will coincide with the races. Put an extra $5 on their ticket to cover entry into the Races."

John laughed but agreed to give it a go.

*

When home, I wrote many heartfelt letters to all the appropriate places, mentioning how the country people were doing it tough and how they looked forward to this once-a-year race day.

"If we make it extra special, it will be enough to lift their spirits until next year." I pleaded.

The sponsors' favourable replies were forthcoming. Thank you to all those mentioned above, including Myer Melbourne, who gave a generous voucher to the winner of the best-dressed gentleman in the second year. They wrote, but don't quote every word!

*We have never donated to functions like this. However, your letter was sincere and to the point, especially how the outback families have relied on Myer Catalogues for the past hundred years to buy their Clothing, Manchester, etc. It brought the ticket home. Congratulations.*

Our convoy of cars and mini-buses were packed, and we hit the road to Hay, an eight-hour trip! I'd placed the Champagne onboard a minibus with our junior team, including Monique Miller, our foreperson, Samantha Ehmann, our apprentice jockey, and our teenage children, Daniel and Lisa. Plus our farrier, Jim Middleton, etc., etc. Our junior team had swigged most of the champagne by the journey's end. I then had to search for country pubs that sold Yalumba champagne?

There were none!

When handing a bottle of Great Western champagne to one of the Fashion entrants at the races, a well-spoken lady who'd not been chosen in the final said indignantly. "This is not Yalumba!"

With a slight push to her shoulder, I said, "oh well, they donated it anyway. Thank you for entering."

She looked at me strangely. I didn't blame her.

I had suggested that John hold a contest for the male contingents. 'What about a You Bute Ute' Contest.' I said. 'Only thing is, the Race Committee will have to find the prizes. I'm too busy."

They took the initiative and found a local Tyre shop whose owner supplied a new set of tires for 1st. A local mechanic gave a grease and oil change for 2nd, and the Royal Pub supplied a case of beer for 3rd.

The Ute competition on that day was so popular; that it began the now-famous Nationwide U Bute Yute Competition! Or, The Ute

Roundup, some are called.

Finally, with all things accounted for, our first resurrected Hay race day appeared to be a great and civilized success until John Clarke, over the loudspeaker, called for all contestants in the Ute competition to drive into center field. When all assembled, he yelled into the speaker.

"Right, you lot! NO BLOODY DONUTS!"

Of course, there's always a naughty boy - or two who dismissed John's plea and generated incredible donuts! To say we were all covered in horse shit and bulldust would be an understatement. Many entrants had not taken it seriously. So we attested to Utes that looked like clay models. The only requirement to drive safely was a clear windscreen where the blades had done their job. Some, of course, were highly polished with Roo Bars out front and giant aerials. Plus, aluminium crossbars sat back of the cabin, placed there for shooters to rest their guns.

Later in the day, the official Race Caller needed to leave before the last race at Hay to be on time for the Trot Races at Shepperton. He'd asked a good mate to call the final race, unknown to anyone else. His mate, *Dear*, I think his name was, and his wife, named *Love*, did their best, which was nearly hopeless. It went like this. Not exactly. But never ruin a funny story with precision!

"Right – the horses are behind the barriers. Hey love, can you help me out with the colours."

We weren't supposed to hear that, but obviously, *Dear* didn't know to put his hand over the loudspeaker when he needed to. We listened to the lot.

"Now they're racing and. Oh, what's his bloody name. Who's that in the pink and green colours, love?"

"That's Storm approaching, Dear."

"Thanks, love. Storm approaching won the jump, and he's leading. I think it's Fire Trail sitting second because he's got the red colours on!"

"No, it's not, Dear, it's Flaming Hot."

"Oh well, same bloody thing, love!"

"Shit, they've gone behind the shed, and I can't see a damn thing! Here they come, and Storm Approaching is still in front, with Blue Boy sitting second. Is that right, love?"

"Yes, Dear, that's right."

"They're nearing the home turn, and we've got a different leader.

While I was lookin the other way, Flinders Parrot spread his wings and flew past Storm Approaching!"

"That was excellent, Dear. Very clever!"

"Do you think so, love? Maybe I should be a race caller, ha, ha, ha. Oh shit, they just went past the winning post, and I think Flinders won with Storm Approaching running second. Or did the one with the green and gold colours pass him? What was his name, Love?"

"That was Giant Slide, Dear."

"Jesus, I'm glad that's over. But I reckon I did a pretty good job. Don't ya reckon love?"

"Yes, you did, Dear."

We, the so-called city slickers, supported the Hay Jockey Club for many years. It's difficult to leave the memories of 'The Resurrected Hay Race Day,' where over three thousand people attended, and fifty-five ladies entered the Fashion Contest. However, we did return with our contingent remaining true blue.

It's 150 years since the first race meeting at Hay, November 2020. Drought or no drought, a busload of us city slickers will no doubt return to help the country folk celebrate.

I retired from being their project manager after five years of what has become a great success. From the initial 350 patrons to now 3,500, or more, it gives me great satisfaction to think I helped with the resurgence. I must add the Batchelor and Spinster Ball, held the same night in the shed on the grounds of the Hay Jockey Club, sported a huge recovery party held the next day at Tabratong, John Clarke's property. And if the racing scenario hadn't catapulted me back to my jillaroo days, then that party certainly did!

*The line-up of the Fashion in the Field. Kim Loy,*
*Tom and Mary Loy's Daugher, first on the right.*

101

*Left to right, Susie Bookahill, the winner of Fashions in the Field,
John Clarke, and me, his old jillaroo.*

*Drinks and a barbeque after the Hay races.
Wade, with Magge, and John Clarke.*

'Merriola,' John's property, has since been handed over to
Cameron, John, and Maggie's son, a fabulous, fun-loving, hard-working
bloke. I've stayed with Cameron and Lynn, his beautiful wife, and

enjoyed reading my Wicky Wacky Farm books in the primary schools to which his three delightful children, Lanta, Lachlan, and Ben, attended in Hay.

Another funny moment! Wade and I drove to Deniliquin when Daniel was five and Lisa 2. The plan was to meet Mum and Dad there, and then the kids and I would go with them to Rye Victoria, where they had retired. We met at a Motel in Deniliquin Friday night, and Wade suggested we go to Jerilderie Races the following day.

At the races, Wade wandered off, as he does, and found a few old jackaroo mates. A little later, I bumped into Bluey, the young, or now more aged roustabout who many years before had caught and saddled the horses for us to ride after we'd first met Wade in the Conargo Pub. Bluey seemed delighted to see me, and of course, I asked, "have you seen Wade, Bluey?"

"Yep, I have! He said eagerly. "You should go and say hello he's over at the bar talking to Smithy. I reckon Wade'd be real pleased to see ya after all these years."

I laughed.

"Bluey! He's my husband, and these are our two children!"

"Well, I'll be buggerd. Last I heard, Wade was gonna marry that other sheila. But I'm real happy he married you instead." Bluey said with a dip of the head and the shyness of someone unfamiliar with giving compliments.

*

I now return to when I left Merriola. John had secured for me another jillaroo position. And one evening, before his parents arrived home, John and Maggie drove me to 'Bullawa,' sitting forty miles southwest of 'Merriola.'

Dudley Rob was the manager. His lady friend, and jillaroo, Jane, lived on the adjoining property owned by her parents. Jane was a gentle person, softly spoken; however, the atmosphere was nothing like I was used to at Merriola, and Dudley certainly did not treat me like family. However, my favourite chore at 'Bullawa' was feeding the poddy lambs three times a day, and they'd follow me around like *Mary had a Little Lamb*, hence my new nickname, Mary. I didn't stay long - six months from memory. I was lonely.

*Jillaroo, on Bullawa after feeding the poddy lambs,*
*accompanied by two adorable red kelpy pups.*

# Chapter 12
## Jillaroo - Part-time Cook - Singer....

I'd found another jillaroo job with George Francis and his lovely wife; sorry, I can't remember her Christian name or the name of his property; it may come back? Nevertheless, it was close to the Conargo Pub. I liked working with George. He taught me invaluable lessons on caring for the land and stock and how to skin a rabbit.

The day I arrived, George handed me a pony named Dolly. She was a charlatan, sweet as a lamb until we were a mile away from the homestead, then she'd lay it on! Around and around in circles before giving almighty bucks! She'd get me off most times. Then I'd have to walk home, slowly following Dolly! If I approached, she'd take off. Or sometimes, after she'd pelted me into the dirt, she'd nudge me as if to say, 'get back on.' I'd laugh through the pain. Funny old tart she was.

*Dolly, my Charleton stock pony.*

George set rabbit traps throughout the day, and we'd drive around and retrieve the rabbits every night. Mrs. Francis, I'm sure, had a hundred recipes on how to cook rabbit. We ate our main meal at lunchtime, and most days, it was rabbit stew, rabbit pie, crumbed rabbit, rabbit curry, and roast rabbit. Mrs. Francis even minced them to make rissoles!

We spent a lot of time clearing the paddocks of fallen branches, throwing them onto stumps that needed burning. I didn't particularly like that chore; I'd rather be out riding. And now, whenever I clear paddocks at Windermere, it reminds me of George.

George's property bordered Billabong Creek, a small arm of the Murrumbidgee River. An array of fish lived in the creek, and George constructed fish traps. He was a trap man. Therefore, we enjoyed fish and chips at least once a week, a welcome alternative to eating Rabbits. Occasionally he'd kill a lamb or a steer, also a pleasurable change.

George built a full-size tennis court using coarse sand for the surface. Surprisingly, it was good to play on once raked. We shared many games; then we'd go swimming in the creek to cool off. What a life. No wonder I loved it. I stayed until I had a better offer from Mr. Clapton.

Basil Clapton was a renowned sheep judge who traveled around Australia, attending shows. He'd advertised for someone to keep house and move his cattle about on his property, 'Sandridge.' What attracted me most was Basil had Australian saddle ponies that needed breaking in, or what I prefer to call, joining up. This coin of phrase comes from the world-renowned Monty Roberts, Horse Whisperer. Not that I knew about Monty then, but I had the same instinct about getting a horse to trust me before putting a saddle on its back.

I liked old Basil and his lady friend, Mrs. Holt. Our introduction came weeks after moving to 'Sandridge' and being naive about politics. I assumed Mrs. Holt must be the Mrs. Holt, wife of the recently drowned Prime Minister Harold Holt. December 17 / 1967.

I did my best to have everything perfect for her visit. I cleaned the silver and the windows, vacuumed under beds, and polished the furniture. Plus, the bathrooms. I scrubbed hard until Basil said, "Oh, you didn't have to go to that much trouble for the old dame."

I was shocked! Fancy calling our First Lady an old dame and a recent widow. He laughed when I relayed my thoughts.

"She's not *that*, Mrs. Holt. She's just an old friend. But I'll grant you. She is a widow."

Basil's Mrs. Holt brought a pear-shaped dark green fruit with a rough exterior. I'd never seen one before. She showed me how to present the exotic Avocado on the plate by cutting them in half, taking out the large brown pip, then sprinkling the flesh with salt and pepper, olive oil, and vinegar. "Food for a king," I said after savoring my first mouthful. And I'm still hooked.

I delighted in her telling me stories about her travels worldwide, usually over a pot of tea. She'd describe the countries and places in romantic detail, to the point where I could visualize being there. Mrs. Holt finished her storytelling before she left with good advice. "No matter how wonderful your travels may be, Doreen, no place feels as good as home. Because that's where your heart is." How true.

I was thrilled once again at having free reign to cook for Basil. And living nearer to Wade meant we became close, especially sharing the same interests. Horses, food, and gardening. Even our dislikes, football, car racing, and other variables were the same.

Wade phoned me at Basil's the first Saturday after I arrived and said. "Do you want to come to the barracks Dor (Jackaroo living quarters)? Mrs. Wilson (the cook) has a new chocolate cake recipe. We could cook the cake, and then we could bottle some peaches. The orchid is full of them."

At first, I thought, '*oh yeah, this is a good way to get what he wants.*' But no, Wadey only had chocolate cake and peaches in mind. I loved it. We were friends, plus I was sick of fighting zealous boys off all the time. Wade seemed like a breath of clean country air. Not to say that we didn't snuggle up on occasions.

Basil often travelled interstate to judge at sheep shows; he was well respected Nationally. It left me alone to take care of 'Sandridge.' However, one time, before Basil was about to go away, he asked, "would you like to fill in as cook for the Jackaroos on Wanganella Estate. The cook is going on her annual holiday, and it will fit my plans."

'Why not.' I said.

On arrival, I was shocked. The kitchen and pantry were filthy. And all the Cook dished up for the boys' at dinner was chops and three veg, or roast lamb. Sweets? A packet of pudding whisked with milk and served with tinned peaches. This I was told by a jackaroo, who secretly liked to cook.

It took me a week to get the kitchen and pantry back to sparkling clean—the rubbish and the out-of-date stuff I chucked away filled a forty-four-gallon drum.

To my delight, I found an old-fashioned meat grinder, the type you screw onto the table. Legs of lamb were perfect for mincing, so I turned the mince into rissoles, spaghetti Bolognaise, and curried mince. I soaked the lamb liver in lemon juice overnight and crumbed it or cooked it with bacon, onions, and tomatoes. Crumbed lamb cutlets were a favourite with the Jackaroos. As were my lemon meringue pie, apple pie, and chocolate cake. You name it. I made it. They never ate the same meal twice. I made toffees, coconut ice, and chocolate caramel slice for snacks to quench their sweet tooth. Some of the *not-so-bright* Jackaroos shoved the sweets in their trouser pockets. Well. Didn't that provoke a snarl from the laundry lady? She came at me like an angry bulldog.

'What the hell were you thinking, giving the boys those sticky lollies! They put them in their back pockets, and now I can't wash them out! You bloody idiot!'

"I didn't put them there! They did! So bugger off with your insults. Yell at the boys if you want!'

The poor old girl threw her arms in the air and marched off. Later, when things cooled down, I did say I was sorry for her dilemma.

I became the live-in hairdresser. Even the boss's son, Simon, liked my styling, so he joined the queue. It was fun, and they were a good mob of young men who appreciated my efforts to cook a variety of food. Especially spaghetti Bolognese, most had never tried it before, and they loved it. I was disappointed when the older cook returned, and my time was up.

Obviously, I love to cook. Like Wade does.

It was the time between working for George Francis and Basil Clapom, plus cooking at Wanganella, that I spent many nights at the Conargo pub. 'The meeting ground.'

When Wade and I were an item, a group of Jazz musicians arrived one night. They were in the district to play at the Deniliquin Jazz convention, so they'd come to experience the famous Conargo Pub. Lodgy had placed his piano against the back wall, and one of the musos straddled the seat and began to play twelve-bar blues.

The blues always moves me. Past life? So I joined the piano player and began to sing. Before long, a crowd surrounded us. Except for Wade. I sang for hours, it seemed, and when I turned to find Wade, he was nowhere. One of the Jackaroos told me he'd been embarrassed by my singing, so he'd left. I must have sung okay because the band leader asked me to sing at the Jazz Convention, and I did. Though first, I had a row with Wade, who said, "If you sing at the Jazz Convention, then that's the end of us!"

I said, "Okay. But let me tell you. You! Or no one else will ever tell me what I should or shouldn't do!"

I don't know what it is with Wade. You'd think after having parents who were more than happy to put on a dancing show that he'd accept me singing in public. Oh well.

After my performance, the Bandleader invited me to join their Jazz Band. 'We have a great time traveling Australia.' He said.
However, they were mainly based at pubs along Victoria's Mornington Peninsula. I thought about it. For *one* minute. Then I said, "no, thank you."

I'd become a real bushy!

One hot, memorable summer night, the Conargo Pub bulged to the seams with thirsty patrons. However, one Jackaroo seemed more dehydrated than most and immediately demanded two jugs of beer! His order was thrown over the shoulder of a big truckie bruiser, who turned around and said, "wait, ya fuckin turn, mate!"

A fight erupted between the two, which ended up outside. Eventually, and before one of them was about to die, six-game men pulled the fighters apart. The truckie went back inside and calmly finished his jug of beer while the Jackaroo sped off in his Ute. I must add that the jackaroo was notorious for his short fuse.

Most men bought their beer in a jug at Lodgy's; it was the best Beer on earth, and a seven-ounce glass of beer amounted to one swallow for these thirsty bushies.

About thirty minutes later, the Jackaroo returned with his loaded shotgun and fired bullets through the bar window. He aimed high so as not to kill anyone. We assumed. He just wanted to show off who had the upper hand. I think. Bloody hell, I flew to the ground, as did everyone else. At the same time, an inebriated Lodgy sat perfectly still in his usual chair behind the bar and said in his beautifully spoken Queens English. "Who's letting off the fireworks? Oh, fuck them. I'm going to bed. Will one of you gentlemen put the till takings in this bag and place it under my pillow when you lock up. Here are the keys. Thank you." Lodgy then threw both items on the counter to nobody visible. We were all flat on the floor.

The next day the Police reported that they'd found a bullet hole resting where Lodgy *always* sat behind the bar!

He was a lucky bugger.

I stayed at Basil Clapton's for around eight months before I desired to try my hand at training racehorses. I looked in Melbourne newspapers for a Stable Hand position and saw an opening at Angus Arminasco's

Caulfield stables. I applied and got the job.

It was hard for me to leave Wade, but I was not ready to settle down, even though I did love him.

Angus Arminasco was a collar and tie trainer. We, the staff, would see him twice a day. Early morning at trackwork, looking splendid, then again at the afternoon feed up, still looking splendid. Angus was calm and pleasant, and he'd never avoid the questions I continuously fired at him. I'm exaggerating a little, but it came to a point where I thought he was evading me, so I laid off and just listened for any tidbits of knowledge he may divulge.

Then there was 'Roy the boy', Roy Higgins, who hailed from Deniliquin; Anguses' number one jockey. Roy and I had many discussions about his hometown, where I had been a Jillaroo, so we became good buddies. He taught me how to count time when riding horses in trackwork. Half pace – 17 seconds to the furlong. Three-quarter pace -15 seconds to the furlong. And working gallops were 13 seconds.
Roy was a gentleman, and I loved it when he'd ask me to make his breakfast, "half a cup of black tea, no sugar. Thank you, Doreen."

I had bacon and eggs every morning (poor Roy). I remained seven and a half stone. However, one day, I cooked rabbit stew for Roy. It was just after the old guy who'd worked with Angus for over thirty years began reminiscing about the rabbit stew his mum cooked, so I volunteered to match it. The old guy said, after the first mouthful, 'it's fairly good.' And winked. 'But nothing ever tastes as good as Mum's cookin.'

Roy disagreed and said my rabbit stew was the best he'd ever tasted! Whether it was or not, it made Roy happy. And me.

We, strappers cum track riders, shared a small communal kitchen and a basic bathroom, though we had our own tiny bedrooms. I survived. I was there to learn. One thing did bother me, though, especially after working at Merriola. The racehorses stayed in their boxes twenty-four-seven except for being ridden in the morning and then taken out for a ten-minute pick every afternoon. We'd lead two horses at a time. Each strapper had four horses to care for, so it was twice out and often became a nightmare. Imagine two fit racehorses raring to go and one skinny strapper trying to hang on to both horses who rarely picked a blade of grass. Especially when the wind whipped in, causing an old wooden fence to rattle and bang. It sat at the end of a narrow laneway, separating the racetrack. (Now, that is where I have begun my fifth novel, named, 'Wrong Side of the Fence.' )

So, I had another scathingly brilliant idea! There was one decent-sized round yard on Angus's property, plus loads of room to build six-day yards. Which meant, if done, it would give every horse at least ten minutes of playtime before we took them out for a pick of grass. I'd worked there for about two weeks when I took the initiative. I'd come back to work before start time, so I had time to bandage my horse's legs. This was to combat injuries if they kicked up in the round yard. After their playtime, the upside was that my horses never mucked up when I led them out for a pick.

The Forman (not a nice bloke) fumed when he discovered what I was doing. Common sense is the only sense I follow; to my mind, he had none. Therefore, I went to see Angus and told him what I was doing. He agreed that it was a good idea. So I offered him some advice.

"If I were you, Mr. Arminasco, I'd build six decent day yards. Over there." I said, pointing. "Then each horse could have a little freedom at allotted times. It would keep them calm and happier when we take them out for a pick."

"I'll think about it," said Angus. Then smartly closed the door and *probably* said, 'little up-start!'

Years later, I discovered that Angus had built the suggested yards.

Many years later, I had the pleasure of meeting with Roy Higgins. Wade and I had horses racing at Hawkesbury( it was well after Roy retired.) A crowd of admirers surrounded Roy, but he kept looking my way, seeming to remember me. So I approached and said cheekily. "Do you think you know me, Roy, or I'm a good sort?" He laughed. "A bit of both, I'd say."

I laughed, too, then went on to explain our past connection. Roy genuinely remembered me.

"Yes, of course! And that rabbit stew you made, Doreen, was the best. I'll never forget it because I had to pay to ride overweight the next day."

Now that was a memorable afternoon, catching up with Roy. What a great jockey Roy Higgins was, but even more - a great man.

# Chapter 13
## Volatile Marriage

While working for Angus Arminasco, Wade wrote and told me he'd found another girlfriend, or should I say *she'd* found him. It broke my heart, especially when I heard they were engaged.  Six months later, Wade phoned to say he was traveling around Australia with his sister, Joetta and Jim Wheel, his friend

"What happened to your fiancée?" I asked.

"Oh, we split up. Can I come and see you?"

Of course, the answer was, 'YES.'

Wade and I patched up our differences. He then went to a remote region of Western Australia, where he worked on the pipelines for 'Nelson Stud Welding, USA.' His father Herman was the managing director. Being American, I suppose, helped.

*Working on the pipeline in Western Australia. Wade on the right.*

We'd planned to marry, and Wade's substantial wage would give us a start in life, and it did, as Wade saved all his money. Later, we had two children, just as I'd predicted when first seeing Wade in the Conargo Pub!

*Lisa and Daniel are in their early thirties. Christmas at Windermere.*

I became Chief Instructor and District Commissioner at Chelsea Pony Club during our separation. It was there I met my dear friend, Margaret Mooney. It came about through my young second Cousin Wayne (Graham's son) joining the club with his mare Princess. Gee, I bet there are more horses named Princess than any other. Whatever we did, we laughed, including camping out with our horses and taking a trip back to Conargo Pub—attending important Pony Club meetings, which we found most amusing. Shame on us! I have never laughed as much with anyone in my entire life.

Margaret later lived with Wade and me for twelve months when we'd first moved to Windermere Farm Wilberforce NSW. Margaret had decided to take a gap year before going to Uni, where she intended to study English. Thank God she did, as she's been a great help, unjumbling my sentences.

Wade and I went to New South Wales to live after the pipeline job finished.

I always say, 'Wade and I have everything in common, but we argue about everything we have in common.'

I suppose it's still a volatile marriage. Nothing much has changed. However, I'm sure the many who have placed bets on us divorcing would have lost their money by now.

We went to a counsellor once. Not for OUR marriage guidance - though we should have. We had problems with our son Daniel after separating from his wife, Teona. After the counsellor had listened to our story, he said to Wade, 'I'll play a game with you. You pretend to be Daniel, and I'll be you. Okay?'

Wade agreed. However, after the counsellor asked several questions (pretending to be Wade), Wade couldn't handle being Daniel. Instead, he argued that he wouldn't say this or that to Daniel. The arguments kept them busy for a while until the frustrated counsellor yelled.

'WILL YOU JUST LISTEN TO ME!'

I laughed and said, "ALLELUIA!" That's what I've been telling him all my life!' When we finally left. Kicked out, I think. The counsellor said to me. "I know what's kept you two together all these years."

'And what's that?' I asked.

'Your sense of humour!' He was correct.

Teona, with their two children, Nicholas and Arianna, remained in the home Daniel built. That was a massive consolation as we became even closer. Teona has a wonderful sense of humour and is a loving mother and beloved family member.

I've lost count of how many times I've packed my bags intending to leave Wade. However, I remember one day being a little tired of doing so. Nevertheless, I still needed to get my point across, including packing my bags. *I'll just pretend*, I thought, yes, I'll pretend. So I dragged my heavy–empty suitcase across the kitchen floor with great effort, yelling.

"I'm leaving you, and I'm never coming back!"

To his surprise, Wade grabbed the suitcase and flung it easily up in the air. "You're not lea…You've got nothing in this case." He said, bewildered.

I laughed.

During another heated argument, I charged from room to room, collecting clothes from every cupboard and tossing them into a suitcase while Wade followed, trying to talk me into staying. Then suddenly, he said, "Christ, you've got clothes in every cupboard!"

I laughed.

Wade had gone to the races one sweltering day, and I stayed home to look after the horses. Due to the heat. When he returned, there was something insignificant I hadn't done, and he noticed.

I was busy bending over, treating our horses' feet with a mixture of Stockholm tar and oil. I stood up hot, tired, and sweating, listening to Wade's unreasonable load of shit until I'd had enough. So I swung the tin of tar around and around. I must say, Wade looked rather dapper in a white shirt with a red tie, grey trousers, and shiny black shoes. It was a shame to let go of the tin, which hit him square in the chest. I watched as tar oozed down his shirt, tie, and trousers, then dribbled over his shoes.

"Well, you'll just have to wash them!" Wade said indignantly and marched off.

Do you think I washed them? NO! I burned them all!

The weather can be boiling in Northwest Sydney, though most afternoons on Windermere Farm, a south-easterly breeze floats up from the Hawkesbury River, giving welcome relief. On one such day, I'd been out and about from 10 am to 4 pm, attending Wade's errands. As we did in the old days, I'd fetched horse feed from our ever-obliging Frank Robank, drove to the Hawkesbury vet Clinic collecting medicines, and nominated horses on handwritten forms I'd delivered to Hawkesbury Race Club. Among many other chores mapped out by Wade.

I'd left our home spotless. However, on my return, it looked like a herd of wild horses had run through it. Jennifer Davies, a young friend who worked with us, had decided to cook Crème Caramel, and she'd burnt every attempt in every saucepan I owned. Clients had visited, and as we do, Wade had offered them coffee, tea, or alcohol, accompanied with cake, cheese, biscuits, etc. The remains were everywhere. Cushions lay scattered around as if they'd had a pillow fight. Luncheon scraps sat on dishes covered in flies, given passage through the screen door that nobody had closed. I seethed!

Wade and the staff had finished their work in the barn, and horses were fed and happy in their stables. Morning feeds had been mixed, and the tack room was neat and clean. The temperature; still extremely hot. But not as hot as me! I rampaged through the barn, flinging saddles and bridles to the floor, tipping feed bins, and throwing horse rugs around, yelling!

'If you bastards ever leave my house like a pigsty again, I'll mess the barn up. Again!"

Ray Skinner, our apprentice jockey, turned the hose on me while saying. 'She's gone fuckin mad! She's gone fuckin mad!

Yes, I was mad. Therefore, Ray appropriately hosed me down like a mad dog, or I should say, bitch. I enjoyed the cool water. He did me a favour—bloody dill. Wade stood transfixed with his mouth open.

When I'd finished my destruction, I stormed off and drove Daniel and Lisa to Windsor, where we ate fish and chips on the banks of the Hawkesbury River. We returned home at nine-thirty pm when the temperature and I were much cooler. The kids loved it, and I relaxed.

I wrote a warning sign and left it on the fridge the next day.

'If you lot DON'T clean up YOUR mess in MY house, I will mess up the barn!'

Visitors would inevitably read the note, which remained on the fridge. They'd ask, 'what does that mean?'

Wade would say, 'please don't ask!'

*Jennifer Dawes, dear friend and the saucepan burner, with Wade.*
*I cannot remember the horse, but it obviously won.*

I must admit, after acknowledging my quick temper. The best compliment Wade has ever given me was when I asked him a question about the movie 'Indecent Proposal. The controversial subject was a popular talking point. So I asked Wade whether he would take a million dollars for me to sleep with another man. Wade thought for quite a while before he said.

"No, I wouldn't." Bless him. xx

I laughed, saying, 'well, if a woman offered me a million dollars to sleep with you. I'd take it!"

"You'd have to warn her. There are no refunds!"

Said my darling, Wade

\*

Back to Ray Skinner, our apprentice Jockey. Ray came to us, an illiterate teenager from Forbes. His parents held high hopes of Ray becoming a jockey, and we needed an apprentice. Our friend, and jockey, Clarrie Buckley, had heard about Ray's natural horse sense and his ability to ride. So Clarrie passed the information to us, and we signed Ray up. However, Ray needed to learn reading, writing, and arithmetic, or he would not be permitted a Jockey's license.

Robyn, a retired schoolteacher and Jennifer's mother, came to tutor Ray. But, on the odd occasion, she almost quit when Ray thought he knew more than Robyn. He'd argue with the tenacity of a Fox Terrier. For instance, Ray said to our four-year-old daughter Lisa, after he couldn't get something right, and she had made an innocent comment.

"Well, you think you're so smart, Lisa. I'll give you a SUM to do! SPELL Horse!" Lisa looked at him dumbfounded, and Robyn cried laughing while Ray said.

"I knew she couldn't do it. Smart arse kid!"

What Ray lacked in intellect, he gained with cunning.

He had trouble with his weight mainly due to his addiction to Tim -Tam biscuits! We were unaware of the stash he'd kept hidden under his bed. Wade, with concern, had witnessed Ray refusing to eat because he was trying to lose weight. It saddened Wade, as Ray was a well-above-average rider. So, Wade took him to the doctor, explaining that Ray needed a script for diet tablets. Sanorex, I think they were. At the same time, Wade experienced nervous dyspepsia owing to the pressure of maintaining his winning percentage. Our doctor had prescribed Wade, Serapax, which helped him relax and sleep. Not reading too well, Ray mistook his Sanorex with Serapax until Jennifer noticed.

"I find Ray asleep in the stables all the time." Jennifer said, "I've been mucking out the front shavings boxes, and when I return to the barn, he's snoring on the straw! I thought he might be allergic to straw. So I told him to do the shavings boxes, and he still fell asleep! There's something wrong with Ray."

We donned the Detective caps and soon understood Ray had

overdosed on the wrong tablets! He was taking the sleeping pills.

Unfortunately, Ray had bad habits deriving from his cunning nature. At first, I was impressed when he'd clean the stables as I, too, had been told by former bosses to stack the straw so high we needed to raise our knees to walk inside. Jennifer soon smelt a rat when very little soiled straw was piled on the heap, which eventually would be taken away by the local mushroom grower. Ray was simply spreading clean straw over the old straw. Cunning! No wonder the boxes stood sky high!

After Ray received his ticket to ride in races, we asked him to ride our best horse, Shamrock King, on a Saturday at Rosehill. A huge compliment to Ray, but we were confident he would ride Shamrock to instructions.

"Let him trail the field, Ray. But when you make a run in the home straight. Take Shamrock to the outside. Don't let the top jockeys coax you to take an inside run. Just stick to the outside fence. It's the only way Shamrock will win. He needs a clear run. Got it?" I asked.

"Yep, I got it!" said Ray determinedly.

Near the end of the race, the announcer called.

"And Shamrock King's pruning the roses down the outside fence! Ridden by the boy with his thumbnail dipped in tar!"

The famous Banjo Patterson phrase ran the Gauntlet. It appeared in all the Sunday papers to emphasize Ray's humble beginnings. Ray had also won the prize for 'ride of the day,' a giant bottle of Johnnie Walker Whisky, much to Wades' delight!

Later, Ray told us how Ronny Quinton had coaxed him to take the inside run.

"I'll let you in, Ray. Come on, boy! Said Ron. "But I said
No thanks!" Ray's face shone with pride.

On another occasion, when discussing our choice of jockey to ride Shamrock King. Part-owners Betty and Murray Evans voiced their concern about who to trust. Meaning, what jockey wouldn't pull Shamrock up for money? It was when Nobbling, plus taking bribes, were ubiquitous. I put a bid in for Ray.

"Ray wouldn't take money," I said. Then thinking about it. "Maybe he'd take Tim-Tams, though." We laughed.

I'm sorry to say. Ray went off the rails after finishing his time as an apprentice with us. Although I must give him sympathy as a con-man in the guise of another apprentice jockey duped Ray out of forty-five thousand dollars. They hit the road in Ray's car, which he'd purchased when the AJC reimbursed his allotted money. Ultimately, Ray's swindler left him destitute when the money ran out. One can only imagine what adventures they had.

We then heard that Ray was living with a group of Aboriginals. And sometime after that, we heard he'd married a wealthy businessman's mentally challenged daughter.

When Wade told me, he said. "I hope they don't have children!" I'm sure he meant it in a caring way. Dear Wadey.

Ray had an impediment in his speech. And years later, to my utter surprise, he turned up at Windermere with his new wife. I couldn't believe it. However, I did when Ray introduced her. "This is me, wife, Oreen." (I was Oreen, Ray could not pronounce Doreen).

The young woman smiled, stepped forward, and proffered her hand, "preased ta meet ya, Oreen." She said.

With a warm smile, I welcomed them in for a cup of tea. Well, what do you know? Ray and his wife had the same speech impediment. Amazing.

I don't know where Ray is now, but I hope he's okay.

\*

With the utmost respect, I must now tell of our dear friend, Don Jones. Don was a fourth-generation Wilberforcean, as we named anyone born in Wilberforce, at least two generations before. Don's father, Harold, had trained trotters (standardbreds) on Windermere Farm long before we came, and Harold was a constant fixture in the barn. Sitting back in his old, tattered cane chair, he kept us entertained, telling tales about the people who'd owned Windermere before Donald Daisley. Some stories were hilarious. At that time, Harold had one horse in training, and when it was ready to race, he couldn't think of a name. I think it was Margaret who suggested 'Pigs,' a play on pigs trotters. Harold decided the horse may not be good enough to race but named him anyway. I suggested he register him as 'Pigs Might Fly.' And so it was.

Harold introduced us to his son Don, who married Nora, another Wilberforcean. They had three children, all of whom became endeared to us. Don drove a truck that delivered Brewer's grain (leftovers from Beer making), which he'd sell to local dairies.

Later down the track, we stood a Standard Bred Stallion on Windermere, named 'Legality.' Legality had a substantiated record of being a man-eater. He was one of the most frightening horses I have ever known. Legality would walk on his hind legs and roar like a lion when he approached our terrified broodmares, and they'd throw themselves on the ground or kick out with back hooves until they were exhausted. I'm sure most mares thought he was about to murder them, not serve them.

Then our saviour arrived. Don Jones suggested he leave a small amount of Brewers Grain. "It'll help wid the feed bill and keep em calm. Brody, good stuff, this Bwewers Gwain!" He, Like Ray Skinner, had an impediment in his speech. Bless him.

And Don was right. Legality and his harem became constantly inebriated after scoffing down the B. Grain like a crew of wharfies on a Friday afternoon. I'm sure you get the picture. After that, we had no trouble with Legality or his ladies, as they were all drunk.

Don decided he'd like to earn a little extra money working part-time with us, and we welcomed him. He mainly bred and trained Greyhounds apart from driving the B. Grain truck. His Greyhounds, I must add, he treated as well as he did his own family.

Don would have the occasional bet on our horses, but there was one he could never catch. Don never bet on Kutzbah when he won - only when he lost. "Dat Hutzbah' s a broddy fustwatin orse!" He'd say.

We owned an ugly green horse truck, the only one we could afford at the time. I remember the day vividly when Don sat in the passenger seat; he and Wade were going to Rosehill Races with Kutzbah, who was fit and ready to take on a top race field. Don called out to me as they drove slowly down the driveway. "If dat Broddy Hutzbah wins taday, I'll be shitin on the woof all d' way home!"

The vision had me laughing all day. Sadly we were not blessed to see the sight even though Kutzbah did win!

I could go on and on with endearing Don and Nora stories.

Oh, what the heck. Just one more.

I was a constant weight watcher, and Nora, who was as round as she was high, asked me how I kept so slim. Apart from not eating greasy chips as Nora did while sitting at her kitchen table reading Mills and Boons books, which I didn't say. I told her about Weight Watchers.

"Oh, really, it does sound good." Said Nora. "After all, I do have a few pounds to lose." Bless her.

I talked her into buying a new dress that would flow over her lumps and bumps. Don hated the dress, "I rike t' see her curbs." He said.

After four weeks of going to Weight Watchers, Wade asked Don if he'd noticed any difference in Nora's weight.

"Broddy oaf. She's rost it in her pwivate parts." He said with a wink and a nudge.

No disrespect meant—just a loving memory.

# Chapter 14
## Muddled Memories, As Most Chapters Are!

Before our Windermere days, we'd leased a ten-acre property in Kellyville. An overgrown garden surrounded the two-bedroom cottage. Nevertheless, it had great promise, so I delivered it back to its former grandeur with a green thumb and hard work. The resurrected garden and newly painted home astonished the owners. And after meeting them, we invited them for dinner and to collect the rent -every fortnight. They were a childless couple who enjoyed cuddling baby Daniel. We'd built the property up by also adding new fences and stables. When established, we pre-trained Racehorses for Mr. Joyce, a long-time friend of Wade's.

We'd purchase undernourished ponies and feed them up. I'd then educate them into show ponies, and after they'd earned enough points at smaller shows, they were eligible for The Royal Show. That's when we'd sell them for good money.

It was a sad day when we left our home at Kellyville and our lovely new friends. But a much better offer came our way. Dick Evans, who worked for Wade's dad, Herman, at Nelson Stud Welding, introduced us to his friend, Donald Daisley.

Donald, since 1960, had owned a sixty-acre property, Windermere Farm, situated on the banks of the Hawkesbury River. Donald's second son, Ross, had tried his hand at running the property as a Dairy Farm, but the handsome young man decided it was not for him. Therefore, Donald dismantled the dairy and hired a personal trainer to train his Standardbred horses (Pacers). When no luck came Donald's way, he decided to turn the farm into a Stud Farm for Standard Bred's.

Unfortunately, the Stud was unsuccessful, so the property stood empty after the stud ceased functioning. Therefore, the paddocks amassed with three-foot-high improved pastures. With no stock to eat it down, Donald purchased around twenty ponies to do the job. When Dick Evan's told us about Donald wishing to sell a few ponies, we showed interest.

One Saturday morning, Donald and Dick collected us from our Kellyville Cottage and drove us to Windermere Farm, Wilberforce. Once again – I had a premonition. I knew we'd live and train racehorses there. Donald took an immediate liking to Wade and me and offered us a home in return for looking after the farm. I jumped at the offer, but Wade felt concerned about the River flooding and how he could get to work.

"Well," I said, "you stay at Kellyville, and I'll live here and train racehorses!"

I liken myself to Yogi Bear and Wade to Booboo Bear.

The optimist and the pessimist! As Yogi would say, 'Let's go get the picnic basket Booboo!" And Booboo would say, "Oh no, Yogi, we'll get into trouble if the ranger catches us."

Just after we moved to Windermere, a significant flood hit! I shut my mouth and prayed that Wade would not leave once the water subsided!

I still loved him.

Not long after we'd moved to Windermere, Wade was retrenched from Nelson Stud Welding. One disgruntled staff member said it was unfair for the Director to hire family members. The company's American CEO agreed, so Wade left and went to work for his mother, Joyce. Her correct name - is Doreen Joyce. She managed an Opal shop at Chatswood for a lovely Korean - American couple, Toni and George Owens. They excavated opals at Cooper Pedy before polishing them to sell in the shop.

Now I'll tell you something remarkable. We are the only Slinkard family in Australia. Surely it must be a world record to have a unique surname throughout an entire country. And to think my mother-in-law's name was Doreen Slinkard is even more extraordinary. I recently Googled the surname Slinkard, which appears to be one of the first families to settle in England. Assuming the name initially came from the Netherlands around fifteen hundred when the Vikings first secured land in Great Britain. Slinkard has become a well-known surname in America, and many notable people share the name, including Politician Mary Lou Slinkard, born in 1943, four years before Wade.

I didn't work outside Windermere; I stayed home and trained the ponies we'd bought specially to make money – and we did – lots!

Both Wade and I had a good eye for a horse, and we'd heard on the grapevine that a truckload of registered Australian saddle ponies had just arrived at the Rouse Hill knackery. After suffering from drought and a tick plague in far North Queensland, they appeared in terrible condition.

However, one gelding stood out, having perfect confirmation, a pretty head, and a deep chestnut coat, not that there was much left. Queensland itch had taken most away. We'd brought a saddle and bridle and asked permission to ride the pony through his paces.

Later I said to Wade. "This is the best pony I've ever ridden,"

The pony was extremely poor in condition, but we knew he'd furnish into a beauty. We named him 'City Lights. A name Wade had always liked. We paid considerable money back then -$200. Well, it was to us.

But when ready, 'City Lights' repaid us by winning every Show Ring event we entered him in, including many champions and supreme champion rosettes.

*At Castle Hill Show, me riding Corioole in his show debut. He became Barastoc Pony of the Year after furnishing into an even better-looking pony.*

After a couple of years, we sold 'Little Red;' (we'd nicknamed him) for $5000 to the Hooley sisters, Tania, and Margaret, who re-named him, Corioole. They took him to the Royal Sydney Easter show, which

I'd already qualified him for, as was our aim when buying potential show ponies or educating hacks.

Corioole had a bad habit of shaking his head when I asked him to halt. Eventually, I solved this problem by taking pressure off the bit straight after stopping him. Tania must have forgotten the trick.

Sadly, in the final workout at the Royal, Corioole shook his head, preventing him from being awarded The Supreme Champion Pony over the all-time winner, 'Baby Doll.' 1975.

The Hooleys then sold Corioole for big money to our friend and horseman extraordinaire, Tommy Loy.

Tommy purchased Corioole for his teenage daughter Kimmy, and within six months, they'd won almost all their events around Victoria, including the Royal Melbourne Champion Pony. Tommy then took Corioole to Western Australia and entered him in Barastoc Pony of the year. It is the piece d 'resistance for Show ponies, who, if they win, are crowned the best pony in Australia, possibly the world. Corioole won, and Tom was offered a ridiculous amount of money. $25000. Corioole was not a child's pony; he could be a devil sometimes. Tom explained this to the would-be buyer. Who said.

"I'll pay anything you ask. I want my daughter to have the best pony in the land."

Tommy tried to convince him that Corioole was not suitable for his daughter. But the man insisted.

"I'll return the pony if he isn't right. And you won't have to pay back the $25,000."

It was a heap of money in the late seventies. Plus, it was an offer too good to refuse!

As you've guessed, Corioole was shipped back to Tommy about six months later with no cash refund required.

Corioole was unbeatable, so Tommy retired him, as he felt sorry for the children who owned lessor ponies. Corioole then enjoyed his retirement with Tommy. Not bad for a pony doomed for the glue pot! Remember the champion from the knackery 1961?

Tommy owned a small property, 'Pretty Pines,' not far out of Deniliquin, where he trained a few racehorses and filled the rest of his day as a general roustabout cum Jackaroo. He was a top horseman and coached his daughter Kimmy to be an A Grade show jump rider. Kimmy now trains racehorses in Queensland.

Tommy and his wife Mary are long gone from this world - though never forgotten. I would need to write another book about all their achievements, but I must say that Mary was captain of the Australian Ladies cricket team in 1963. Her maiden name was Mary Allitt. The team travelled to England to fight for the world championship. Before playing for the Ashes, Australia won nine out of seventeen games around England. Before England won the third and final test, the first two tests were a tie. To be Captain of such an elite cricket team is something to be proud of; however, Mary took no comfort in pride.

Tommy, later in life, wrote his memoirs, 'Down by The River.' It's a moving story about the hardship of growing up with twelve siblings, all living in a tent by the Edward River. Tom's memoirs take us on a journey to his later life and include many achievements. A must-read - if it's still available. Tommy was a respected gentleman and admired by all who knew him, as was Mary, a fine lady. Besides being an integral community member, Mary was an invaluable leader and riding instructor at the Deniliquin Pony Club.

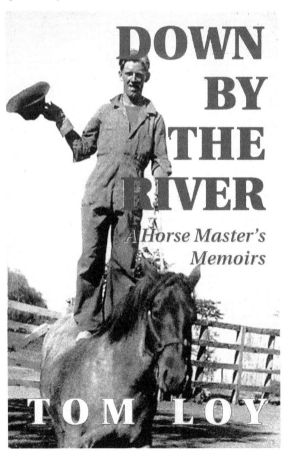

*Dear Mary Loy. It was the last time I saw her at her home in Deniliquin, and she was delighted to receive one of my children's books.*

# Chapter 15
## Trainers Licence

Windermere Farm is a sixty-acre property and boasts the best soil around, as do most Hawkesbury River properties. It sports a half-mile sand track next to the river where we worked our horses. Its undulating paddocks are perfect for building muscles and stamina, and lush pasture improved vegetation offered an ideal diet for our four-legged friends. An enormous heritage barn holds such an incredible atmosphere that you can feel the presence of horses and people long past.

The barn leaks - and we patch it. It leans - and we push it up. Never will it be demolished, we hope. It's a treasure. Not only did it house our horses, but it also gave cover to our saddling up, etc.

Including some memorable parties in 'ye old barn.' My fortieth birthday, to name one! The theme? 'A Hippy Happening.' One hundred and sixty people adorned in kaftans, love beads, and wigs. Friends and relatives, aged eight to eighty, partied the night away to the sound of Janis Joplin, Bob Dylan, and the Rolling Stones dancing under a disco ball. We decorated the barn walls with signs painted on calico, Ban the Bomb! Burn the Bra! Make love, not war! Peace, brother, etc. We should take heed today!

I'd like to stay at that party for another chapter, though I dare not, for recrimination may follow! Although I must add, and I won't name names. A mother phoned the morning after, looking for her thirty-five-year-old daughter, who by all accounts had an incredibly romantic time with a young man in a nearby tent where my younger cousins *tried* to sleep.

The mother said. "She has to work today, and she'll be too tired."
My mum Betty, knowing the story, replied.
"Yes, you're right. She's absolutely rooted!"
Good on you, Mum, never short of a quip.

*

*My family at my Hippy Happening party.*

I remember the day I said to Wade, "Windermere is perfect for training racehorses." Alas, Booboo bear was reluctant to accept the idea of becoming a Racehorse Trainer. 'It's too risky,' he said.

The following sentence changed his mind.

"Okay. Then I'll get my license, and *you* can help me!"

He argued. "They won't give a woman a trainer's license!'

I think he was right, but I came back.

"I'll move heaven and earth to get it. You mark my words!"

Wade knew I'd give it my best shot, so he relented.

How naive we were.

Wade made an appointment to meet with the Committee of the AJC, albeit with good references, but having no horses to train and not enough money to set up a training business, Wade was denied his Licence.

Not to be beaten! I had an idea. Hopefully, if we pre-trained a big team, we'd be given a few cast-off horses that weren't good enough to win in the city. Wade could then re-apply for his Trainers Licence.

We had a meeting with Donald about using Windermere to spell racehorses plus pre-train. Thanks to dear Donald, who paid to have Spelling yards built, everything came to fruition, and we acquired many horses to pre-train. Plus, we purchased ponies and horses to sell and made more money. No free lunches, they say. So Donald asked that we pay rent. Understandably.

We were *terribly busy*! Wade decided it was near impossible to travel so far to work. Remember Chatswood, the Opal shop? He needed to find a local job, preferably shift work, so that he could help with the horses. He secured a position as a barman at Windsor Golf Club. There, he endeared himself to the local golfers, who laughed when Wade would say through clenched teeth, "I can't serve you now. The race is about to start!" And he'd turn the radio up, so they could all listen.

No one complained; instead, they formed a punting club with Wade, the tipster. It was a great success, and they promised Wade that when he obtained his trainer's license, they'd purchase a yearling for him to train. Very funny. Although some were true to their word, namely Sam Ghantous, Wassim Gazal, and his father Maurice, a true gentleman and loyal friend.

I was flat out working on the farm, having a toddling Daniel to care for, promising show horses to ride, plus pre-training racehorses. Not to forget caring for the horses who came to spell. Thank God Margaret decided to take a gap year before she started Uni. She brought her pony, Prina, a piebald mare, smart as a whip. If Margaret whistled, the pony would come running. Sometimes Prina would be head down grazing when Margaret called, "stand Prina.' Margaret would then take a few running steps and leap from behind onto Prina's back. What did they call that in Physical Education? Mounting the horse – wooden, of course, I could never do it - no spring in this little black duck. Margaret rode Prina bareback using a hackamore bridle (no bit in her mouth). She looked like a stolen white child riding her Indian pony.

*Margaret Mooney and me at Chelsea Pony Club.*

We experienced many floods together, which could be interesting, as the Farm became islanated. I know that's not a registered word, as Race Caller extraordinaire John Tapp pointed out when interviewing us. However, if you lived there in flood time, you'd appreciate Windermere Farm becomes an island. The main house and the cottage are both built high on a ridge. So are the stables – yards - and 'ye old barn.' So, before the property flooded entirely, we'd bring the horses up from the river paddock and then push them up and over the small bridge covering a natural watercourse. Sometimes we were too late. (flash floods happen when they let the water go out of Warragamba Dam, maintaining a safe level). If we didn't make it down to the back paddock and back over our small bridge in time, we'd herd the horses around and through the next-door property, bringing them out onto Wilberforce road, then we'd turn right to get them home the long way. This happened on more than a few occasions.

And one such time, Wade stood looking at the torrent of muddy water gushing over the bridge after a flash flood. He wore a heavy Dryazabone coat, covering many layers of clothes, gumboots, and an Akubra hat. A few of us, including Mark Tolhurst, our friend and next-door neighbour, had followed Wade down to see if we could push the horses through the floodwater.

"I'll test the water, see how deep it is," said Wade.

'It's a pity he isn't related to Jesus,' I said after Wade took two steps, missed the bridge, and sunk into the abyss.

His Akubra hat was the only thing visible. I panicked when Wade didn't come up straight away, but Mark said. "Don't worry. He'll come up - soon."

We waited about a minute - two-three, then just as I was about to dive in, out came a soaking - bedraggled Wadey.

"I'll just go and get changed." He said calmly as he sloshed past. Mark and I looked at each other and burst out laughing.

We then decided to herd the horses the long way around.

Many *not* desirable items came our way in the floodwaters. I'll never forget opening the lid on a small iron drum and finding a load of shit! Lovely! I should have known better! Although, we did score some good things, like a fabulous antique dining table. Chairs of many descriptions, plus a beautiful Jersey cow mooing her lungs out until she found safe ground on Windermere. She then let out an audible sigh of relief. We named her Moo. Old copper kettles, tools, and mattresses landed or went floating by. One memorable day, we found a tightly lidded wine barrel. When we pried it open, we found it filled with pornographic books.

"Burn them immediately!" I said.

But Mark's wife and friend, Jane, giggled along with Wade. Both agreed they should keep the books to see if anyone came looking for them. And they did. Two shady characters knocked on the door a couple of months later and asked Wade if he'd found a barrel of books.

'They floated away in the flood,' one degenerate drooled out.

Oh really, was there a flood? You F whit! I would have said.

Plus, given him a piece of my mind. But fortunately for them, I was not home. Wade simply showed them where to find the barrel. Not funny! But very funny. (I'm not a prude.)

While we still enjoyed the pleasure of Margaret's company, she and Wade were walking along the driveway towards the hay shed when a man, completely nude apart from being scantily covered in river weed, strolled past. 'He seemed surreal,' they said, 'but he did say hello.'

To which they answered, 'hello.'

What else do you say to a madman?

Wade hurried inside and phoned the Police to report what they'd just seen. Funny; no one else in the district had seen the strange - nude man. Or the same apparition? Though I do believe them because, after all these years, they still bring it up in conversation. Maybe it wasn't river weed? But the other kind. You know.

Horses soon arrived by the truckload! A bit exaggerated. Nevertheless, many new clients from the city were drawn to our advertisement and trusted us to pre-train and spell their horses at Windermere. They'd like to drive out of town and see their horses as city folk do. And as country folk do, we'd offer them a cuppa. Being constantly busy (with horses coming first,) we'd run out of milk on the day four gentlemen arrived. That's when 'Moo, the flood cow,' came in handy. Margaret tied Moo to the fence and milked her in front of the clients. Hey, presto! We had milk in our coffee. The city slickers were awestruck, to the point where they had to take a jar of Moo's milk home for show and tell.

Wade's endeavour to secure a trainer's license looked even more promising the day Stan Evans arrived -unannounced.

'I was just out for a drive and noticed your sign on the corner."
Stan said. "It says you have paddocks to spell racehorses, and you pre-
train. Is that right?'

'It certainly is,' we both replied before offering him a cup of tea
or something more robust.

We gave Stan a guided tour of the property, including the stables
and the training track. He was impressed, and probably coming from
New Zealand and knowing how the Kiwis train, Stan had visions of his
horses living and being trained similarly.

That day began a long and fruitful association with Stan Evans
in the mid-seventies. He grasped how hard it was to obtain a Trainer's
license, especially without having a few horses to train. So he offered
Wade his first horse to train, named 'Instant.' Stan also suggested we
accompany him to the Inglis Summer Sale and purchase a yearling
together. We did and bought a young colt by Lunchtime out of Bridal
Day. We named him 'Smorgasbord.' Appropriate?

At the same time, Stan's long-time trainer Harold Riley, also from
New Zealand, was forced to retire a young filly that Stan had purchased
at the Adelaide Yearling Sales. Her knees, after little training, had shown
weakness and therefore x-rayed. The photos revealed her knees were in
no condition to race. She had been bred and sold by the Brown family
from the notable 'Nurrung Stud.' South Australia. Stan made a deal with
the Browns to return the filly in exchange for a suitable type of yearling.
He simply wanted a racehorse, and seeing the filly was well-bred, the
Browns may like her back to breed. So the Browns sent Stan a yearling
colt - passed in at the Adelaide yearling sales—considered too small.

Harold Riley was also at the point of retiring. So to our delight,
Stan gave us the Brown's yearling colt by Boysie Boy out of Aslef
to train. Stan named him 'Cheval De Volee,' meaning horse of flight.
Standing only 14.2 hands, Cheval looked more like a Galloway show
pony than a racehorse. However, the Browns assured us that the smaller
the Boysie Boys were, the better racehorse they made.

"Well, this little fella should be a champion!' I said.

While working our pre-trainers at Hawkesbury track, Wade
struck up a friendship with jockey cum trainer Clarrie Buckley, and he
helped Wade plan for his future training career. After viewing our two
yearlings, Cheval and Smorgasbord, Clarrie offered to break them in.
Later he proclaimed. 'I reckon you have two outstanding racehorses,

Wade.'

Both horses later proved Clarrie right. It didn't take long for him to offer Wade a deal.

'You train them, Wade, and I'll get my jockeys license back.'

And so it happened; we became close friends with Clarrie. Every night before a race, he'd come to discuss the tactics, and Wade would have the scotch whisky ready. Together, and in all seriousness, they'd try to fathom the speed map. Funny because Cheval and Smorgasbord led in every race. Later in the night, Wade would pick up an inebriated Clarrie and lay him on the spare bed. When we woke, Clarrie was gone, and Wade would later find him riding work at Hawkesbury Racetrack, none the worse for wear. A tough contender, our Clarrie, but he has a heart of gold.

*Clarrie Buckley riding Cheval De Vollee. Painting by Ross Daisley.*

\*

I worked a few evenings a week at the Tourmaline Hotel, Magrath's Hill, where Horse Trainer Tom Sewell lived on the Pub's acreage. He was also a part-owner of the Tourmaline Hotel. And one evening, not long after Wade had struck up the deal with Clarrie Buckley, I overheard Tom complaining about a new bloke who'd almost brought his good horse down because he was slow cantering his horse on the fast track. I knew who that was, so I apologized to Tom, which he accepted with grace, as was his nature. Little did I know then that Tom would become a valued friend and client some forty years later.

Of course, with a few good horses to train, Wade received his Trainers Licence, and Clarrie returned to being a Jockey. Wade soon trained Cheval De Volee to win the Tiny Tot Stakes at Rosehill. It was Chevy's s first start in a race.' He went on to be among the top ten two-year-olds in Australasia.

'Smorgasbord,' however, had problems too numerous to count. Therefore his racing career was short-lived. But his most memorable win was The Quicksilver 2 yr. Old Stakes at Hawkesbury. Hc raced six wide in a top-class field and won by four lengths.

Smorgasbord then contended a listed two-year-old race at Wyong. Clarrie was suffering from boils down the inside of his legs. An excruciating situation, especially if riding in a race, which Clarrie insisted on doing. Smorgasbord duly won, and after passing the winning post, Clarrie collapsed off the horse. From standing up cheering in the grandstand, I ran down the steps and weaved my way under and over fences to be at Clarrie's side within a minute. He was awake but groaning in agony, clutching his inner legs. Feeling relieved that Clarrie was still alive, my sense of humour kicked in.

"Who do you think you are, Clarrie. National Velvet?"

"Oh, don't make me laugh, Dor," He said, laughing and moaning simultaneously.

Yes, he's bloody tough, alright.

# Chapter 16
## Our Racehorses

After a long and enjoyable training career, it would take another two books to write about all the talented horses we've trained, and each horse has a story, be it funny or sad. However, I shall tell some of the most memorable stories beginning when we flew to Adelaide yearling sales. Cheval was reigning supreme, and after being bred and sold in South Australia, Cheval was a bit of a hero there. And we were minor celebrities.

While looking for a special yearling to buy in the viewing stand, I listened to an old fellow sitting next to me reeling off who - was - who with the yearlings on offer. Plus, which one would not stand up because of different faults, and which yearling came from honest and talented stock. I thought he was talking to the bloke next to him, but when that fellow got up and walked away, he kept on with his outspoken spiel. So I asked him, "how do you know so much about the horses in the ring?"

He told me he'd been breeding racehorses most of his life and held incisive knowledge about S.A's bloodlines.

He then offered his name, 'Arthur Smith,' along with a sandwich.

'I grew the beef myself.' Arthur said with pride, 'and the wife pickled it. Oh yes, and her fruit chutney would win at the Royal show!'

How could I knock back a sandwich with such a credential?

I needed to find the Lady's room a little while later, so I introduced Arthur to Wade. On my return, Wade, on Arthur's advice, had bought a magnificent filly by 'Boysie Boy.' The same sire as Cheval De Volee.

'She's a bit straight up and down," said Arthur. "but don't worry, her mum was too, and she stayed sound. Yep, a real honest mare she was. And I reckon this filly will be better because the mare's a good nick with the stallion. This Filly should be a cracker!" Arthur finished with authority.

We said goodbye to Arthur with the promise to keep in touch and inform him how the Boysie Boy filly was going, which I did faithfully. But before I tell you one of the highs and lowest of lows we have ever experienced in racing, I must explain what a character our darling Arthur was.

He was up before dawn seven days a week and worked until sundown on his dairy farm in Meadows, which also homed his thoroughbred yearlings plus a large herd of cattle. Later, when meeting his son, Ken, and his wife Helen, they told us about Arthur's enigmas. Even after a long hard day at work, Arthur was never tired when he jumped into bed with his wife, if you know what I mean.

We'd write to each other regularly, though I phoned him when my last letter was unanswered, and Mrs. Smith answered. 'I'm so sorry, Doreen, but Arthur has had a terrible accident. He's been run over by a tractor.'

'My God, is he dead?' I asked in shock.

'Oh, no dear, he's in hospital. He asked me to phone you and let you know, but I've been very busy and forgot. I am so sorry. Please forgive me.'

Of course, I did when I got over the shock.

'How is he now?' I asked.

'Well, he must be alright because he's up to his old tricks.'

'And what are his old tricks?' I asked.

'Chasing the nurses around the hospital dear and pinching them on the bottom.' She said with a giggle.

*Our dear friends Ken and Helen Smith from South Australia.*

Ken, Arthur's son, could never outrun his father to work no matter how hard he tried. Arthur would always be waiting for him, no matter what the time.

"The days half gone, son!" Arthur would say.

One morning, around four o'clock and well before dawn, Ken thought he'd wait in the work ute and say the same to Arthur.

"The days half gone, Dad."

Never to be caught napping, Arthur was already in the ute.

"Would you like a cup of tea, Son?" Arthur asked with a sly smile, and the thermos tilted.

Funny old bugger he was. God rest his soul

We named the beautiful filly, purchased on Arthur's advice, 'Belle Pouliche.' French for 'beautiful filly.' She developed into an honest, classy racehorse. We syndicated her, and the owners, including Ross and Peter Daisley, Donald's sons, were treated to many great wins.

There was only one way to ride Belle Pouliche, letting her settle back in the field. If you gave her a clear passage in the straight, I think she'd match it with Bernborough. Sometimes she'd be running last, especially in a fast run race. Racing the way she did, we thought it a good idea to see if Belle would stay, especially after her 1900mt win at Canterbury. So, we trained her for the Oaks at Randwick. Peter Cook rode her and told us later how pleased he was with her effort in running a close sixth, particularly after being afforded no luck in running.

Belle Pouliche had subsequently earned the right to run in the 2800mt Saint Ledger, a race Peter Cook said she could win easily.

Excitement was fever pitch in the Grandstand when Peter Cook rode Belle to the front in the home straight. She was doing it easily when Peter looked behind to see her competition struggling. YES! Belle Pouliche was going to win The Saint Ledger! No doubt about it!

Then tragedy struck. Halfway down the straight, Belle put her foot in a hole and snapped her leg. I cannot explain how devastating it was to see this beautiful-natured, honest horse try powerlessly to stand after she'd fallen. Peter Cook returned to scale with tears gushing. He was unable to talk.

We later received condolences like we'd lost one of our family members. It felt just as bad. Sometimes you can be lucky enough to own such an endearing Racehorse, and they're like good people who never stop trying.

Now a funny tale to lighten the reverie. Shamrock King, we purchased from our good friends Ron and Val Langsford, who resided in Kumeu, New Zealand's North Island. Stan Evans had known Ron and Val for many years and first introduced them to us. They had bred and trained many top horses; 'Isle of Man' was one. And, of course, 'Shamrock King.'

They would stay with us at the farm whenever they brought a horse to race in Australia. And one day, we accompanied Val and Ron to watch 'Isle of Man' win the Canterbury Guineas. The celebrations lasted for days until they flew home to New Zealand!

*Off to the races with Ron Lagsford left of me, Val right,*
*and their next door neighour from Kumu, New Zealand.*

Shamrock King was a real character, but unfortunately, he had soundness problems deriving from flat feet. It began a chain reaction, causing other complications, which inhibited his performance in what would have been a long and fruitful racing career. His stable name was Wally, and if a horse could make you laugh, he would. One of his tricks was to unlock his stable door and walk outside to graze around the barn. He'd stroll back into his stable and smile if he heard you coming. I kid you not.

Shamrock's first start was a Saturday race at Randwick. That gives you a clue to how good we thought him to be. On returning to scale, his Jockey, Ronnie Quinton, said, 'I think you've got a damn good horse Wade; he just needs gelding, plus give him time to mature.' the speed Shamrock showed when he tried to catch the filly in front of him was phenomenal!" Ron laughed as he walked away.

Shamrock was gelded, and then he rested in one of our lush, shady paddocks for twelve weeks. He returned to win a string of good races, including a Group 2 race, and he was also Group placed. Shamrock was such a promising stayer that we nominated him for the Melbourne Cup. Twice! However, the problems deriving from his flat feet kept him from starting in the MC. Even though we did employ the best farrier around, Albert O'cass, who tried everything to overcome Shamrock's feet problem. We were lucky to have a make-do swimming channel on the next-door property, and it did help. Albert had also suggested swimming.

The day remains vivid when Shamrock King won the 2400mtr Mannion Cup 1978. Due to torrential rain, the races were postponed from Saturday to Monday. Shamrock had been the fourth emergency but secured a run due to numerous scratching's. Shamrock was a mudlark! Yippee!

On the Monday morning of the race, I'd parked our car behind a small truck outside our local Post Office. I walked inside to collect the mail, and the truck driver passed me on his way out. He nodded, 'gidday.'

Next, I heard a crash and looked out the window to see he'd reversed his truck into our car. He was irate, ranting, and raving. I walked outside to inspect the damage, and he yelled, "you've parked too close to the curb! You're illegally parked!" I was speechless. Unusual for me.

He phoned the Police, and they came.

The younger Constable asked our names, then smiled, 'are you Wade Slinkard's wife?'

'Yes,' I said.

'Well, we have a punters club, and we've made a heap of money on his horses!"

The truck driver looked defeated, obviously with the familiarity surrounding him. So, I tried to brighten the predicament.

"I'll give you all a tip,' I said, looking directly at Mr truck driver, 'if you put your money on Shamrock King today in the Mannion Cup, I reckon he'll win, and it will solve all your problems!'

The Policeman wrote it down, 'you seem confident, Doreen,' he said, eyes remaining on the paper.

"I am because Shamrock loves the mud, and he's working fantastic."

Mr Truckie became even more agitated. "What are ya gonna do about her. She's illegally parked!" He said, poking his finger at me.

The young Constable shook his head, then paced out the line to the corner from where I had parked. Keep in mind that my car had shifted due to the inertia of the bang. However, it was still within the boundary—poor Mr truck driver. I waved him goodbye and yelled, 'don't forget! Back Shamrock King! He'll be big odds, and you'll ...... (What Mr Truckie, I'm sure, did not hear) 'have enough money to pay for the damage!'

*My cousin Betty and me at Rosehill races on one of her many visits.*

Our Vet, Alan MacKay, was a gregarious and clever man. He was at Rosehill on the day and told me in his Scottish brogue. 'You know there are only three mud runners in this field, Shamrock King, Star Dynasty, and Vivartchie. You should take that trifecta.'

'You're right,' I said.

But it was the old days, no money machines at the races, and I hadn't had time to go to the bank because of the hold-up with the accident. Therefore, as mothers do, I added up what I had in my purse to buy something for dinner. Not enough left over for a $6 trifecta, plus have an each-way bet. So, I took a standout quinella with Shamrock to win, and Allan's tips to run second or third = $3. Two dollars to spare on another bet, so I went all out and backed Shamrock to win! Five dollars in total. Bloody idiot! What would a dollar buy!

We settled in the trainer's stand and directly behind us sat Bart Cummings, his son, Anthony, and the best sports journalist ever (in my opinion), Bert Lilly. The barriers sprung open with Shamrock, as usual, running last. BUT! With his incredible length of stride in the home straight, Shamrock moved outside the field and gobbled up his opposition in what seemed like four bounds to win by a neck! While this scene unfolded, I stood against etiquette and screamed, 'Go, Wally! Go, Wally, go, Wally, go! He WON!" I yelled.

Bert Lilly and Bart laughed, with Bert saying, 'well, at least we all know who Wally is now!'

Wally had won at odds of $200 to $1!

Alan MacKay shook me like a rag doll repeating, 'YOU GOT IT! YOU GOT IT!

"Yes! Wally won!" I cried.

"No! I mean, you got the trifecta!"

"No, I just got the quinella and had $2 to win.

He shook me again, "you silly woman, I told you to have the trifecta."

I simply laughed. I was utterly overcome with joy and elation; I didn't care who said what. We'd won!

But why didn't Alan take the Trifecta? Silly bugger.

Bart Cummings was still laughing at our pantomime when I turned to say. 'Shamrock could win the Melbourne Cup! What do you reckon, Bart?"

He replied with a broad smile. "I hope he does, Doreen."

141

Now the bad news. The TAB, off course, had broken down just before Shamrock raced, causing heartbreak to some of our dearest friends. Including the young policeman, who phoned me the following day to inform me the accident had been sorted.

'Plus,' he said. "I had the most frustrating day ever. I was in line at the TAB, with $100 ready to place $50 each way on Shamrock, then the TAB broke down. I stood feeling helpless watching Shamrock win! I'm telling you, it was torture!"

Of course, I had to ask. 'Don't you know any SP Bookies?'

And to this day, I still kick myself. For one more dollar outlaid, I would have had the only winning trifecta ticket, which paid, Vivarchie, Star Dynasty, and *any other horse* fifty thousand dollars! I would have scooped the pool. Who knows what it may have paid - a million$ or more?

So many wonderful horses now gallop into mind, but I'll try only to choose the standouts. I don't want to bore you. I simply want to entertain with what has been the most intriguing, rewarding, and sometimes heartbreaking of all professions.

Kutzbah was a strong-minded horse. The word should be spelt Chutzpah. (I'm pleased I'm not the only one who can't spell.) In Yiddish, it means intestinal fortitude, audacity, courage, etc.

With a smile on his face, Wade will never forget the day he stood alongside friend and client Ross Daisley, plus others on a cold rainy day in New Zealand, to discuss the purchase price of the then two-year-old Kutzbah. This New Zealand-bred horse had heaps of Chutzpah to spare. They watched him go through his paces, ridden by a young Mauri lad on a property south of Christchurch. Around and around and around, they cantered on a muddy track. And again, and again, in the rain, until Wade realised they'd been going for about thirty minutes. He stopped the show, and the horse came back without a blow. Now that rhymes! They wanted to buy a stayer! Well, say no more! When the deal was completed, home to Aus flew our misspelled Kutzbah, named, I'm sure, after his heroic effort.

Kutzbah had many peculiarities. One was he detested being shod. Fortunately, at the time, we were lucky enough to have one of the best farriers ever to grace an anvil, Bruce Fox. He was a massively built bloke who could handle any horse. However, Kutzbah held Bruce over the coals. It's supposed to be the other way around. One day, I walked into the barn to see a calm, calculating Kutzbah viewing his carnage. Wade was rolling around on the concrete floor, obviously in pain. Bruce moaned in agony, nursing his ribs. Our apprentice Jockey was bent double, holding his groin, screeching in pain.

"What happened?" I asked while I tied Kutzbah, the conqueror, up to the rail where he'd broken away. It took time to receive an answer, as all injured parties were beyond coherent speech.

We didn't use Ace tablets back then, meaning a mild tranquilizer. I wish we had because Kutzbah took four days to shoe. One hoof each day! We were lucky, though, as most times, when Kutzbah put the same fight into his racing, he'd win like a champ.

The Hawkesbury Gold Cup, 1985, was held on a heavy track, which Kutzbah did not handle. I suppose he gave the impression he did when he'd churned around on a quagmire track in NZ. Though he was only cantering then, it makes a huge difference when a horse fully extends on a wet racetrack that either sinks or shifts beneath them.

The night before the Hawkesbury Cup, we'd experienced one of the worst storms I'd seen. A massive deluge of rain fell like a waterfall from the sky. Trees toppled with gale-force winds that could hurl anything over. It's a wonder we all survived to see Kutzbah race.

Our mood was sombre.

"We may as well race him, I suppose," said Wade. "He's been set for this race. Shame about the track, but if we're lucky, he might finish 5th.." Decent prize money paid to 5th place in major races.

For reasons unknown, I felt confident about Kutzbah winning. Another premonition or gut feeling? So I laid a big bet, for me, twenty-five dollars each way. However, my mind told me that Kutzbah winning would be impossible due to the heavy track. Kutzbah started at eighteen to one. I also took a four-horse trifecta, which cost me twenty-four dollars. It was the most significant outlay of my life. Marietta, Ross Daisley's wife, and I sat together in the Grandstand. We were shocked to see Kutzbah running last in the field when the race began. He usually led or was on the pace.

"Well, there goes my premonition,' I said. 'He can't possibly win from there! Not on a heavy track!"

Kutzbah took up the chase one hundred meters before the home turn and rounded it, the widest runner, then in the home straight, he gathered his rivals in like they were pegged to the ground. Marietta and

I stood and screamed until Kutzbah passed the post two lengths in front! Yeh!!!

I'd taken a tiny handbag to the races. Consequently, the enormous amount of money I'd won, including the trifecta dividend, would not fit. So, I asked Marietta to hold most of the cash in her *big* bag. The Trifecta paid thousands!

That night we rejoiced at a local Chinese restaurant. Our friends Ray and Pat Selkrig joined the party (Ray had ridden Shamrock King to victory on many occasions). Troy Phillips, at the time, was apprentice jockey to our friends John and Linda Holgate. Troy, a gregarious young man, decided to show off his unique rap dancing towards night's end. The Chinese waitresses and kitchen staff had never seen anything like it. They stood with shocked expressions before deciding Troy was taking some sort of fit. Soon a bucket of water appeared and was about to be thrown over Troy while he was in a spectacular spin on the floor. It was unexpected, as nobody had understood their animated Chinese language. It was hilarious—just another memorable event to finish a great day.

Two weeks later, Wade backed Kutzbah up in the Orange Cup.

Ross and Marietta, part owners of Kutzbah, had stayed at Windermere the night before, making their trip to Orange easier. Early in the morning, Kutzbah and Wade began their truck journey. I was to stay home due to not feeling well. One hour later, just before Ross hopped in his car, I had another premonition, I had to go, or something terrible might happen. I made myself comfortable, lying down in their back seat, resting my head on a pillow. I slept for most of the journey, but thank goodness I woke suddenly. We were in the midst of the Blue Mountains, and I sat up just as we were about to enter a sharp right-hand turn. I could see a truck overtaking a small car on the wrong side of the road. I screamed, 'SWERVE LEFT NOW!' If I hadn't, and Ross agreed, the truck would have collected us. It must have been our lucky day because Kutzbah won the Orange Cup with a leg to spare!

When Kutzbah began to suffer soundness problems, his performance regressed. We decided it best to sell him at the William Inglis Tried Horse Sale and claim him only to be a riding horse. We also disclosed his difficult temperament and, most importantly, his unsoundness to race anymore. We thought all was good. However, we were unaware that an undercover agent for a disreputable trainer bought Kutzbah. And at the same time, an undetectable wonder drug, 'Elephant

Juice,' was being used. The drug was ten thousand times more potent than morphine. So powerful that a horse could win on three legs.

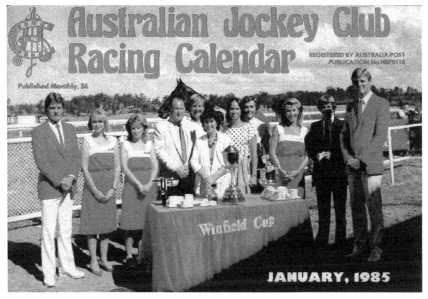

*Wade, me, Ross and Mariette amongst the officials after Kutzbah won the Hawkesbury Gold Cup.*

*Kutzbah winning the Orange Gold Cup.*

Not only did Kutzbah win two races while being given Elephant Juice, but he was also backed off the map on both occasions at starting odds of 80/1.

Immediately after, Kutzbah was sold to an honest trainer in Victoria for huge money. You may guess the outcome. Kutzbah raced poorly before he broke down irreparably. I later spoke with Steward Larry Morrison about the scenario, but unfortunately, he could do little, as Elephant juice was undetectable.

Times have now changed with the total care of our retired racehorses, organized by Racing NSW. Plus, allowing another Trainer to race Kutzbah after we'd declared his un-soundness should not have been allowed. Thankfully, it would be outlawed today. All conditions must be disclosed by the seller and adhered to by the purchaser.

I was at Randwick the second time Kutzbah raced for the new trainer and after the race, I went to see Kutzbah and noticed he was highly distressed. His heart rate was beyond the sky, and his breathing was erratic. I was about to call for help when the Course Vet arrived. Kutzbah, by then, looked like he was about to die. However, Khutbah's blood test later showed nothing abnormal.

Unfortunately, the story belongs to the old adage.

*'The lure of easy money!'*

Eventually, Elephant Juice was detectable and hit the headlines like a tidal wave. Previously, the blood of winning racehorses, specifically the horses who had performed uncharacteristically, including Kutzbah, had been frozen at the AJC Laboratories.' When the advanced procedure and equipment became available, their drops of blood were re-tested to find that many racehorses had tested positive for the drug—founding my suspicions. Kutzbah had been a victim.

# Chapter 17
## Trials and Tribulations

Back to Cheval De Volee.

Cheval won his first race start, The Tiny Tot Stakes, without an official Trial. Racehorses were not required to Barrier Trial before they raced back in the seventies. He won by six lengths and therefore sent a message to all that he would be a serious contender in the Golden Slipper. His dominance of the field was remarkable. Mum and I watched Cheval win from the Grandstand at Rosehill and almost fell over the rail with shock. Later, when standing in line to collect our winnings, the fellow in front said to his mate. 'I can't believe you backed that horse. He's only as big as a pee!'

He was right. Cheval stood only 14.3 hands.

After that win, Cheval was put out to spell, and he returned to win 'The Pago Pago Stakes' by five lengths. Cheval's success offered him a ballot-free start in the Golden Slipper. However, the nomination fee had not been paid by the owners, including my dad, who, after Cheval's first win, had bought a 50% share from Stan Evans. Unfortunately, in Stan's opinion, Cheval was bred to stay, so Stan insisted that Wade train him as such.

I said, 'you should take it as it comes, Stan. Cheval's a sprinter!'

My opinion was based on Cheval's blinding barrier speed, then seeing him settle and sprint again over the final two hundred meters. Incredible! He'd won both sprint races in record time. I reckoned we had the best two-year-old sprinter in the land! How on earth did Stan think Cheval would stay?

My dad, Tom, agreed with me and offered to pay the late entry fee into the Slipper. The endless arguments for and against began, generating headaches, alcohol binges, and crying. They all came to nothing. Stan Evans (the senior partner had his way.)

Even Ken Calendar and John Tapp, when speaking on TV

the morning after Cheval's Pago Pago win, proclaimed Cheval as the favourite for the Slipper. "If only the owners would pay the late entry fee," said Ken.

Newspaper Journalists hounded Stan and Wade, asking for a good reason why Cheval should not start in the Slipper.

"We'll wait for the Sires Produce. The distance of 1400mts will suit Cheval better.' Said Stan, with stupid authority.

It was the worst decision made in our history as racehorse Trainers.

Manakato won the Golden Slipper that year after traveling up from Melbourne, and Cheval, two weeks later, raced against him in the Sires Produce. And he beat Manakato to the post!

Now I shall tell the story leading to this battle.

Murphy's Law!

The heavens opened for over a week leading to the Sires Produce. Windermere Farm flooded to the point of us being trapped. (*Islanated. My word for it.*) All we could do was walk Cheval up and down the driveway, which lay hip-deep in floodwater. Today they have mechanical water walkers, not back then. So we all took turns, three times a day, walking Cheval through the floodwater.

Early on the morning of the Sires Produce, we cut the boundary fences and led Cheval through the neighbouring property ( also underwater) to reach King Road Wilberforce, where a horse float awaited. Cheval was a good traveller on a truck but terrible on a two-horse float. (No trucks available). It took four and a half hours to trek Cheval over and around the Blue Mountains to reach Randwick Racecourse. Cheval, on arrival, was a lather of sweat, suffering badly from the trip. Luckily they landed three hours before the race, as Wade could walk Cheval and hose him down. Wade repeated this routine until Cheval finally settled enough to nap before being saddled. Courageously, Cheval led all the way in the Sires Produce until he was swamped on the line. Manakato had fought with Cheval over the final two hundred meters, with Cheval getting the better of Manakato to run fourth – Manakato ran fifth.

I recently read another take on the saying. 'Everything happens for a reason.' 'Yes, everything happens for a reason, but sometimes it's because we make the wrong decision!' How true in this case?

*Cheval De Volee, in the Group 2 Sires Produce. Still in the lead!*

Cheval went on to win many Metropolitan, Group, and Stakes races before retiring too soon. His early retirement was triggered by a track accident. The load of soil delivered to top-dress the course proper at Hawkesbury Racetrack held a few rocks. What chance that Cheval would gallop on one and shatter his sesamoid?

Cheval was operated on by a well-respected local Veterinary Surgeon, The Late Jerry Rose ESQ. Jerry meticulously drilled pins and screws through Cheval's multi-fractured sesamoid. Jerry was not entirely confident the new age operation would work. Fortunately, after Cheval had been stabled in the barn for three months, he healed well enough to stand at stud. Thanks to the brilliance of Jerry Rose.

Not once did Cheval become agitated. What helped, I'm sure, was all the love and attention Cheval received from us, plus he was able to see horses being saddled up in the barn. He'd watch them go in and out all morning, neighing to each other. I can only imagine what they said.

We had offers from well-known Studs to stand Cheval. However, Stan Evans thought it best we stand him at Windermere.

More money to him. But bloody hard work for us.

We all, except for Stan, toiled hard for many Stud seasons. We were lucky when Mum and Dad came up from Rye Victoria to help during the Stud season. Mum was the cook cum housekeeper and Dad fed the broodmares morning and night.

Unlike the well-known studs, we had limited time and limited mares. However, Cheval did produce many city winners. He was the Great Grand Sire of 'Calaway Gal,' the Golden Slipper winner (2002). We'd trained her Grand Mother, 'Calais Girl,' by Cheval De Volee.

One of my first horses to train by Cheval was Cheval D'clare. He was a firecracker and could gallop just as fast. At first, I thought him to be as good as his dad or better. So I entered him in the first two-year-old trials at Randwick. If he won or ran a place, he'd be a good chance of getting a run in the Breeders plate, the first two-year-old race for the colts. The Gimcrack Stakes is for fillies.

Monique was leading D'clare around the mounting enclosure at the trials, and I'm sorry to say, she had a very relaxed hold on the horse, whose attention was drawn to the horses already out on the track. Jockey Adrian Robinson approached and suddenly flung himself on board D'clare, who took fright – and flight. He dropped Adrian like a hot scone and broke loose from Monique. D'clare then jumped the fence separating the mounting enclosure from the Oaks Bar.

Our friend, June Truscott, was sitting in the Oaks Bar reading the barrier trial program and feeling guilty about sipping on a gin and tonic at eleven am when she felt a gush of hot breath streaming onto the back of her neck. When she turned to see a horse standing behind, quietly overlooking her program, June almost passed out. She later said, "It was even funnier when the Clerk of the Course calmly rode his horse into the bar and collected Cheval D'clare like nothing had happened."

I begged the Stewards to allow me to run D'clare in another barrier trial on the same day, mainly because I understood what had gone wrong. "Or," I said, "allow me to leg the jockey up again and lead the horse around the enclosure. I'm certain we will complete the procedure without a problem. And then we'll never have trouble in the mounting enclosure again. If only you would let me do this, Gentlemen."

Their answer was "NO!!! You, Mrs. Slinkard, have to trial him on his home track- Hawkesbury! You may then take him to a country race meeting. If all goes well."

D'clare returned to Hawkesbury, where he won his first barrier trial by ten lengths. The next venture was Orange, where he raced in a significant two-year-old event. Our Apprentice jockey Kevin Harpley, who knew the horse well, rode him. Plus, I'd asked a few good mates to assist with any problems we may have in the mounting yard.

## Youngsters try out their trackwork tricks

THERE were thrills and spills when new-season two-year-olds showed their potential in barrier trials at Randwick yesterday.

Cheval D'Eclair, a gelding by Cheval de Volce from Would Ever, decided against giving punters a preview of his racing prospects.

Cheval D'Eclair tossed apprentice jockey Adrian Robinson in the mounting yard as he was about to go on to the track.

After breaking away from his strapper, Cheval D'Eclair hurdled the fence and headed full gallop for the nearby Oaks bar.

An official cornered the youngster near the bar door and led him back to the stable area through the members reserve.

Stewards decided, because of Cheval D'Eclair's "barfly" antics, to scratch him from the trial and he will have to undergo further education.

Flighty filly Marks Gain (Biscay-Golden Ban) gave jockey Gavan Duffy two heavy spills before running unplaced in the 13th heat, won by Houdini.

Duffy had to scramble from under the flailing hoofs of Marks Gain after being heavily dumped, but remounted to finish unplaced.

While Duffy appeared to escape injury, he had one more unplaced ride before complaining of a sore knee.

The tough little jockey vowed he would be fit to ride at Rosehill today.

— ROD GALLEGOS

ABOVE: Marks Gain takes to the air while Cheval D'Eclair (right) is grounded.

Pictures: DAVID HICKSON

*My naughty Cheval D'Clare, at Randwick's first two-year-old barrier trials. It's not him raring up, it's Cheval on right hand side below being led out of the Oaks bar by the Clerk of the Course.*

Tim Walsh, a fantastic horseman, accepted the challenge, as did John Holgate, an excellent horse trainer, plus Wade (I cannot praise him too much, haha,). Wade was there to take the Steward's attention away from us. Wadey loves a chat, so that was easy.

Tim led D'clare around the enclosure until they faced the small bar at the back of the parade ring. This is where John Holgate proceeded to leg Kevin up. However, D'clare suddenly swung away and, in doing so, he stomped on Kevin's foot. "He's broken my toes!" Kevin cried. John Holgate, through clenched teeth, said, "if you don't get back on, I'll break your dick!" And with that, the grimacing Kevin was legged back up on D'clare. The horse then dashed toward the fence separating the bar from the enclosure. Oh no, not another bar entry! With heels dug firmly into the ground and a grip to match Tarzan, Tim fought D'clare to pull him up just before he jumped the fence, with Kevin still on board. Thankfully.

Meanwhile, Wade held the attention of the Steward by pointing to a horse out on the track, "That horse is lame, Sir." said Wade. Of course, the steward had to study the said horse, taking his concentration away from what was happening behind his back.

D'clare won the race by five lengths - in a canter.

The next day, I phoned the chief Steward and announced excitedly, "Cheval D'clare won by five lengths at Orange, Sir!"

"That's good, Mrs. Slinkard," he said and promptly hung up.

Our friend and jockey Neil Campton agreed to ride D'clare on a Saturday at Randwick. From memory, the deal was that if D'clare behaved in the country, he would be permitted to return to the city. All went well. Neil was safely mounted and made it out of the saddling enclosure onto the track when the loudspeaker blasted a deafening blow. D'clare spun around so fast he almost dislodged Neil, but he hung on for dear life while D'clare charged back into the enclosure and raced towards the weighing room. He was pulled up just in time by the clerk of the course, who gave a sudden tug on D'clare's reins, and with that, Neil lost his balance and fell, breaking his wrist badly. Poor Neil, such a lovely friend. Well, he was before that. I'm only joking.

Later I was called into the stewards' room.

"Please take a seat, Mrs. Slinkard. We have discussed the matter of your *unruly* horse, and we declare that Cheval D'clare is too dangerous to race."

I stood up, thumped my fist on the desk, and almost yelled. "Well, gentlemen, let me tell you! Cheval D'clare has broken world records on the track! (plus a few bones. But I didn't say that). And you're telling me that you're banning him from racing because of no fault of his own!"

"How do you figure it's no fault of the horse?" One Steward asked, more quizzically than seriously. So I told them the story from the beginning. "If I'd been permitted to leg up the jockey in the enclosure later in the day of the Barrier Trials, I strongly believe all would have gone well. Plus, today's loudspeaker spooked Cheval D'clare and caused patrons to place their hands over their ears until someone adjusted the sound!"

The Stewards listened to what I had to say and then asked me to leave while they deliberated. I waited ten minutes before I returned for their judgment.

"We've taken into consideration what you have said, Mrs. Slinkard. And we have agreed. You may race the horse. But only in-country and provincial races. Never at Metropolitan meetings."

Cheval D'clare had won 52 races by the end of his career, though not all under my training. We sold him later to Lorry Manzelman from Mackay. Lorry would sometimes race D'clare in the first and last on the same day, and he'd win both races.

The best part about that story is that Lori was involved in the Mackay Pony Club, so D'clare and all of Lori's retired racehorses found good homes. Lorry, over time, bought from us around twelve horses who'd out-weighed their ability in our area. And every horse won at least three races around North Queensland

*Cheval D'clare with a happy, relieved me after his win at Orange.*

\*

I stop again to bring you into the present.

It's April 13, 2019. The Saturday afternoon when Winks claimed her 33rd victory - in a row. A perfect Autumn day at Royal Randwick provided the stage for Winks to perform yet another brilliant performance. She has just won the Queen Elizabeth Stakes beating Happy Clapper and Hartnell. What a heartbreaker 'Winks' has been to her rivals. But a heart starter for the crowds who have witnessed her total dominance.

God Bless her.

Her regular jockey, Hugh Bowman, admitted to the Press when they echoed the foregone conclusion, 'Winks will now retire, Hugh?'

"Yes, she will, and I'll have my life back." He replied.

But how much richer for the experience Hugh? And what memories to share with your great-grandkids.

My connection with Hugh began when he first rode Festive Knight, a horse I'd bred and trained. Festive was out of Celebration Star by Sir Dapper. I've told the story one hundred times to friends and family about how Festive Knight only cost me $20. But now, '*It is written.*'

We, the Hawkesbury trainers, organized an annual 'Hawkesbury Horse of The Year Ball,' including a raffle. We sold tickets for the chance to win services for mares to various stallions, all donated by generous Stallion owners. My raffle ticket was drawn first on our inaugural night (definitely not rigged). I chose Sir Dapper, the Golden Slipper winner, 1983, and probably better known for his running second to Emancipation each time they met.

Excited at the prospect, I sent our mare, 'Celebration Star,' to 'Sir Dapper .' She gave birth to a perfectly conformed colt eleven months later. When he was a yearling, I gave away shares to friends, and we named him 'Festive Knight.' I did so to keep costs down when Festive was ready to join up. (Break in.) And what fun we owners had, especially when I decided to race him for the first time at Randwick. It was Festive Knight's first start back from a spell. This race began his second preparation. In his first preparation, he'd won a maiden race at Hawkesbury. Festive then ran second in another race, and I put him out to spell.

The race at Randwick was ('*No more than one metropolitan win.*') Not only was it a strong field, but it had been raining, and Festive didn't handle the wet. I had doubters left, right, and center hounding me not to start him. But I knew in my heart; that Festive could do it - if the track were okay. So I phoned the Randwick Course Curator after their track gallops on the morning of the race. By then, he would have determined the track condition. "Yes," he said, "it's a good track. But I have to class it soft because there's a couple of soft patches on the fence."

Before this, I'd heard of a new Apprentice Jockey who had a natural feel for a horse and was bound to be a top jock one day. His name was Hugh Bowman. I engaged Hugh and claimed the 3kls off Festive's back.

The time arrived to collect the saddle, and I stood patiently in the weighing area, waiting for my jockey. Jockeys came and went after handing saddles to trainers. Then all went quiet, leaving me standing like a shag on a rock. I wondered where my jock was even though I had the company of a rather tall skinny young fellow, wearing only a singlet and jodhpurs, holding a number '1' saddle blanket. So I waited, and I waited. Festive was number 13. (number 3 was hidden under the fold)
Becoming anxious, I asked the steward. 'Where's Hugh Bowman, Sir?'

"He's standing right next to you." Said the Steward with a smile.

I gave Hugh a whack on his arm. 'Why didn't you say something?' I demanded.

'Because I didn't know who you were either!' Said Hugh, flinching.

So funny! I still laugh at that memory; it seems like yesterday.

Once saddled and ready in the mounting enclosure, I gave Hugh his riding instructions.

"Festive will jump well. But don't move. Just let him find his feet. That should see you in the first four or five. Hold your position. When in the home straight, wait until you've managed the hill and the dip; just keep him balanced. Okay?" Hugh nodded. "Then, at the final 200, ride him like a shark's after you. But hands and heals only. Don't use the whip. He'll give you his all."

Festive Won! NO whip!

The scribes later surrounded Hugh, declaring. 'What a brilliant ride, Hugh. Well beyond your years. You showed considerable patience waiting for the final two hundred. And no whip mate!'

The innocent, lovable Hugh said while pointing his finger at me. 'She told me what to do, and I just did it!"

I've mentioned the doubting Thomas's before Festive raced on that day. Well, a part-owner of Festive thought I'd gone totally mad, running him on a rain-affected track, especially first up in a high-grade race. The same young, inexperienced owner had taken time off from his City office job to watch 'Festive' race at Randwick. Before the race, he stood on the other side of the horse stall fence and gave me a mouthful.

" It's a bloody waste of time, running Festive on a heavy track! I don't know what you were thinking!"

I tried to explain calmly what the course curator had said about the track and how well Festive had worked. But the young part-owner wouldn't listen. He came back at me with,

"Festive should have gone to Bathurst or Orange, where he's sure to win! This race is far too hard." '*silly bitch*', I heard him whisper.

Dear friend, Jane Tolhurst, also a part-owner of Festive, stood beside me and was horrified at this young man's behaviour. Even when Jane is angry, she's still soft, and you can't help loving her.

I ignored my sledger and began talking to a professional Punter I knew standing nearby. He said to me quietly, and I quote. "I disagree with that mug. I reckon if Festive's come back only one length better, he could win this race." I agreed.

And I must add, he'd give you a sling if you gave him a tip.

I then coped another scoffing from the young troll. I'd had enough, so I told him to "piss off!" And he did.

Punter then asked, "who was he?"

"He's one of the owners," I said.

He laughed.

After Festive's win, we all gathered in the celebration room. Champagne and chicken sandwiches awaited and the young troll stood proudly boasting what a great horse HE owned. So I wiped the corner of his mouth with my napkin.

"What did you do that for?" he asked, surprised.

"I just wiped the egg off your face!"

Success is the sweetest revenge!

*Festive Knight's great victory at Randwick. Janie Tolhurst is on the right of Festive. You may guess who the young fellow is behind me.*

*Festive Knight, Hugh Bowman on board.*

Hugh was later suspended, but not for his ride on Festive. I told Hugh he may as well come out to the farm and spend a day with us. 'I'll cook you steak, eggs, and chips. I've heard it's your favourite meal, and I've gathered a nice wad of money for your winning ride on Festive Knight.' Hugh took up the offer, and after eating an enormous steak, I suggested he looked tired.

"Lay down on the couch and have a snooze, Hugh."

What makes me smile now; it's the same couch I'm sitting on today, April 13th, 2019. And where I have just watched Hugh ride 'Winks' to victory. I could say Hugh had 'Forty Winks' on the same couch many years before. A great bloke, our Hugh, and a true horseman. He listens and compromises with horses and knows, they know, exactly what the job is. Whether you jump horses or train them for Dressage, Harness race them, or whatever. Horses will happily learn their trade. All we have to do is kindly relay the message.

# Chapter 18
# Opporunities

I applied for my Trainers license when Lisa and Daniel were both in high school. I thought Wade would protest. But NO.

"I think it's a good idea, Dor. It'll keep you out of my hair."

Instead, Wade tried to mess with mine!

As Wade does, he thinks his way is the only way, though he would say the same about me. I know. Wade and I have everything in common, though we argue about everything we have in common! STILL!

My first horse to train was a filly named Misty Tempo by Charmande out of Chilli Pettine. Misty was offered to me by the late Irwin Ormsby, a Lawyer, good friend, and generous owner. His offer came the day before I was granted my Trainers license.

I shall now give credence to my first interview with Racing Steward Larry Morrison, an old Jackaroo mate of Wades. Larry knew my long history with horses. So we simply chatted, laughing about the old Jackaroo - Jillaroo days. Consequently, the Licensing board of the AJC was informed by Larry that I had impeccable references and I was experienced enough to Train Racehorses. Two weeks later, I received notice to go before the Committee of the Australian Jockey Club for their final approval. Hopefully!

The interview appeared to be a very serious matter. I was on trial. John Shrek, the Chief Steward, sat to the left of Mr. Ryan, the Chairman of the AJC, with other Committee members to the right, and after they had viewed my cache of references. Including one from Trainer Angus Arminasco. The Pony Club Association of Victoria, etc. Also, a reference from Wade, saying I was a vital part of his training business. Mr. Ryan dipped his head, glasses sitting precariously on the end of his nose, looked me in the eye, and asked.

"Is your Husband going to teach you how to train, Mrs. Slinkard?"

"No." Said, smart arse me. "I taught Wade how to train!"

I could see John Shrek choking down laughter.

I was then asked to stand in the hallway while they considered. Little time elapsed before I returned and was granted my Trainer's license. Yippee!

Upon leaving the building, John Shrek walked toward me with a wry smile, "Good call Mrs. Slinkard." He said and walked away – still wearing a grin.

John Shrek still holds my respect. He was consistently fair and above board when delivering fines and suspensions to Jockeys and trainers. He also retains the ownership of hunting down and bringing the culprits who devised the Fine Cotton affair to justice - for those who don't know.

At Doomben races, 18/8/1984, a speedy horse was switched with a slow horse named 'Fine Cotton,' who was out of sight and far away on the day. On the morning of the race, an amateur make-over job was executed upon the speedy unsuspecting horse. He was given a white blaze and three white socks. Sadly, the paint began to dissolve when the horse sweated. The only right thing the offenders did, was win.

But it didn't take long before 'RING-IN!' Was called, from Doomben to the far reaches of Australia. The search then began for the culprits, and it became, I'm sure, Australia's most colourful racing story. John Shrek consumed himself with hunting down the perpetrators. It took him twelve months before he accumulated all the evidence needed to put the dummies in jail. Yes, the dummies, who were paid to take the wrap for a few well-known identities. End of story? NO.

Long before that day, we'd had our share of nobblers, whom we called the low grades, who, for money, would sneak around racing stables specifically to dope horses before they raced.

It was rumoured that a gelatine capsule containing carbon gas was administered to the chosen horse approximately 12 -14hrs before it ran. The thickness of the case surrounding the gelatine capsule ascertained approximately when the gas explosion would occur. The horse would then experience excruciating stomach pain while still trying to race. Cruel! Neither element left a trace - an ingenious but not without risk business.

It was first known to us when a Sydney detective contacted Wade. They had been informed and captured a group of nobblers who had infiltrated Trainer Des Lake's stables. They were about to drug one of his good horses, who, like our Shamrock King, had put in some un-characteristic bad runs. Meaning they'd started favourite and ran last. I'd say on numerous occasions after our horses were made favourite by the Bookies and went terrible. "He ran like a ruptured duck!" It wasn't far from the truth.

After putting a dragnet around Des Lakes property and catching the culprits, the Detectives warned Wade that the nobblers had a map of Windermere Farm in their possession. They knew precisely where Shamrock King was stabled. Cheval De Volee was also on their list, but not that evening.

So began our nights of sleeping in the barn - or trying to. Wade soon came up with a scathingly brilliant idea! We would create our own *Fine Cotton*. We changed names on the stable doors, and Wade strung fine black cotton around the front of the stables, plus the windows. It did the trick. Anyone trying to get to our horses would surely break the cotton. From then on, things did quieten down.

There were some big names behind the nobbling sting, and the Detectives did point the bone, but for obvious reasons, I will not divulge their trust.

*

I will now bring you into the moment. I have just watched the Chanel 7 Crime Investigation. March 20-2022. What's that saying? The truth will eventually come out. David Waterhouse, son of Bill Waterhouse, claimed his father instigated the Fine Cotton racing affair and, more upsetting, trainer George Brown's brutal death. It was the same accusation or truth about what the Detectives had told Wade in the mid to late seventies.

*

I'm returning to my first horse to train, Misty Tempo. She was a real challenge! So highly strung that I could not stable her or even train her from a yard. She'd pace up and down all day, so I trained her from a small but decent-sized paddock where she'd gallop whenever she felt like it. It took a few disappointing runs before I realised I was overtraining Misty. While scratching my head, trying to fathom why she'd go like the clappers then stop in her races. An acquaintance, Angela Field, told me, "the Charmande breed cannot take a lot of galloping. Only once, seven days before they race is sufficient."

I took Angela's advice.

Each morning, I'd watch Misty race around her paddock. If I

160

thought she'd done enough work, I'd say to Wade.

"I'm not riding her today; she's done enough."

Wade would have a heart attack. Almost.

"You must work your horses! You have to ride them!"

I didn't listen to him. I listened to my horse.

Horses will tell you what's what. And all you have to do is observe.

Before Angela's advice, I'd gallop Misty three furlongs, three days before she raced. A hard-held working gallop, of course. Misty had won the jump and led in all her races until she'd compound over the final 200mts. When I trained Misty differently, ascertaining if she'd done enough work in her paddock and only galloped her 7 to 10 days before she raced or backed her up without fast work, she'd settle just off the pace and either win or run exceptionally well. She was no champion but an honest contender, always sticking on until the finish. My first horse to train could not have been better. I learned so much from Misty Tempo.

*Lisa with Wade after Misty Patches' win at Canterbury,*
*and while Lisa, a schoolgirl then, spent her day at being a Race Steward*
*for Work Experience. She dobbed Wade for not changing the race form*
*after Misty was gelded. He was shown as a Colt in the Race book.*
*The Stewards laughed and only warned Wade to change it.*

161

I am not taking anything away from Wade's ability to train. He was an excellent trainer. We simply have different ideas, and like all trainers, we do our best. I felt I had to tell 'The Misty Tempo Tale,' as it may help others appreciate, per size and strength, that horses are only one-third as strong mentally and physically as humans. And that is a proven fact.

Soon after acquiring my trainers' license, I flew to New Zealand to search for a future Melbourne Cup winner. I stayed with friends Val and Ron Langsford, who'd asked around on my behalf. "Does anyone have a staying-bred horse for sale?" Snowy Upton from Palmerston North put his hand up. He had a three-year-old gelding *not* broken in by 'Palm Beach,' out of 'Grande Countess.' The mare, to her tribute, was related to a New Zealand Darby winner, New Zealand Cup winner, and New Zealand Oaks winner, not to forget The Grande National Steeple Chase winner. Hardly a bad relation in her pedigree.

It was a sunny winter day when Val and I travelled south to Snowy's property. No refreshments were offered, just a big burgundy bay gelding with a thick white blaze. I fell in love at first sight. Therefore, on looks and breeding, I paid the asking price. I did so on behalf of clients who held confidence in allowing me to choose a Melbourne Cup contender!

Once home on Windermere, I held a long lunch for the part-owners. After enjoying countless wines and fine cuisine, we all placed our chosen names for the horse in a hat, and I picked up 'Hungry Dawson.' Geoffrey Robinson then told the story about Hungry Dawson, who'd desired the name. Geoffery was married to Sandy, a stunningly beautiful American girl. And so Geoffrey's accent is unique, a mixture of Aussie / Yankie, trimmed with the vernacular of a nasal race caller.

"Once upon a time, there was a Horse Trainer named Dawson. He was a true legend, traveling around the Australian bush, camping under the stars with his talented racehorse, Hungry." Geoffrey told his captivated, inebriated audience. "Hungry won every race, Dawson entered him in. It was said that Dawson would tell the horse, "if ya don't win taday mate, we'll both go hungry. Hence the name, 'Hungry Dawson."

True or false, I won't spoil Geoffrey's story.

Australian and Kiwi equestrians have forever claimed that horses bred and raised in New Zealand hold incredible bone strength. "It's

162

the limestone," they say. "Buy an NZ horse, and you buy strength and soundness!" Well, let me tell you, Hungry Dawson had bones like chalk! He went shin sore three times before standing up to a solid preparation as a three-year-old. And when he did, Hungry showed just how promising he was by winning his first start, a 1400mt maiden at Hawkesbury. When he won a 1900mt race, mid-week Canterbury meeting, excitement brewed even more. We thought we were underway for a Melbourne Cup preparation. However, in that race and on the bend into the home straight, Jockey Adrian Robinson felt compelled to forcefully hit Hungry with the whip. Totally unnecessary! Hungry had never been hit with a whip, particularly with such intensity. Therefore, he overreacted, causing his body to whiplash. We later found that this action had put Hungry's back out. And so lay the future for many problems. Hungry, I decided, needed to swim, particularly in a straight line due to his back issues and fragile bone density. It became another argument between Wade and me.

"We don't need a swimming channel! Anyway, we don't have the money!" Argued Wade.

*Hungry Dawson was one of the most challenging horses I have ever trained. This is after his win at Canterbury with some of the owners, including Susie Bookalill far left.*

163

# Chapter 19
## Fashion Pays

As luck would have it, Fashion Plate ME entered the Hawkesbury 'Fashions on the Field' contest and won! First prize; a trip for two to Hawaii. Value, $4000. Plus $500 spending money. Our friend and fellow Horse trainer cum Race Club committee member, Geoffrey Heikman, stood beside me in the enclosure when it was announced I was the winner. He asked quietly, "do you want to take the prize or the cash instead?"

I immediately thought about the swimming channel and agreed to take the money. Later, a notably elated Wade suggested that Lisa and I go to Hawaii because it was too complicated for Wade and me to take a holiday together.

"I'm not taking the holiday," I said.

Wade's shocked expression made me laugh until I told him we could have a swimming channel built with the cash I'd won.

*Winning the Fashions of the Field at Hawkesbury. I'm far right.*

There were great prizes back then, which continued for quite some time.

I intended to plant a palm tree at the end of the channel to *remind* me of Hawaii. That I didn't means I have never forgotten. However, I later travelled to Hawaii, but only in my imagination. I created a beautiful young woman in my first novel. She was half Hawaiian, half English. Sound like a Pizza?

That memory leads to some thirty years later when Jane and Mark's daughter, Amanda, our Goddaughter, accompanied me in the 'Mother and Littlest Daughter Fashion on the Field' at Randwick. It was the AJC Autumn Carnival. Amanda was an avid eight-year-old punter, addicted to party pies, especially those sold at the races. Hence her nickname, '*the pie-eating punter*.' We'd take Amanda to the races whenever we could. She loved it. Plus, she picked nearly every winner!

This particular year, I suggested to Jane that she and Amanda dress up and enter the 'Mother and Littlest Daughter Fashions on The Field.' Unfortunately, an important business issue arose at the last moment concerning Mark and Jane. So I shepherded my disappointed, beautiful God Daughter Amanda, dressed like a princess, to Randwick and promised we would enter the contest together. I thought we wouldn't win because most ladies spend thousands and take it seriously. When we lined up before the judges, I browsed our opponents and thought, *yes, we have a chance of winning*. So I whispered to Amanda. "If we win darling, and they ask you your name. Say, Amanda Slinkard."

A bit naughty. But it was fun when we won!
Cameras flashed from every direction, and journalists approached us, asking Amanda her name.

"Amanda Tol…Slinkard." She said with a frown and then a smile.

"That's an unusual name." One Journo said.

I jumped in.

"She was just going to tell you her middle name."

"And what is it?" He asked.

"Oh, don't worry!" I said. "It's complicated."

The following day our winning photo almost filled the back page of every Sunday newspaper. I received phone calls from people I hadn't heard from for years, saying, "I didn't know you had a younger daughter."

"Well, she is my Goddaughter. The same thing, I reckon!"
That was my defence.
I must add most of the prizes we gave to charity.

*One of my happiest memories. Our Goddaughter, Amanda, and I won Mother and Littlest Daughter Fashion at Randwick, Autumn Race Carnival. Take a look at the faces of the women standing behind. Not happy Jan!*

The charity donation came about because Monique Miller, who'd worked with us for the past five years, was chosen to enter the Miss Australia Quest. Monique was and still is tall, beautiful, and gracious. Therefore she proved a good choice.

Monique, many years later, married Horse Trainer Terry Robinson. They remain happily married and have two delightful children, Matilda and Tom.

After the Miss Australia Scout approached Monique at Hawkesbury Races, Monique asked me about entering the Competition.

"As long as you enter for the right reason, Monique. And that is to raise money for the Spastic Center."

So that is where most of Amanda and my prizes went.

Monique became Miss Metropolitan Fund Raiser, with over forty thousand dollars in tow. We held a celebrity-packed dinner dance at Hawkesbury Race Club, raising a considerable amount of money, plus many more great fund-raising events. The whole scenario was time-consuming and challenging but rewarding, and we had loads of fun.

*Monique giving her speech at the Miss Australia Quest.*

*Our darling Monique is such a hard-working, loving person.*
*She is an inspiration to us all.*

It was also worth the effort to hear Monique's answer when the Miss Australia judging panel interviewed her. They asked.

"And who is the Australian you most admire, Monique?"

"My mum." Said Moni without hesitation.

In my opinion, Monique should have won Miss Australia with that answer.

Not to be retired in the Fashion stakes just yet. At age sixty, I'd purchased a lovely *in-vogue* black dress for Lisa to wear in the Hawkesbury Fashions on the Field 2011. Lisa hated the dress, which was a faithful rendition of a 1950's number. High collar, nipped-in waist, figure-hugging until it blossomed into a ballerina skirt around the thigh. I loved it. It was flattering, and I had a stunning Carol Mayher hat to compliment the dress. A wide-brimmed, white straw hat with black trim. "No, Mum!" said Lisa, "I'm not wearing that dress. Though I do love the hat."

It came about that Lisa did have an opportunity to change her mind. On the Saturday before the Hawkesbury Fashion Comp, Lisa arrived at the farm to accompany Wade to Rosehill races. Before they left, Lisa noticed a stain on her pink silk dress.

"Oh no. I was so looking forward to going. I can't go now. I have nothing to wear!" She cried.

I suggested Lisa wear *The Black Dress* to Rosehill. Reluctantly, she did.

On returning home, Lisa relayed how many compliments she'd received at the races from admirers of THE BLACK DRESS!

Well, I need to say no more. Apart from proving my good taste prevailed, the following Thursday, 'Ladies Day at Hawkesbury,' Lisa decided to strap our racehorses on the day. And I decided to wear *The Black Dress.*

Even though I was slightly inebriated after drinking too many champagnes, I did my best to stand up straight and look elegant in front of the Judges. It must have worked because I won! Just as well, they didn't ask me to walk a straight line down the catwalk.

A group of handsome young Firemen had the pleasure of sashing the winners. I watched through blurry eyes an attractive young man strutting towards me carrying an enormous sash.

"Oh, no, I'm too old for that," I said.

He said, "No, you're not," and threw me back in his arms before planting a kiss on my lips!

The onlookers approved with woof whistles and applause. YAH!

When I had recovered enough to stand and pose for the photo shoot, I saw our horse, 'Hamberg,' trained by Wade and owned by Tom Sewell, racing past and leading the field by two lengths. He maintained that distance to win The Ted Macabe Cup!

What a day!!

*Me, left, winning the Hawkesbury Fashions on the Field at sixty years of age. I would have chosen the organge flower. What about you?*

It would be remiss of me not to mention my beautiful and talented friend Suzie Bookallil, Horte Couture', who designed and made for me, plus women of importance (that's not me) the most amazing outfits. Suzie, from age sixty-eight, began suffering from Alzheimer's and is now cared for in a Sydney Nursing Home. So very sad for her family, and us, her friends. Far too young, far too talented, and far too beautiful a person to suffer this prolonged life-taking disease. Her husband, Stewart Lawlor, is Suzie's rock, and his arms will remain her haven. Bless you, Stewart.

So many happy memories Suzie and I have shared, and now a special one springs to mind.

Suzie agreed to be Fashion Judge at the Hay races and joined our annual pilgrimage. Being the primary judge of the fashions, Suzie was seated at the judge's table, looking divine in a pale blue suit with black trim. Her pillbox hat sat jauntily, adorned with black netting, which I'm sure helped keep the flies away. A little boy wearing a large Stetson hat, jeans, checked shirt, and riding boots strolled up and stood close by. He stared at Suzie for some time before he approached and asked.

"Hey, lady. Why you got chook wire on ya hat?"

A priceless memory

# Chapter 20
## Clients

Client and friend Chris Lawlor, founder of International Animal Health, came along around 1998 from memory. We began training his handy to extremely competitive horses, all named Ausbred something or other. Most derived from his 'Blue Bird' mare, 'Stormy Zephyr.' Her chief offspring would be Ausbred King. However, he did take time to become a racehorse, but when King finally learned his trade, he was a fierce competitor. He went on to win 9 races, 10 seconds, and 11 thirds. And like most horses, if he'd had more luck, he'd have won 30 races! His main claim to fame was winning the Listed Nevil Selwood Stakes at Rosehill on April 4-2009, with Kathy O'Hara on board.

King had won three races straight before the Neville Selwood. His final in the trilogy was a Saturday race at Randwick.
Ausbred King retired into the loving care of Dayna, one of our valued staff members.

Chris also supported us by buying some lovely yearlings around Australia. One such time was at the Melbourne Inglis sales. It was my birthday, and Chris said, "happy birthday Dor. Now choose a horse, and I'll give it to you to train."

With deliberation between us, we selected a lovely little athletic filly by Hussonet, out of, The Roscoe Rose. The obvious name was 'Ausbred Rose.' She began her career trialling in the first two-year-old barrier trials at Randwick. A tenacious little striver. Rose then participated in the Gimcrack Stakes. The first two-year-old race of the season. Definitely not disgraced in the Gimcrack; Rose then went out for a spell. However, when she returned, it was to a shaky start. It took time and heaps of patience to settle her down at the races. I thought about the problem before we trucked Rose to several race meetings where she could stand for a couple of hours without racing. Therefore, Rose would never know when she would or would not race. My plan worked. Rose became happily confused, and eventually, she accepted her fate peacefully.

Rose raced from the Gimcrack distance of 1000mts to race in the Oaks 2400mts, where once again, she was not disgraced, especially since it was an extremely heavy track - which she loathed. I had a milkshake bet with late Trainer Guy Walters that Ausbred Rose would beat his filly, 'All Black Miss,' in the Oaks. When the race was over, Guy approached and asked: "what flavour would you like, Dor?" Guy loved a joke and a chat; he was a great horse trainer and a Gentleman. Such a sad parting to the horse world. And our world. RIP, Guy.

Rose retired to Stud after a short career, winning three races, including one city win over 1600 and two provincial over 2100mts & 2300mts consecutively. Her six minor placings were unlucky runs. Unfortunately, Rose has not yet bred a horse as good as herself, but it's not over yet. Bless her.

*

Mark and Jane Tolhurst, our next-door neighbours, dear friends, and sometimes clients, introduced us to the now late Jamie Mackay. Jamie was a true gentleman and one of Australia's top polo players, and Jenny, his wife, came from a prominent racing family. Her great grandfather owned the 'Braeside' property at Mentone, which Harry Telford previously bought after Pharlap had earned him the funds.

The late Anne Raymond, Jenny's Great Aunt, was the daughter of Jenny's great-grandad. Anne, or Aunty Anne, owned 'Sledgmere Stud' in the Hunter Valley - at Scone and later bequeathed it to Katrina, Jenny's daughter, Anne's great-great Niece.

Katrina remains running Sledgmere as a successful and well-respected nursery where thoroughbred foals are born and raised. And her mother, Jenny, is a breeder of many fine thoroughbreds. She sells the colts at William Inglis Sales, plus the Magic Million, and keeps most fillies to race before sending them to stud.

Trainer Guy Walters had trained for over thirty years, Anne Raymond's horses, and Jenny's more recently. Jenny took the liberty of asking an unusual request of Guy. Would he go against his practice of race training to prepare a two-year-old gelding, which she'd entered in the William Inglis, Ready to Run sales? I presume Guy agreed as a reward for Jenny and Anne's loyalty.

When at the sale, I took a quick look at the gelding and loved the type, strong, well-muscled, with a determined look in his eye. One thing was slightly askew, though. His head seemed to lean to one side. I didn't get to ask Jenny if something was amiss before he was sold.

Wade needed to buy fillies for clients to race before sending them to Stud. So a gelding was not on the list. Nevertheless, Jenny's horse did take my eye.

*A fabulous weekend at Dungog, staying with Jamie and Jenny Mackay on their Horse Stud. Later that day I spotted Shenanigan (Noddy) in the paddock. Jamie in red shirt far left and Jenny far right in the spotted top. Harvey and Nola Woodhouse mid photo. Wade and I near the tree.*

After knowing Jamie and Jenny for some time, they asked us, plus a group of our friends, to stay for a weekend at their fabulous Property near Dungog. It is where Jamie's Scottish ancestors had lived for the past six generations. When staying at Jenny and Jamie's property a few weeks after the sale, Jenny showed us around, and while inspecting her yearlings, I spotted the horse I had admired in the sale ring.

"Isn't that the horse you sold at the ready-to-run sale?" I asked, a little surprised.

"Oh yes, that's right. They sent him back, saying he was a wobbler."

"May I catch him and take a closer look?"

"Yes, of course."

I approached the horse, talking to him sweetly, and caught him with no trouble. I then asked Jenny to hold him by the headstall. No lead.

"When I say go. Let go." I said, 'I'll give him a hard whack on the bum to make him run. If he staggers, you have a wobbler; if he doesn't, he's not a wobbler."

It was evident to me; that the buyers had made up a story. Because Noddy, we nicknamed him, had a crooked head, plus Noddy was a bit of a maniac. Therefore, the buyers returned him quickly and got their money back.

When I hit Noddy on the rump, and Jenny let him go, he ran straight as a dye at a hundred miles an hour. I offered to lease him because I didn't have the forty thousand the previous buyers had paid. Jenny soon rustled up a few friends, and we all shared in the lease of ownership.

Later, Jenny told me that Noddy had flipped over backward while being broken in. The breaker thought Noddy had killed himself. When he was about to confirm Noddy dead, he sat up, sporting a crooked head, which plagued him for the rest of his life.

Noddy had many quirks and various problems. Consequently, Jenny named him 'Shenanigans.' Nevertheless, Noddy held above-average ability. He won eight races, his first at Hawkesbury, leading the entire journey and pulling up without a blow. He was a tremendous winded horse.

Unfortunately, at the end of his third preparation, Noddy raced like a drunken sailor. We, plus the Stewards, witnessed after the race that Noddy had bled from both nostrils. The Stewards banned him from running for three months.

When the time came for Noddy to return to work, our stables and yards were full of horses, so he remained grazing down the back paddock until we had room. All up, he spelled for nine months. Besides that, the other lessees decided they would not take up Noddy's lease again even after he'd won four races. Their decision left me alone to keep the faith. I didn't tell Wade I held the lease on my own. He would have said NO! He would have suggested I give Noddy back, remembering he was a tough horse to train and even harder to handle, let alone a bleeder.

I had before this read up on legally administered coagulants. Strawberry tea was an old remedy for women experiencing menstrual trouble and haemorrhaging after birth. So, I boiled water, added a cup of strawberry tea leaves, and allowed it to brew. I did so every morning and night, then added it to Noddy's feed for the entire time he was in training. He loved the tea, proving so by licking his feed bin.

I knew it worked because I'd done the same for Hungry Dawson, who had a minor bleed from one nostril. We'd only noticed the bleed when Hungry was unloaded off the truck after he'd raced and won. I kept him in work but treated and trained him as a chronic bleeder.

A professional study of bleeding using hundreds of racehorses has shown seventy-five percent bleed to some degree. After being given strawberry tea for some months, our vet scoped both horses and found no scarring of the lung tissue and no sign of new bleeding.

I chose not to trial Noddy before his first start back at Warwick Farm. Instead, I galloped him a thousand meters with another horse ten days before. And to be safe, I gave him a Lasix injection to help stop the bleeding. I'm sure it was legal ten days before the race, just not on race day.

Noddy – Shenanigans started at $26/1. Janie Tolhurst was with me on the day, and we had a small wager, as we usually did. The late and great trainer, Max Lees, trained the odds-on favourite, which was declared unbeatable in the same race. However, as they say. *'there was only ever one certainty. But it got beat!'* And Shenanigans beat Max's certainty by a length and broke the course record. That was Shenagans most impressive win. And it was noticed by chief steward John Shrek, who said, "That was an outstanding training effort, Mrs.Slinkard. I noticed Shenanigan hadn't raced for over twelve months. And without a barrier trial? Great effort!"

*Yep, probably my best. I love a challenge.*

Noddy's head had almost seized up near the end of his racing career. Fortunately, we had a brilliant chiropractor, Ken Butler, who had kept Noddy on track throughout the years. On this particular day, Ken declared, "I think he's done for, Dor. His head won't move. It's riddled with arthritis."

"Mmm." I said, "well, I believe in magnets and celery juice. I'll give both a go."

I removed the plastic sights off a set of blinkers, stitched magnets onto a cloth, then attached it around the top of the blinkers, so the magnets ran around Noddy's head and behind his ears. With that and a large volume of celery drops daily, Noddy's head became subtle, and he seemed to stretch out in his work much better. Noddy went on to win three more back-to-back races before running a close second at Randwick on a Saturday.

Magnets work!!!

*

While writing about remedies, our friend and client Linda Filewood was diagnosed with Lymphoma cancer and given three months to live. Linda decided she didn't want to go through the usual chemo, radiation, etc. She would brave it out and live life to the fullest. However, as they do, a friend of a friend told her about a Guru curing people with cancer. His small farm was situated in Western Australia, and Linda would need to live there for three months, which was the only condition. Off she went, and along with other people living with cancer, she participated in the Guru's deep and meaningful self-discovery therapy. 'We prayed a lot to Buddha,' Linda said, 'and we all drank a small amount of extremely salty liquid every day!! And we only ate organic self-grown food.'

After three months, Linda felt amazing and decided to stay another three months. Six months elapsed before having her cancer checked to find no sign of cancer. Amazed and convinced it was the salty liquid she drank religiously, Linda asked the Guru to tell her what it was.

"Yes, of course.' He said. "I believe the cure for cancer comes from the sea. The liquid you drank was the syrup derived from de-salination of the purest seawater on the South Australian Coastline."

Linda asked whether he would mind if she went ahead and had it tested at the Government laboratories in Canberra and perhaps market it. The Guru had no objections.

Linda was the first to market and promote 'Sea Minerals.' Though only for animal use. Too many tests needed to be done, possibly taking years before being sold for human consumption.

And miracles began to happen. Under Linda's instruction, we took no notice of the animal use sticker, and every one of my friends and acquaintances suffering from cancer received a bucket of the stuff from yours truly. The first person I suggested using it was Anthea Crawford – Brading. Ant phoned me one night approximately 30 years ago and told me. "The doctors say I have three months to live, Dor. I'm suffering from Lymphoma cancer."

I'd had too much to drink with friends and declared with the confidence of a drunk, "That's bullshit! I've got some stuff that will cure you for sure."

I then told Ant the story about Linda, who had the same type of cancer, and how she'd produced the Sea Minerals that she believed had cured her and then sold them commercially. Also, how she'd had the liquid mixed with petroleum jelly to make an ointment.

"I know your mum suffers from skin cancers," I said, "so to help prove it works, tell her to put it on her skin cancers and watch how they react and disappear."

Ant is still alive, and her mum, after using the cream, never needed to have another skin cancer burnt off.

We trained a horse called Star's Ego at the time, with a cancerous growth in the corner of his eye. Our vet, Trevor Robson, explained that Star would need an operation. But the horse was winning races then, so Trevor said he would wait and operate on Star once he'd finished his racing prep.

"For what it's worth," I said to Trevor, "I will faithfully give Star the liquid through a syringe into his mouth and apply the ointment to the growth three to four times a day."

I did, and the growth disappeared within six weeks.

By the time Star had finished his racing prep and was ready to go out for a spell, we could not see where the cancerous growth had been.

Later, when Linda presented her Sea Mineral products at a Natural Health Remedy Conference, she asked our Vet, Trevor Robson, to write a statement saying that to the best of his knowledge, Sea Minerals had been given to Stars Ego twice a day. Plus, the Sea Mineral ointment had been applied to the cancerous growth several times a day. The result was a complete cure. If it weren't, Trevor would have had to operate. Of course, there was no denying the result, so Trevor wrote the letter.

At the same time, we decided to give a large capful to our racehorses every day. We raced thirteen horses within twelve weeks, and they all won! With something so unbelievable happening, you convince yourself it is *impossible*! Now that is stupid.

The unfortunate part of this story is that Linda Filewood died (not from cancer.) It was when her 'Sea Minerals' were becoming a great success. Her son, Dean, was making the most out of their good fortune; therefore, he was not interested in taking over the business when his mother died. Regrettably, he sold Linda's Sea Mineral Company.

However, other companies have since emerged to sell Sea Mineral products. I still tell people about *Australian-produced* Sea

Minerals. And the miracles keep happening.

*

Wade will not let me rest unless I mention Mr. Yamano, our delightful and generous owner from Japan. Mr. Yamano would visit us twice a year to watch his horses race and inspect his breeding stock at Harvey Woodlouse's magnificent property, 'Amber Park,' Kulnura, NSW. On one visit, Mr. Yamano accompanied Wade to Bathurst races to see his horse, 'Aragarto,' race on Anzac Day. Unfortunately, she was beaten by a nostril to run second. When Wade said how sorry he was, Mr. Yamano replied. 'Never mind, vely difficult for Japanese name horse to win on Anzac Day. Aso."

*Mrs. Yamano is in the middle of her Japanese Tea Ceremony at Windermere Farm. Notice the green shagpile carpet?*

So many clients have become friends and will never be forgotten or cease to be appreciated for their loyalty and generosity. If they choose to read my memoirs, they will know who they are. To name them all would run the risk of leaving some out.

During our final years of training racehorses, Tom Sewell had been our business's savior and, on occasion, our sanity. When Tom died, I was asked by his family to write something about Tom, which was easy as he was one of the most generous people I have ever met. I tried to do him justice in the poem below. Written 13/10/2018.

ONE word encompasses Tom Sewell.

**INTEGRITY.**

I - stands for the _Ingenious_ ideas Tom brought to fruition.

N - is for the _Never-ending_ love and empathy he gave to his family and friends.

T - is for the _Tenacity_ Tom showed for all he believed in.

E - is Tom's amazing _Energy_ for life.

G - is for Tom's enormous _Generosity_ seldom shown in any person.

R - is for Tom's eternal passion for _Racing_.

I - is for Tom's _Intuition_ which he never failed to follow.

T - is for _Tolerance_ and understanding of others.

Y - is for - forever _Young_.

Tom is sadly missed, and his passing is one of the reasons we retired when we did.

*Tom and Una Sewell, after Hamburg ran to victory at Hawkesbury.*

# Chapter 21
# The Daisley Family - Owners of Windermere

I should now explain a little more about how we became extended family to the Daisleys. (Before I run out of paper and ink.) We moved to Windermere when Donald and Sylvia's children were married and pregnant. So our children virtually grew up together. Every weekend, Ross, with his wife, Marietta, Helen (the only daughter of Donald and Sylvia), her husband, Rod, and sometimes Peter, the youngest Daisley son, Kathy, his wife, and their children, would come to stay at the farm. We rarely saw Donald junior and his family. Except when Sylvia brought their two children to the farm.

Every Sunday night, after the usual barbeque, Ross, and Marietta, with their young daughters, Sascha and Savannah, would come over to the cottage, and Wade would make pancakes for dinner.

We would then play the card game '500,' and the kids would play bull under the rug. It was great fun for all. But Julie, Helen, and Rod's eldest daughter would cry all the way home because Rod wouldn't stay. He wanted to get home and watch the news. Spoilt sport. I always felt sorry for you, Julie.

Our fabulous, shared holidays were unforgettable. Especially our trip to Ayers Rock. I stand corrected Uluru. Ten adults and eleven kids journeyed to the red center of Australia in 1987. We had the wonderful and unique experience of 'riding camels to dinner,' which was hilarious.

Climbing Uluru was awe-inspiring; it felt like we were standing on top of the world. Although I agree with our indigenous people, their sacred rock should have never touched the millions of feet climbing its surface. I suppose we were lucky to have climbed the rock and written our names on a piece of paper which we left inside a Milo tin. Maybe someone has kept it as a record for future reference. I now feel guilty, but the Aborigines had not complained about us climbing Uluru back then.

*The Windermere Wackers at Uluru.*

'Windermere Whackers' we named our group of the fun-loving holiday-makers.

Queenstown, New Zealand, was another memorable trip. On our first day skiing down a snow-clad mountain, Mariette, Ross, Dina, and Kent, plus anyone else in our group who was a competent skier, left Wade, me, and Lisa with a troupe of mostly children and a patient ski instructor. We had never skied before. Daniel was working and couldn't make it, a shame as he was a brilliant skier. Dan had impeccable balance. He walked when he was eight and a half months old.

After the lesson, Wade left me struggling while he plodded over to the café to relax and enjoy a hot chocolate. Notably upset that she could not ski, Lisa was ushered away by the two compassionate sisters, Sascha and Savannah.

Determined me, stayed on after the lesson, trying to master the art of skiing. After a while, I thought I was doing okay, and my improvement was later noticed by the other, 'Windermere Wackers,' who were all expert skiers.

"You're ready to ski Dor," said Dina, "We'll take you up the mountain and help you down." What did that mean?

185

Oh well, as I always do, I had a go.

Rising to the top of the mountain looked easy, especially when a young man assisted me onto the bum lift, a long pole with a bar at the end where one places their posterior.

"If the pole goes down and you lose contact with the bar under your bottom, please remain standing. It will come up again. But you must let go and separate yourself from the lift if you fall." Said the young man sporting a knowing grin.

The poshly-spoken lady who sat on the lift directly in front of me turned slightly and said condescendingly.

"You will be fine if you do as the man says."

Halfway up the mountain, the pole suddenly dropped, leaving me without the bar attached to my bottom. The only trouble was, it never rose, well, not quick enough. I lost my balance as the pole began to swing, and I fell unceremoniously. But was I going to let go of that pole? NO! Particularly when I looked down to see the dangerous depth. Then I looked up to see the massive height. So I hung on while hearing a chorus from Mrs posh.

"Let go! Let it go! Let go of the pole! Let it go!"

"I'm not letting any f.n… thing GO!" I said.

Dina sat gracefully on the pole in front of Mrs posh and laughed her way up the mountain. Finally, battered and bruised from the rocks I'd been dragged over and belittled by the punishing looks I'd received from Mrs posh, I eventually regained my dignity. Dina, I'm sure, wet herself laughing before recovering breath enough to tell the others what had happened. When their laughter ceased, I concentrated on skiing down the mountain. Holy shit, it was steep! I noticed the outer side of the mountain fell a vertical five miles, so I kept well away. Kent, Dina's husband, had been an international ski instructor, and so he explained just how I could accomplish descending this monstrous mountain safely.

I began skiing with Kent's instructions, a little wobbly, and then I got the gist.

Now, this is where I will tell you about the outfit. I'd borrowed a gold sequined ski suit, a white fur hat, and diamond-studded pink ski glasses.

Not the outfit one wears when learning to ski.

Well, what do you know, I was actually skiing. FASTER. FASTER!

Kent, an expert skier, skied backward and, simultaneously, videoed me.

The 'Aunty Dawn and Uncle Arthur' skit was well-known on 'Comedy Company.' Kent did the voice-over while videoing.

*"And here comes Aunty Dawn in her beautiful gold ski suit. She's skiing like a champion! There you go, Aunty Dawn, there you go!"*

I don't know if it was my laughter or the speed I'd accumulated, but the skis suddenly crossed, and down I went headfirst into the snow. I couldn't see, but I could hear the laughter before Marietta said, "Isn't someone going to pick her up?"

I hoped so because I couldn't move and was about to suffocate!

The story does not end there!

I decided then. I was not ready for the monster mountain, so I skied carefully to the next slope, designed for intermediate skiers. Yes, that's more like it! I spotted a conveyer belt, or whatever they call it, where you hang on with one hand while it tows you up to a higher level. Smart arse me grabbed the handle but missed and fell. The thirty or more people behind me fell like dominos, one on top of the other.

I was not popular.

*The ever chic, Ross and Marieta, and brilliant skiers, no less.*

After our morning ski lesson, Wade made a wise move. He'd taken the first bus to leave the snowfields. Back in the comfort of our Hotel room, he enjoyed a hot shower, lay on our luxurious bed, read a book, and drank Scotch and coke. WE, expert skiers, stayed on until dusk.

Ross was notorious for holding up the works wherever we went and did so on this occasion. We provided excuses to the Bus Driver on Ross's behalf, especially as it was the last bus taking skiers down the mountain.

Eventually, and not before, a few disgruntled passengers protested. "Leave him behind. The bloody cheek of him!" Ross appeared carrying a tray laden with hot drinks, chips, party pies, and sandwiches. Oh yes, and chocolate bars. The driver physically stopped Ross from entering the bus. "You're not allowed to bring food and drinks onto the bus. Sorry mate."

Never to be outdone, Ross, with our help, argued the point until the Bus Driver relented. He, too, wanted to be home with his family, sitting by a warm fire. We hadn't travelled far down the mountain when we heard an urgent radio call.

"Do not proceed! Hear this. Do not proceed! Bus hanging over mountain edge!"

'SHIT!' Was the general reaction.

*Our NZ skiing holiday. On the homeward bus with Dina-Lee, Kent, me,*
*and the beautiful Sascha, who is going to hate me for this pic!*

Ross, always the gentleman, shared his food with fellow passengers. The ones that hadn't moaned, that was. The bus driver was allowed first choice. Two and a half hours later, we arrived back at the Hotel with stories to tell and one of the funniest videos I have ever watched. At least twenty times, we all roared laughing at my fall from Grace in the bedazzling ski suit, head planted firmly in the snow. I must add there was nobody injured in the hanging bus fiasco.

*

A recent visit from our dear friend Dina Lee in May 2022 had me agreeing to include a funny story about when Dina came to help Wade make melon jam at the farm. So I am in the present again, writing about the past.

It was a humid summer evening in 1985 when Dina Lee came to help cut up three humongous jam melons under Wade's persuasion. As Wade does, he delegated Dina and me to do the chopping while he placed the sugary lot into what looked like an orphanage boiler. He then left us to watch television; occasionally, he'd return to stir the pot. The phone rang in the kitchen, where Dina and I sat dutifully cutting up the melons. Wade answered. It was a call from a disgruntled horse owner, threatening to take his horse to another trainer if Wade did not follow instructions. All trainers have this issue from time to time. Even Bart Cummings would say to his clients, I charge $100 a day to train your horse, but if you try and help, it's $200. (Don't quote me on price)

I could hear clearly what was said, so I fumed while Wade tried to appease the man, making me madder. I voiced my opinion, hoping the man would hear me. Wade kept placing his hand over the phone piece, telling me to shut up, making me even madder until I stood with the giant carving knife in hand, waving it about like a sword. I needed to go to the toilet, situated at the end of the veranda. I took the knife, and halfway to the bathroom, I poked my head through the open window into the kitchen and gave Wade a mouthful on why he should not take shit from anyone while shaking the knife at him.

"Where are you going?" Asked Wade.

"I'm going to the toilet!"

Dina remained silent with her head down, chopping the melon.

Once relieved, as I'm sure Wade was when I'd disappeared. I returned to see Dina still chopping and Wade calmly stirring the jam pot.

"What happened?" I asked.

"We will talk about it later, Dor." Said a calm Wade, but I still seethed. Poor Dina Lee, I thought. However, she'd witnessed Wade and me fighting before. Plenty of times. But I calmed down for Dina's benefit. Wade, the delegator, continued watching television while we two enslaved women made little progress on the gigantic melons. Dina laughed while relaying the last scene, saying, "I thought you were about to stab Wade with the knife. But then I thought, no, that's just Dor. A born actress."

I saw the funny side, as I always do.

I looked at the time, which was getting late, when Dina said, "we'll be here all night, Dor cutting up those melons."

We'd accomplished quite a pile, ready for the next jam lot.

"No, we won't," I said, gathering the uncut melons and throwing them outside and over the fence into the horse paddock. Wade returned to the kitchen and looked at the empty space where the melons had been.

"Have you cut all those melons up already?" He asked, a little surprised.

"Of course we did. And we'd have been much quicker if you'd helped!" Said I, who won't take shit from anyone.

So there you are, dearest Dina, a story you have never forgotten. I hope I've done it justice.

*

Now I will give you a fine example of Wade's adage.

*'We all need help coming into the world and leaving it.'*

Sylvia Daisley, the wife of Donald, mother to Donald Junior, Ross Peter, Helen, and dearest friend to us, had open-heart surgery at age eighty. After the operation, Sylvia had what appeared to be an epileptic fit and was prescribed a drug called Epilim. From then on, Sylvia went into a downward spiral. So much so that the family thought it best to place her in a nursing home. Lisa was at University at the time, studying to be a nurse, and could not bear the thought of Sylvia, her surrogate grandmother, living in a nursing home. Lisa suggested Sylvia live with us, and Lisa promised to rally her student friends to help care for Sylv whenever we could not due to our workload.

The Daisley family delighted with the idea, so Sylvia moved in with us. At first, she seemed okay, although she slept most of the day. I'd heard of the drug 'Epilim' through my cousin Betty. When she was seven, her daughter, Jane, began having epileptic fits and was given

Epilim. It had the same effect on young Jane; she literally slept most of the time, so the drug was changed appropriately. Therefore, I believe Sylvia's medicine also needed to be changed. After all, it had made a huge difference to Jane.

Plus, I knew Epilim was too potent for Sylvia because she'd lay down and sleep for hours whenever she took a single aspirin for a headache!

I asked Ross if I could take Sylvia off Epilim, especially when I had to administer it in liquid through a syringe, as Sylvia was too non-compass to swallow tablets.

Ross said he would ask the doctor about changing the drug.

"She may have another fit and die." Said the Doctor.

I shook my head at his stupidity. Sylvia was not living, only surviving.

Sylvia slept so soundly; that she'd wet the bed, which meant changing her pants throughout the night. A terrible ordeal. (You ask why I need to tell this? The funny part is coming.) So we invented a 'wee-wee pad.' Helen, her daughter, stitched them together. They were square pieces of plastic with super absorbent material sewn on top. I'd check it once or twice through the night, and if soaked, I'd change it with a dry one. Sylvia never woke; it was a simple pull and push motion to change it. Still, I knew this was unnecessary - the drug was the problem. I became so frustrated when people wouldn't listen to me that I threw the Epilim in the bin! Voila! Three days later, Sylv, who needed a wheelchair and rarely spoke, began walking and talking almost back to normal.

When Sylvia was still in her incoherent state and sleeping ninety percent of the time, her family paid for carers to come at 9 am to shower and dress her. Plus, they attend to other needs, e.g., doctor appointments, going to the movies, anything she felt like doing, until three pm. Then we'd take over. Monique's sister, Belinda, was one of Sylvia's angels, I would hear them laughing all the time, and nothing was too much trouble for Belinda. She cared for Sylvia with all her heart and soul. Thank you, darling Belinda. Sadly, Belinda later died of a heart attack aged forty-five, and I know she is amongst fellow angels. We miss her very much. Sylv had other angels, Jenny and Sue. Thank you, ladies, for your kindness and compassion.

Sylvia's extra care was given during the first year she moved in with us. However, after I threw the Epilim in the bin, Sylvia showered and managed most things herself. The Doctors had given Sylv twelve months to live after her operation. But she beat the odds! For nine years, we loved having Sylvia live with us.

Sylvia was true blue. She never mixed her words and gave everyone many shards of good advice, EG: "make yourself happy don't rely on anyone else to do it."

She was also my partner in crime. I'd buy a new dress and hang it in the middle room of the main house. Donald and Sylvia stayed there almost every weekend until we moved from the cottage to care for Sylvia. The first thing Sylv would do was to check what I'd bought. So when Wade would question me like a school principal. "When did you buy that dress, Doreen? You know we can't afford to buy new clothes all the time!"

I'd say. "Ask Sylv. She knows. I've had it for ages."

And dear Sylv would back me up. "Yes, it's true. Dor has had that for ages."

Not a lie.

I'd look forward to a quiet chat and a cupper on most Sunday afternoons with Sylv. But Wade always came looking for me, probably to do something he could have done himself. I'd hide under the kitchen table, and Sylv would say, "Dor's just left, Wade. She must be hiding somewhere." We'd laugh our heads off.

When Sylvia was coming out of her Epilim stupor and still occasionally needed her wee-wee pad ( now the funny part), she had a habit of ringing her bell several times throughout the night. It was supposed to be a warning that she wanted something done, or something was wrong.

However, and unfortunately for us, she'd ring the bell at 2 am to tell us things like, "I'd like to go on a holiday. Can you please phone Ross and ask him to arrange it." Yes, it was funny. Most of the time. But at this stage, Sylv was still a little non-compos, so Wade warned her.

"Okay, Sylv, don't ring the bell unless. The house is on fire. Or we're being robbed. Or you're about to be raped!"

Of course, we laughed. But it worked; Sylv never rang the bell through the night again. Yes, she was getting better every day.

About a week had elapsed since Wade's warning, and I was asleep on the couch. I think it was the only time Wade understood how exhausted I was. So he put Sylv to bed, which entailed pulling her nightdress up and placing her bottom dead center on the wee-wee pad, then lifting her legs up and onto the bed. (While he looked the other way.) He pushed and pulled to no avail; he just couldn't get the knack of getting Sylv's bottom in the center position of the wee - wee pad. So he stood on the bed and straddled her, thinking he could do it that way.

"Should I ring the bell now?" Sylvia asked.

"Why," he said.

"You said if I look like being raped!"

We've shared many a chuckle over that story.

Apart from Mum, Sylv was the funniest lady I've ever met. She had a dry sense of humour, and like, Mum, she didn't suffer fools or flatterers. One of Sylv's pieces of wisdom. "They may have a stone to grind, and you may be their grindstone."

Another night, just after the tragic September - Eleven terror attack on the Twin Towers in New York. We slept in the furthest room away from Sylv, and as is our habit when first going to bed, we were reading. We heard Sylv's walking stick, clunkedy clunk, clunkedy clunk, down the hallway. Sylv popped her head through the doorway and said, in her usual croaky voice, (she had nodules on her throat).

"The television's on fire!"

Wade and I thought, *oh, she's just watching the news*.

"No, Sylv, that's just the news on the Twin Towers. Go and turn it off." Said Wade.

Two minutes later, we heard the same clunkedy clunk, clunkedy clunk.

"I'm telling you; the television's on fire!" She said indignantly

"You'd better go take a look," I said to wade.

He moaned, as he usually does when he's inconvenienced.

A minute later, I heard Wade call. "Quick, Dor, the TV's on fire!"

I ran down the hallway to see Wade standing statuesque, hands in the air, not knowing what to do. So I told him – as I usually do.

"Pull the plug out and throw the doona over the TV. Quick! Pick it up and throw it out on the lawn."

Black plastic dripped over the green New Zealand wool carpet as he hurried outside with the melting TV.

"Great." I said, "we'll replace the carpet! The home and contents are insured."

Now let me tell you, the carpet was a mid-green indestructible shagpile and hopefully irreplaceable, *Thank the good Lord*, I thought.

But Wade loved the carpet, so the next day, unbeknown to me, he'd cut the melted plastic off the abundant shagpile.

"See," he said, "I've saved the carpet!"

Bloody dill!

*Enjoying a barbeque breakfast at the farm while Sylvia lived with us. Left to right, Ross, me, Sylvia in her wheelchair, Geoffrey Robinson, part owner of Hungry Dawson, with his darling wife, Sandy. And Wade the cook as usual!*

When in 2019, potential buyers came to inspect Windermere, I'd say. "The home IS NOT heritage listed. But the carpet is!"

That received a few horrified looks until they got the joke.

Giving the carpet, it's due. You could spill anything on it, red wine, blackberry juice, coffee, etc. And after mopping it up, not a trace could be seen.

During Sylvia's time with us, we were fortunate and honoured to have the world-renowned Monty Roberts, 'Horse Whisperer,' come to the farm for a day. The reason for Monty's visit? Monty was looking for a rustic horse barn to produce a video with the Reverend Bill Crews and his band of homeless and abused teenagers. Our friend Rob Horne, also a remarkable horseman, worked with Monty on his horsemanship shows

194

around Australia, so Rob suggested our barn.

The video was to show Monty's gentle methods on how trust and respect between horses and humans can be established. The old barn at Windermere was a perfect dwelling to showcase this! It felt surreal to have Monty, and his lovely wife, Pat, in our home and watch Monty's magic when working with horses and children. We cooked them a sausage sizzle on the barbie and were delighted to be part of this once-in-a-lifetime experience.

Whatever happened to the video, I'll never know. But the most memorable moment was at the end when Sylvia approached Monty with a Novel in hand, asking in her endearing croaky voice.

"Monty, would you mind signing my book."

Monty assumed it was his 'Horse Whisperer' book and said.

"Why, ma'am, it would be my honour."

When Sylv handed him a copy of 'Gone with the Wind,' Monty said. "That's not my book!"

And Sylvia said, "I know. It's mine, but you can sign it."

Well, Pat Roberts split her sides laughing, as we all did.

*Sylvia with the famous horseman, Monty Roberts.*

*Priceless photos of Monty Roberts, featured with the Reverend Bill Cruise and a couple of the troubled boys, bought to the farm for the day to learn Monty's methods on how communication with horses can also work between humans.*

\*

Later, while Sylvia was still living with us, my dear cousin Betty suggested that my mum and dad needed to sell their home in Rye, as they were reaching the age when they needed help. Of course, I agreed, and we made arrangements for them to come live nearby. My brother Wayne helped with the move and drove them up to the farm. The following day Mum became quite ill and was admitted to Hawkesbury Hospital. The tests revealed she had a ruptured bowel. After the bowel operation, Mum suffered many minor strokes, reeling her into dementia. When her condition did not improve, we sadly needed to find a good nursing home, which we did. Dad visited her every day, staying from morning to night, and eventually, his loving care brought her around. It took almost twelve months, and although Mum was a bit doolally, she was happy and funny.

Dad spent those twelve months waiting for Mum to mend with us at the farm. Sylvia and Dad loved the races, and Dad would push Sylvia around in her wheelchair (she could walk, but it was a lot easier to move her when we went out.) They got along well, though sometimes Dad played practical jokes on Sylvia that she always took in good humour. One day at the races, I heard Dad and Sylvia laughing, so I walked over, and Sylvia said,' your dad just backed the wrong horse in Melbourne. He kept the ticket because he said it might be lucky. And the horse has just won at $100 to $1. He had five bucks each way!"

Dad and Sylvia were the perfect pair, being Taureans, I suppose. Together they'd read the newspaper from front to back. Seeing them chatting on the veranda about current events was a pleasure.

When Mum healed enough to return home, she decided to live in a nearby retirement villa. They were there for almost three years before Dad died from an aneurysm. Mum died a year later from many ailments. They were the most loving parents any child could wish for; we were indeed blessed.

One funny story, I must tell. Mum feared being cremated and demanded that she would come back and haunt me if I did. Dad privately told me he wanted to be cremated, and his ashes spread with Dawn and Ernie into the ocean at Safety Beach Victoria. "I don't know how you'll get around this with your mother if I go first." He said.

Luckily Mum had never fully recovered mentally from her minor strokes. It left her with slight dementia, so it wasn't difficult to cover up Dad's cremation. Later I placed his ashes in a cupboard, waiting for the opportunity to take both ashes to Safety beach.

When Mum died, I went against her wishes and had her cremated. After collecting her ashes, I placed them beside Dad's. I needed to go to the toilet. When I sat on the seat, I spoke to Mum. "There you see, Mum. Now your spirit is with Dad. It doesn't matter what happens to your body."

The heavy bracket around the heating lamp on the roof crashed onto my head. "OH, shit, that hurt! You old bitch!" I yelled but laughed at the same time. She'd kept her promise. Funny.

It wasn't easy to care for our older crew and manage a horse training business, especially as it demanded physical and mental strength. I began to suffer from the constant pressures; I had no time. It was all work and no play. That's when Lisa suggested I take some time off and play golf. I'd never played before but knew Dad had been an excellent golfer, so I gave it a go. Lisa drove me to the Nutmans golf course in Grose Wold. Before this, it had been their horse property. And now Wade and I stay in the refurbished Pro Shop, as years later, John Nutman turned the golf course into five-acre lots and then sold them. Lisa lives over the road in a small cottage on fourteen acres, and Sarah, our friend, owns the five-acre block that holds the refurbished pro shop, now their guest house. Sarah insists we stay there. Thank you, darling Sarah.

I have so many humorous golf stories, but it would only bore you if you're not a golfer. Anyway, I took to golf straight away. I had lessons with a professional and dragged poor Dina Lee away from whatever she was doing to come and teach me how to play golf. When ready, I joined Windsor Golf Club, and I can honestly say golf saved my life. I'd practice with plastic balls in the expansive garden of the farm. Sylvia always watched from the veranda, throwing me encouragement. Sylvia was a talented player in her younger years, as was my dad. Thanks again to Dina-Lee Stuart, Mark Tolhurst's sister, for her never-ending patience in teaching and showing me the art and fundamentals of playing golf. What fun we had over many-many years. You are a champion Dina-Lee.

Sadly, after living nine years with us, we lost our dear Sylvia. She lay in Hawkesbury Hospital with an oxygen mask sitting over her nose and mouth, suffering from bronchitis. Wade and I visited Sylvia three times a day, and on her final night, her dinner sat covered on the tray, so Wade took the cover off and gathered food on a fork.

I had a feeling Sylvia would leave us that evening, so I held her hand and took the opportunity to tell her how much I loved her. She returned the sentiment, "I'll see you again, Dor." Meaning the afterlife we'd often speak about, Sylvia placed the oxygen mask back over her face.

Meanwhile, Wade had a plentiful supply of vegetables sitting on the fork. "Here you are, Sylv, eat this. It will make you better." Said Wade.

Sylvia took the oxygen mask off and said, 'you've got to be joking."

Sylv left us that night with one of her best quips.

# Chapter 22
# The Love of Storytelling

My writing began significantly in 1987, I think. The universe called, and I began writing Children's stories. Wade would find me in the wee hours of the morning, sitting at the kitchen table, handwriting my Wicky Wacky Farm tales. The literary experts say if you are going to write, write about something you know. And many funny things had happened on the farm that linked to our children.

And so began my journey. I wrote stories about Wally and Dora and their children, Donny and Lulu, who lived on Wicky Wacky Farm. The names I chose were close to ours, though only one stuck: Wally. Everyone thought it suited Wade better.

When I wrote about Auntie Jane and Uncle Mark, who lived next door, I asked them. "What name would you like me to call you in the stories?" Mark replied. "What's wrong with Mark and Jane?"

Indeed! And I wasn't going to denigrate them in any way. How could I?

They have been an integral part of our lives and are seemingly indestructible, as I will now prove with this little ditty.

On a storm-threatening day, Jane was down their back paddock working their Polo ponies, riding one, leading four, two on either side. It's a bloody difficult job, especially if the horses become fractious, which they did when the predicted storm gushed in. Claps of thunder boomed so loud the four horses Jane was leading reared with fright and broke away, heading for the catching yard. The gate was a post and rail affair that looked old-worldly and was not easy to budge. Jane urged her horse into a gallop. If luck had it, she'd beat the mob before they crashed into the fence, or better still, she'd open the gate and corral them safely. Jane won the gallop, as only Calamity Jane can do. She jumped off her horse and, with great effort, struggled to open the wooden gate. Jane was almost there when the terrified mob galloped towards her in a charge to rival the Light Horse. Over the top of Jane, they galloped hooves connected from every direction; in everyone's opinion, she should have been killed. But not 'Calamity Jane,' as I'd nicknamed her, due to many scrapes she'd gotten herself into. I love Janie to bits, and like me, she never takes life too seriously.

I was out and about checking on our horses when I saw our apprentice Jockey, Kevin Harpley, who'd seen the entire scenario, struggling to carry Jane over his shoulder. 'Help!' He cried.

I ran to them and was horrified to see Jane's injuries. "Just wait here," I said and quickly backtracked to my car, then carefully placed Jane in the front seat. I then drove like Jack Brabham to Windsor Hospital. Of course, I stayed and made Jane laugh. She was lucky to be alive—a reason to celebrate.

In the meantime, Mark had phoned Wade to see where Jane was, and he told him. "Dor took Jane to the Hospital. She'll be okay. She just got run over by a mob of horses. Don't worry. She won't die."

Shocked at the thought, Mark hurried to the hospital and found us laughing. Although, one look at Jane lying in bed with a significant chunk of wood protruding from her upper arm, a large gash across her forehead, and numerous other injuries. Mark passed out on the floor. A nurse rushed over, took one look, and said. "Someone find him a pillow. Next came their daughter, our Goddaughter, Amanda, who went green around the gills and slumped in her chair.

A memorable day among many.

Over the years, Janie and I have taken turns driving one another to the Hospital. Horses can be dangerous!

*At the Polo with Jane, my sister in spirit.*

200

Through cohesion and demand from family and friends, I eventually forwarded the Wicky Wacky Farm stories to Penguin Publishers. Nearly four months passed, and I hadn't heard back. I thought, oh, they've thrown the stories in the bin. But when I phoned and spoke about my books to the receptionist, she said, "I'll ask my boss." She returned five minutes later. "Hello, Doreen. I have to tell you, your stories are on the shortlist, and you will receive a letter soon."

OMG! I couldn't believe it! How does a rooky writer get published first off? Unfortunately, I never did.

However, I did receive what most authors say is not the norm.

An encouraging letter arrived. *Your stories are delightful. However, it is with much consideration that we must decline the publication. Penguin Publishers have cut children's Farm stories by two-thirds. We are looking toward science fiction, as we believe this is where the future market lies.*

Maybe I could have sent the Wicky Wacky family into space to see if they had farms on the moon? No, I'd just stick to the real deal. I've never liked science fiction. Maybe Harry Potter. Yes, I do like Harry.

Years passed, and when my granddaughters, Grace, and Emma, were four years old, Lisa said. "Why don't you read your Wicky Wacky Farm stories to the girls, Mum?"

Lisa was busy, though she could hear me reading the stories. I must say I had a captive audience.

"You should have another go at getting them published, Mum," Lisa said after I'd finished.

The Computer age had hit like magic, and my old typed pages had faded.

"I'll have to re-write them on the Computer," I said. "I'll go online and see what I can find about publishing these days."

I emailed the stories to every known publisher in Australia. None were taking chances with unknown authors, so I began looking overseas. Perhaps the Yanks would appreciate my Aussie Farm stories. And yes, they did. Strategic Publishers from New York put their hand up. They loved the kangaroo, the polo theme, and later Little Thought Monsters.

The CEO, Robert Fletcher, phoned to say he'd placed a sign above his office door, 'LEAVE YOUR THOUGHT MONSTERS OUTSIDE!' What a compliment.

Robert and his partner, Leslie, became our friends, and when in

Sydney, they stayed with us at Windermere Farm. Mark and Jane also treated them to a sailing trip around Sydney Harbour in their yacht.

Robert had hired a conference room in a Sydney Hotel to meet and speak about Strategic Publishing with his Australian Authors. One guest speaker impressed me, though I cannot remember her name. She was from 'Ingram Sparks, Lightning Source Printers,' based in Melbourne. Strategic had set up a deal to print their Aussie books with Ingram Sparks. Usually, it would take two to three weeks to receive our orders from America, plus the postage was costly.

Our saviours had arrived in the name of 'Ingram Sparks.'

Before this event, I'd secured a time slot as a Strategic Author at the Beijing Book Expo. In my excitement, I thought it a good idea to ask a group of friends to join me, and we'd go sightseeing in the bargain. So, Jane, her friend Maggie, our client and funny friend Marie Baker and Chris Lawlor's daughter, Melanie, who stood as my secretary, flew to Beijing. This was the first time I'd traveled overseas, apart from our numerous trips to New Zealand to buy horses.

I packed a bundle of different-sized blow-up kangaroos plus metal bookmarks with a painted map of Australia and Koalas. I went prepared to sweeten the public! No, I wasn't. Nothing could have prepared me for the crowds who gathered literally to stare at the blown-up kangaroos. It was hilarious, but not for the guards who often had to move the sea of Chinese people away.

My first slot *in the booth* proved effective. A Mr. Wang Yongli from CCTV Beijing approached and asked while browsing through my Wicky Wacky Farm books.

"So, how rong it take you to wite TV selies on storlies?"

"Oh, about a week!" I replied.

"Oh, leally?"

"No, I'm only joking. I'd need co-writers, I'm sure. But I'm pretty quick at whatever I do."

(Except writing memoirs.)

"I have your books published in China." Said Wang Yongli. "Then the Chinese Government approves children to read stories in school. When popular, we do TV series. It may take a rong time. You agree?"

"Yes. Most certainly, I agree!"

'May take a rong time – may take a rong time – may take a

rong time.' The sentence kept repeating itself. Has anyone dealt with the Chinese?

Six years later, Yongli had ten Wicky Wacky Farm stories published in one bi-lingual book. He had also secured the stories with the Chinese Government. They agreed, 'Yes! Official reading for Chinese school curriculum.'

Murphy's law stepped in.

"So, Solly. New translation methods just now come to Chinese schools. Name Pin Ying. So no Wicky Wacky Farm books for schools now. Must have translation changed to new Ping-Ying. Then try again.

*Finally published in China, thanks to my friend Wang Yongli.*

As is the Chinese way, a favour is returned with a favour. Yongli needed my help translating and editing a novel he had written called 'Hell and The World.' To say it was a harrowing experience would be a gross understatement. Not only with my struggle to untangle Yongli's English, which I was not then equipped to do. At least at that stage in my writing career. But his story about a little girl who'd witnessed her entire family being slaughtered in the 1989 Tiananmen Square massacre upset me terribly. And the atrocities she perceived and physically experienced, from the time of her survival that night to eventually escaping into a more enlightened and democratic Chinese society, moved me to tears. Often. Plus, I suffered extreme anger and sometimes depression. Something I had never experienced before when writing. Wade told me to give it up, as the story disturbed me too much. But I stuck with it, and Strategic Publishers kept their word and published the book. Yongli had done a deal with Robert Fletcher. If Robert published the book, Yongli would give Robert thirty minutes of prime time on CCTV Beijing.

My only regret is that Strategic did not edit my work. And God knows it needed editing. Sorry Yongli, I did my best at the time. Oh, yes, let me not forget when Strategic Publishing and its authors were packing up to leave the Chinese Book Expo, an ocean of blackheads appeared and stood in front of our Booth.

*Wang Longli's book that I helped edit. A harrowing and troubling story that moved me to tears on many occassions.*

"What do they want, Robert?" I asked.

"They want those damned kangaroos!"

I laughed, yelling to the crowd.

"Okay, I'm going to throw kangaroos at you! But no fighting, or I will stop!"

The guards also lined up. Luckily, I had about ten kangaroos in their plastic bags, so I threw a few out to the crowd. Nobody even tried to catch them. So I demonstrated how to take the Kangaroos out of the bag and blow them up.

"Ahhh, Soooo!" I heard from the mob, accompanied by nods and knowing smiles. Then things got more animated as Robert and I began throwing the bags. Eventually, I handed the already blown-up roos to the guards and thanked them for their excellent work.

"Pity," Robert said, "You could have sold those Kangaroos and made a damn fortune!"

Wang Yongli, in my opinion, should be Prime Minister of China. He is an award-winning writer, a well-respected TV Producer, and tireless humanitarian. Yongli's books of poetry are to be treasured. He loves and protects nature to the point where he would like to receive a Noble Peace prize. Not for himself but to help his fellow citizens understand how essential the Earth's Ecology is to our survival. I hope I live to see the day when Yongli's wish comes true. Now I'm stuck between China and traveling to my next Book Expo, so I think it's an appropriate time to tell you the right Royal story.

I felt inspired to send Her Majesty, Queen Elizabeth 11, a gift for her Golden Jubilee. I Googled; how does one write an appropriate letter to Her Majesty. What better gift (I hoped) than five of my published Wicky Wacky Stories to read to her grandchildren. I'm a bit delusional sometimes.

Following Google's advice, I wrote, in my best handwriting, which I'd won an award for in primary school, though I needed to practice as the art had left me. Nevertheless, I strived to do my best and replay Her Majesty's memory back to 1954, when Her Majesty and Prince Phillip floated along Swanston street Melbourne, sitting in the back of an open Bentley, waving to their Australian subjects. Namely, me- me – me!

I wrote. But I won't quote because I can't find the letter.

"Your Majesty may remember a little dark-haired girl waving to you from the front row of your admirers on that occasion. I do hope your Majesty remembers. I say this because my father had lifted me to sit on his shoulders. I called out, 'I love you, Queenie,' and Your Majesty waved directly at me."

I assume we all know Queen Elizabeth has a wonderful sense of humour. And my piece of cheek would have amused her. It must have because I received a personal handwritten letter of thanks, directed from Queen Elizabeth Herself.

Mrs D Slinkard
Windermere Farm
Wilberforce
NSW 2756
Australia

BUCKINGHAM PALACE

3rd July, 2012

Dear Mrs Slinkard,

The Queen wishes me to write and thank you for your letter enclosing some of the books you have written for children and which you have sent to Her Majesty as a present on the occasion of her Diamond Jubilee.

The Queen was pleased to hear your recollections from her visit to Melbourne in 1954 and Her Majesty was touched by your kind thought in sending her your gift.

I am to thank you again both for your present and your message of good wishes to The Queen in this, her Diamond Jubilee year.

Yours sincerely

Mary Morrison

Lady-in-Waiting

Mrs D Slinkard

*No doubt about me. More front than Myers! As the old saying goes.*

**LULU'S NEW PONY**
Doreen Slinkard

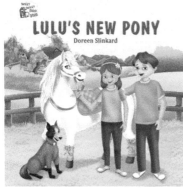

**PEPPI**
**The Polo Pony**
Doreen Slinkard

Wicky Wacky Farm Series Book 4
**The Uluru Adventure**
by Doreen Slinkard
Illustrations by Kaipart

Wicky Wacky Farm Stories
**Peppi Goes to China**
By Doreen Slinkard

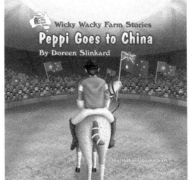

**Little Thought Monsters**
Doreen Slinkard

207

# Chapter 23
# Promoting Overseas

The London Book Expo 2011 was my next mission. I'd turned 60 - on March 6 and took the opportunity to gift myself a significant birthday present. So off to London, I travelled - alone. However, I would be joining the team from Strategic Publishing, whom I knew from meeting in Beijing.

During my final week in GB, I'd planned to stay with friends Mandy and Robert Shepherd, plus their four delightful children, Thoma, Tilly, Bea, and Digby. Mandy, many years before, had worked with us as a strapper cum track rider. At that time, Mandy was fortunate to find passage to England on board a flight carrying Thoroughbred Racehorses when her holidays were due. She was offered a free return if she accompanied and cared for two horses. An offer too good to refuse.

We wished Mandy well, plus I remember saying. "I'd like to be going with you, Mandy."

Three weeks into her four-week UK holiday, Mandy phoned to ask, at some un-Godly hour. "Will I still have my job if I stay in England for three months, Dor? I've applied for a working Visa, and I love it here." Of course, I said, 'yes.'

Mandy was a great girl, and even though she'd turn up late for work most days, she always had the most fantastic excuses. I looked forward to Mandy being late so we could hear her stories!

I love telling this next Mandy story. It's given me great mileage. Mandy began her three-month working stint in a small English Country pub near Salisbury. North Fordingbridge, to be exact. And while carrying a tray full of drinks to a table, the young, handsome Robert Shepherd crossed his long legs and tripped Mandy up. Over went Mandy and the drinks; Robert immediately went to her rescue. And the rest, they say, is history. Mandy stayed in England and married Robert Shepherd. Her triperuppa!

*Cheers Mandy and Rob, always a warm welcome and loads of fun at their amazing property in the UK.*

I kept in touch with Mandy, primarily through Monique, our foreperson back then. Many years later, Monique married Terry Robinson from Berry, where he and his family had lived for many years. They held a fabulous, fun wedding on their property near Berry. Mandy flew from England to attend and bought her son Digby, still in nappies, and a pram. It was the first time I'd seen Mandy since she'd left for England twelve years before. She hadn't changed a bit. However, her Aussie accent had, Mandy now speaks *very posh* English. From that day on, our friendship rekindled. Now I'm smiling at the change in Mandy's vocab, so I must tell the following story.

When going to England for the first time in 2011 and staying with the Shepherds, Mandy bundled her four children, plus their Jack Russel dog, Bindy, and me, into her four-wheeled Land Rover before driving us around their property.

I love that song by Sting. '*Will you lay with me in a field of Gold...*'

We came to a magnificently dense, tall field of golden barley, where we all lay down and then jumped up to surprise each other. Sounds silly, but it was fun. When done, Mandy called to her dog in her posh voice.

"Come, Bindy! We are leaving Bindy."

Bindy, it seemed, was lost in the field of gold.

We were all in the car waiting for Bindy to come.

"Bindy. Where are you, Bindy! Come Bindy." Mandy's calls continued until she lost her temper and screamed in her Aussie accent.

"Come ere Bindy! Ya bloody mongrel!"

I cracked up, and so did the kids, especially when I said.

"It Just proves. You CAN take the girl out of Australia, but you CAN NOT take the *Australian* out of the girl. Your mum would leave Eliza Doolittle for dead! My Fair Lady, in case you didn't know!"

I must now tell one more hilarious Mandy story.

Mandy and her family were leaving for a holiday to the Galapagos Islands on the morning of the night that I was to fly home.

The day before, Mandy asked if I could please drive their Land Rover down the road, or tight laneway, as we Aussies would call their roads. "Tilly will go with you, Dor, to show you where to stop and pick us up."

Thomma, Bea, Digby, and Mandy rode one pony each and led the others to a paddock where the ponies would stay until the family returned from their holiday. I drove to the designated spot and was momentarily stunned. Before us stood an enormous Friesian cow, she stood sideways, so her entire body blocked the lane. I sprung out of the car to see a row of vehicles lined up facing us on the opposite side of the road. The first was a Mercedes Benz with an attractive blond driver. Behind her, a Police car with two baby-faced cops sitting in the front. One was talking into his radio.

The blond woman wound her window down and said.

"Oh, do be careful. We think it's a bull."

I looked underneath the monster cow and saw an enormous udder.

"No love, she's a cow. See, there's her udder." I said, pointing to the mass.

Babyface Cop jumped out of his car, hands in the air. "STOP! Stand easy! Be careful!" He said in *very posh* English.

I had to laugh.

"It's only a bloody cow. What's wrong with you lot." I said in my best Aussie drawl. "Shoo, shoo," I yelled while waving my hands at the monster cow, who duly charged off, crashing through a low-lying fence. It needed mending anyway. Well, it did when she'd finished.

Babyface Cop then strode forward, proffering his hand.

"I say, well done. Yes, incredibly well done."

He had a firm handshake. I'll give him that.

By this time, Tilly was rolling around in the car laughing, and Mandy came running from the paddock where they'd left the ponies.

"What happened?" She asked.

I told her the story, and she joined Tilly in laughing.

The blond then drove up close. "Thank you so terribly much. I was quite frightened, really. You are so very brave. Do you come from Australia?"

"Yes," I replied.

"I see. Most understandable." She smiled and waved goodbye.

The entire trip was fabulous, especially The Book Expo, meeting interesting people from all over the world, plus weaving my way onto BBC TV.

Yes, that's right. I was sitting at my desk, 'Strategic Publishing Booth,' when two well-dressed young men carrying cameras and sound equipment came along and stood in front of me. Hence, they were blocking the crowd from seeing my book display.

I asked kindly. "Please move aside, gentlemen. This is my moment to shine."

"Oh, terribly sorry, Madam. We were just looking for an author to interview for BBC TV."

"Well, mate, you found her! Read the sign." To which I pointed.

'Doreen Slinkard – Author.'

"Oh, I say that would be perfect. Do you mind?"

"Is the Pope a Catholic?"

"Pardon me?"

"Never mind. Fire away."

Pardon?"

"Oh, p-l-e-a-s-e, just ask me a question!"

They wished to interview two authors, so I introduced them to a softly spoken American Author. (Hard to find). They interviewed her first. She spoke eloquently and answered all their questions about Kindle, allowing readers FREE access to the first chapter of any book before deciding whether to buy it. I thought, Oh well, that's me over. She's done a great job. BUT suddenly, the camera swung around. Never a copycat. I had to think quickly about my answer.

"Well," ( I said, my standard beginning), "I liken it to buying a bottle of wine. If you're not familiar with the brand, I think you should be able to taste it before you buy it! Therefore my answer is YES! Try before you buy!"

Imagine bottle shops full of people sampling wine all day. A crowd had gathered to watch the interview, and they laughed. I smiled after realizing what I'd said. And how I'd said it. Not a bad idea, though. The polite, well-spoken, and presumably well-bred young gentlemen gave me their card, and I returned my details. They finished with,

"We will text you in plenty of time if the interview airs on the BBC news. Tonight actually! Thank you, it was a pleasure to meet you, Doreen."

*At The London Book Fair.*

Later that night, I met up with Jen Robinson, the first daughter of Terry Robinson, before his marriage to Monique. Jen was living in London at the time and is a world-renowned Human Rights Lawyer. She represented Julian Assange in the Wicky Leak case. Anyway, in her choice of wine bars, I told Jen about my exciting day at the Book Expo and that I may be on TV. I'd phoned Mandy previously and told her. Within the next minute, a text on my phone said, YES, the interview would go to air in 30 minutes.

Knowing the Wine Bar proprietor, Jen asked him to turn the volume up on the *giant* TV so everyone could hear my interview. I wasn't going to argue with a lawyer, so I shrunk in my seat.

The segment finished with laughter throughout the bar, except for one who said in all seriousness.

"What a damn good idea!"

Meanwhile, at the Shepherds, Mandy tuned into my interview and laughed while Rob sat sipping his wine. "What's so funny about that, Mandy? Good on Dor!" Rob said with a wine glass salute.

*At The London Book Fair. Proud to be an Aussie!*

*

Throughout my memoirs, I have placed some events in the wrong order. And so it was that my trip to Paris came before I stayed at Mandy's Property in Salisbury. We were lucky to know Sandra Tremier, an attractive young French woman who rode our horses at the time. I remember the morning she came for a job interview. I sat talking with her on the veranda of the farmhouse when Wade appeared with a tray overloaded with bacon and

213

egg rolls. "The staff's breakfast," He said.

Sandra's eyes bulged, "Really. Are they for your staff?" She asked in her charming French accent.

"Yes, we give our riders breakfast every morning, and there's a kettle in the barn for coffee and tea," I said.

Sandra begged for the job! And I gave it to her - with laughter.

Later, when I told her about my UK trip, Sandra said, "You cannot possibly go to the UK without going to Paris. I will phone my parents; they will show you around Paris and take you to our family home for lunch. It is near Chantilly. My Mum is a great cook."

How could I refuse?

*

Every morning for three consecutive days, I was collected from my Paris Hotel by Bridgette and Alain, Sandra's parents, and her sisters, Julia or Simone. The two sisters exchanged days due to space in the car. We spent my three days there, seeing and visiting the highlights of Paris, including the Chantilly Racecourse and museum, plus we were lucky enough to attend a world-class show jumping event there. And finally, the dinner and a show at the Lido Nightclub. Then the 'piece de resistance; lunch at Bridgette and Alain's delightful home. Bridgette mastered the French favourites of Duck Confit and chocolate mousse with the flare of a five-star chef. Thank you, Bridgette.

*In Paris with Sandra Tremier's Parents, Bridgette and Alain.*

I fell in love with Paris and Sandra's family. Beautiful City and beautiful people. Sadly, Alain, Sandra's father, was not in good health and died twelve months after my visit. I gave respect to him in my second novel, 'For the love of Freedom.' Alain Tremier became my fictional character, who played a prominent part in the French Resistance.

I did and still do promote my books around Australia. I usually stay with friends and family, reading The Wicky Wacky Farm series at their nearby primary schools. It is great fun; I love every minute.

The words of my English teacher, Mrs. Atwell, kept prompting me to write a novel. She said, and I quote. "One day, you will write novels, Doreen. And when you do, my advice is to find a good Editor. Your stories are brilliant, but your punctuation and spelling are terrible!"

(Sorry, I think I've repeated that.) Why not?

Mrs Atwell was absolutely correct – about the grammar and punctuation. I can't be smug about my stories. When I began writing novels, they flowed so fast I did not - or would not take time to punctuate. Even stopping to space a paragraph was not necessary. I kept writing. Now, many years later, I hope I've learned the skill of punctuation. NO. I'm still learning, thanks to my dear friend, Denise Dorisarmy, who lived close by and would come with her ruler, and if I did not comprehend her lesson, she'd wack me with it. Jokingly, of course. However, we do disagree on occasions, which can also be humorous.

Thanks also to Margaret Mooney, my lifelong friend mentioned earlier. Margaret knows me as well as I know myself.

I am so fortunate to have friends willing to help and give advice, which they have done tirelessly. Sandy Gray is a beautiful friend and always ready to proofread. Thank you all, including Editor Brian Clarke. I was first introduced to Brian when I joined an Online Writers Club in North Queensland. Dee had suggested I pay for another Editor to polish my first novel, 'For the love of Patrick.' So I hired Brian to do his magic before sending the MS to publishers. Brian worked with me, not changing much, just polishing. Which I thought was a compliment in itself. He also made sure my references to History were correct towards being annal. He found only a few mistakes, and I'm pleased he did, as I had done all the research myself.

After six years of research and my never-ending expedition to becoming a wordsmith, I finally finished my first novel. 'For the Love of Patrick.'

In the wake of entering a short story competition, a Who Done it Murder. I'd written thirty thousand words called, 'Beat around the Bush.' Cliché, tut-tut. Wade loved it because I'd based it on and around the Conargo Pub (changed to Conooga in the story). It was where we met, plus the story included a glimpse of his life as a Jackaroo.

Wade encouraged me to turn the short story into a novel. So I began my long and enjoyable writing journey.

Down the line, through dear friends Jacqueline and Phillip Noss, I was introduced to Michael Cybulski.

I must now add that Jacqueline and Phillip owned and ran 'The Villa Delmany' in Kiama. This spectacular and first-class Boutique Hotel's French influence came from Jacqueline being Swiss-French. Wade, and I, along with our friends, stayed many times, enjoying our delightful hosts' fine cuisine and quirky character. We encouraged Phillip and Jacqueline to come and stay at the farm. Wade loved to cook, so we would spoil J & P, as I called them. Eventually, they came, and Wade cooked an eight-course dinner for ten. It was a fantastic dinner party that continued until 2 am. This evening began our eternal friendship.

Now I return to Michael Cybulski, who'd recently set up and registered 'New Authors Collective.' The idea was Michael and his collected authors, through their contacts, would endeavour to be published. Michael eventually found a UK publisher in London who took interest and published my first novel, 'For The Love of Patrick.' Working with them was frustrating and non-profitable. I did eventually break my contract. However, before I did, I promoted 'For the Love of Patrick' throughout the UK in 2018. I expected the publisher to be true to their word and introduce me to various Book Shop Managers, who would invite me to give author talks. This, I assumed, would benefit us both. I never made physical contact with my promotions manager. He was either too busy, had unexpected meetings, a massive workload, etc.

So I travelled the UK promotion trail alone. Well, not entirely. I did have tremendous help from dear friends Brian, and Val Mayson, who organized a book launch at their local pub and welcomed Helena and me into their home-like family. Brian and Val are the parents of Danny Mayson – Kinder, founder of the 'Fly High Billie Charity.' The charity supports mental health studies in youths and promotes kindness and compassion. The charity came about after Danny's twelve-year-old daughter, Billie, died tragically in a horse accident.

*The Baroness Anette and Steven Von Kohorn hosted a Book Launch on my behalf when in the UK. I am still reeling at their generosity and warmth.*

*Another UK Book Launch with Mandy and Rob.*
*I hope that's not a look of boredom on Tilly's beautiful face.*

The Baroness, Anette Von Kohorn, and her charming husband, the Baron, Steven Von Kohorn. (I'm not trying to impress.) The Baron and Baroness are down-to-earth and gracious. They, too, welcomed me into their home. Also, dear friends Mandy and Rob, Shepherd were most supportive. I was invited to stay with both families, and they held fabulous Book Launches on my behalf. Not to forget, Helena, my dear friend who accompanied me on the trip and was my advocate, re-book sales on tour.

Most people who had read 'For the Love of Patrick' would ask.
"So you came from South Australia?"
"No."
"Are you Catholic?"
"No."
"Did you come from Convicts?"
"I don't know?"

Thus began the mystery of where my forefathers came from; I searched and found it in our local paper, *Accredited Genealogist Dianne Williams. Blue Mountains NSW.*

Dianne appeared to have the necessary qualification to trace my family's history. And the cost was reasonable. Dianne traced and substantiated my bloodlines, proving what I had always felt. Spirits from the past speak to me. I am simply their tool.

Dianne discovered that in the 1700s, Dad's, 'Forster,' family were known Jacobites, staunch Catholics, working with Bonny Prince Charlie to restore the Catholic religion to England. Personal letters below prove the intent to bring forth their Catholic restoration plan. Our forebearers were caught in the act of helping Prince Charlie and subsequently imprisoned on their properties.

No doubt - they had some clout!

Furthermore, Dorothy Forster and her husband William owned Bamburgh castle in Northumberland in 1749. However, William gambled away their fortune and eventually went bankrupt. Not to be poor forever, William later purchased an excellent property a short distance from the Bamburgh Castle named 'Hunting Hall.'

How could I travel to the UK with this information and not see the two properties my forefathers had owned?

I was delighted to have found on the Internet 'Hunting Hall Farm Stays.' I emailed Karin and Tom Burn, the owners, and wrote about my distant family, owning the same property a century ago.

We shared many emails, and eventually, on a beautiful day in May 2018, Helena and I arrived at Hunting Hall to Tom and Karin's warm welcome. They insisted we stay in the main house with them, which we did for two nights, and I was honoured to have slept in my fourth great-grandmother's bedroom. And even more fortunate to see her in my dreams. Or maybe it was her ghost? If anyone reading my memoirs feels inclined to visit Hunting Hall, I can recommend it as an experience to treasure.

*Karen and Tom Burns, owners of Hunting Hall, a property that*
*a century ago was owned by my linage of Forster's.*

Helena and I visited many landmarks in the district of Northumberland, which sits Northeast of London and is a significant historic settlement established on what is called the Northumberland Coast. After our self-tour of Bamburgh Castle was complete, I, as all tourists *must*, took my exit through the gift shop. Helena trailed behind, still taking photos. Tempted to buy a souvenir, I stopped to look around when I noticed a cardboard cylinder with 'Forster Family' written outside. I was elated and said aloud. "Oh, look, that's my paternal family tree. They owned this Castle once!"

*Proof of Ownership!*

The saleswoman behind the counter said haughtily.

"Yes. They were the ones who went bankrupt!"

"Oh well, they owned it for a while," I said and laughed.

A couple of American women standing behind me also saw the funny side and said. "Good on ya, mate." Then we all laughed.

Dianne had also discovered Mum and Aunty Dawn came from Irish convicts with the Surname Suitor. I smiled. Yes, I felt a strong connection there! I don't know about the Aristocratic side?

The Suitor family remained in Tasmania after the young and enduring James Suitor survived his seven-year term at Port Arthur. Bg.1839. When released, he married an Irish female convict. .....

They became citizens of Tasmania, and from what I've heard, a small museum in Hobart holds memorabilia of their life and times there. I believe some descendants still reside in Tasmania; I am yet to meet them. I would be thrilled to meet Mum's distant relatives, as I have not yet found Dad's relations in England.

I must add that Dan Brock, a notable Canadian Historian, has since challenged Dianne William's findings regarding my Forster family line. Over the past six years, I have corresponded with Dan, who is still working on his conclusions. However, he was of great help with the story of Mum's Irish Suitor family migrating to Canada from Ireland. And that is where the trouble began: the elder brother was hanged for manslaughter, and his father and younger brother were transported to Port Arther, Tasmania. Another tragic story in itself. They were innocent. It was self-defense, as explained in the local newspaper of the time.

*

My trip to the UK in 2018 was a memorable and exciting journey. In particular, when I touched the walls and slept in a bedroom where my past relatives had once lived.

The moment I reached home, spirits gathered as a guiding light, helping me write the two books concluding the, For the Love of Patrick trilogy.

Book 2. 'For the love of Freedom.'

Patrick's daughter Sally becomes a War correspondent during World War 2 in England. Sally sets out to find a missing female relative who had fallen in love with a Swiss-German Officer. Sally's journey leads her to members of the French Resistance. With courage, Sally never fails in her missions.

Book 3. 'For the love of Justice.'

Patrick's son, PJ, graduates Law in South Australia, then takes time off in the Northern Territory to decide whether he wants to follow Law or become a Horse Trainer. His true passion. PJ meets a Quadroon Aboriginal girl, Tarni, a talented horse whisperer. He saves her life, and Tarni holds a vital role in his horse training venture. The story touches on the stolen generation and racial tension.

A Book Launch for both books was at Jane and Mark Tolhurst's Arunga Polo Club, Arunga meaning 'Red Kangaroo.' The Tolhurst family has been an inspiration from the moment we met. Hardworking, diligent, honourable, and friends to anyone in need. Once again, I feel fortunate and blessed to have such wonderful friends. Adam, Amanda's elder brother, is a remarkable young man, full of good humor and mateship. Adam agreed to model as 'Patrick' on my front cover, and he is a perfect Patrick. Bianca, Adam's beautiful wife, owns the same disposition as Adam and happily volunteered to pose, 'For The Love of Justice.'

The very handsome Tom Norton – Knight,  Amanda's husband, joined Bianca on the same cover.

Sascha, Ross Daisley's stunning daughter, modelled for the front cover of 'For The love of Freedom.' Thank you all, including Danny Mayson -Kinder, who photographed all three book covers. Brilliant job, Danny! I am so fortunate to be surrounded by beautiful young friends.

'Henrietta,' my fourth novel, was a pleasure to write. However, I don't know what possessed me to write about the gay son of an English Duke; in 1897. Though I will say, when I began writing Henrietta, *Henry*, in the first paragraph, writes about his perfect features. Of course, he would!

I knew then that Henry had searched me out because, at that moment, a pop-up ad appeared on my Computer, containing an old photograph of a man dressed in a tailored suit, plus another photo of the same man dressed in a frock. (I had to use that word frock – I just love it). I looked closer at the article, written in 1852.

It read.

*When arriving as an assisted migrant in Australia from Ireland, Ellen Tremayne dressed as a man and lived thereafter in Melbourne as Edward De-Lacy-Evans.*

Ellen Tremayne's facial features, the crossdresser, were remarkably similar to how Henry has described himself. I tell you the truth!

The article above was shown to me via the Internet after I'd written about Henry's features or Henry wrote about himself. Sorry, Henry. Though early enough in my book for me to get the message. Yes, another spirit was with me!

I felt compelled to use the article as a prologue to '*Henrietta.*'

I have left the story of Henri -Etta open to a sequel. I shall see how popular it is first. The front cover of 'Henri -Etta' was painted by the highly talented Pat Lata, who has won numerous art awards.

Thank you, Pat. Not only did you create a masterpiece, but you made sure it was completed on time for my book launch. I cannot thank you enough.

'Wrong Side of the Fence' is my fifth novel and will be published before my memoirs. The story's main character, young Grace Nobel, has aspired to call Horse Races from a very young age, as does her father, Tom. Grace's mother, Nelly, is slightly neurotic, and Grace's brother Walter has minor cerebral palsy. Together their dreams and struggles take many unexpected turns while leading them all on a journey of self-discovery. Like all my stories, it holds a generous dose of Aussie humor.

I have begun another novel, named 'Evie and Me.' However, I would like to first publish my now-finished memoirs in 2022.

At this stage, I plan to publish a novel every year until I am unable to do so.

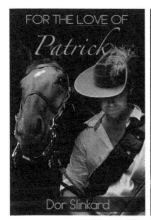

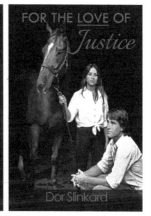

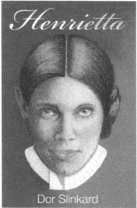

# Chapter 24
## Almost There

One more horse story before I go! It's just another glimpse into the life of a horse trainer! Oh, please bear with me.

Mark Goodwin and his mother Rhonda (whom I hadn't met then) watched Ausbred Rose win a sixteen-hundred-meter Metropolitan race. 27/5/2008, on Television.

Mark, before this day, had been introduced to a dishonest horse dealer directly after Mark had purchased an impressive chestnut yearling by Fantastic Light out of Tilting. Mark was subsequently duped big time by the shady character. Shady, I'll call him, approached Mark, and offered to manage Billet, as the horse was later named. Mark unwittingly agreed. Shady told Mark he would send Billet to a spelling property, where the horse would be broken-in. Shady told Mark not to worry. He'd handle everything; all Mark had to do was pay him money so he could then pay the appropriate people.

Many months passed before Mark, a bit anxious, demanded that he see his horse. He was told emphatically that Billet would not be ready to view until fully broken in. Mark being naive about all things to do with breaking in and training racehorses, accepted Shadey's word until Mark's naivety was indeed tested. Six months had elapsed, and Shadey's excuses to Mark about why he still could not see his horse became unbelievable.

Finally, and unannounced, Mark went to see his horse. He was greatly concerned about the floods throughout the region where Billet lived. His suspicions were founded; Billet was standing in floodwaters up to his belly and appeared too frightened to move.

Mark was intuitive and intelligent enough to have hired a Horse Float, which he'd never towed before, let alone load a horse. It took some doing, but to Mark's credit, and with patience, he secured Billet on the float and took him to another Horse Trainer.

Unfortunately, Mark had paid Shady thousands of dollars for spelling fees, plus the supposed breaking in of Billet. However, shady had pocketed all the money.

Time went by. Again. And the new trainer told Mark that Billet had definitely *not* been broken in, but he would arrange it.

That never happened.

In the meantime, with help from friends, Mark tracked down Shady and re-couped most of his money. Good on you, Mark Goodwin. Great name for a horse owner - Goodwin!

Mark was sick of all the lies, so he searched for a Horse Trainer he could trust. When Ausbred Rose won, Mark phoned the next day after watching my television interview with Richard Calendar. In that interview alone, Mark chose me to train Billet.

"Are you sure?" I said, "I'm usually only given horses to train by our clients or close friends."

"Yes, I'm sure," Mark chuckled. "We were impressed with your interview. And Mum heard you say you'd just finished playing your golf championships, and she loves golf."

Well, Golf, it seemed, was another validation for me to train Mark's fabulous, funny horse, Billet.

After arranging for Billet to be broken in, he arrived on Windermere, an obese, slow-moving horse. Honestly, I could have run faster than him. I found it hard to tell Mark this. The Goodwin family are delightful people, and I felt sorry for Mark after all the trouble he'd gone through. So I prayed the horse might improve after his first barrier trial at Hawkesbury. Sadly, Billet ran last, beaten eight lengths. However, Mark and Rhonda were happy with Billet's effort. I suppose they were simply overjoyed to see him eventually run a race.

Mark's dad, Ray, also interested in Billet, told me, "be patient. I can see something special in this horse." And so I was patient.

Ray is a great bloke who has had a rough trot with many operations on a benign brain tumour. With each procedure, the doctors removed another piece of Ray's brain, leaving Ray a little shaky when walking and with only one eye. His friends called Ray Pirate as he wore a black patch over his missing eye.

And this is where I should tell you that Clarrie's son, and jockey, Grant Buckley, became a valued member of our team, riding Billet to victory on many occasions. Grant is recognised as one of the hardest working jockeys in NSW. Having Clarrie as his father, it's no wonder. We had a lot to do with Grant as he grew up and we admire and love him.

*A most memorable win with my favourite jockey Grant.*
*Well, he was on that day when he rode  Haute D'clare in brilliant style*
*to win The Hawkesbury, Return Soldier's Cup.*

Anyway, the main thing with Billet, I thought, was to get the weight off him. Never one to cut back on a horse's feed, I began my kill or cure campaign. After his first trial, I worked Billet harder than I'd ever worked any horse in my life, and to my surprise, he relished it. He would have made a great warhorse. The only thing preventing this, Billet was frightened of water. Not surprising, after standing belly-deep in water for God knows how long?

However, I knew swimming would lessen the impact on his joints, as with all the hard miles he needed to train to stay, it would cause soundness problems. I simply had to get Billet in the swimming channel. However, the time Billet had spent petrified, standing in the floodwaters, gave him what we thought was a permanent phobia. Then slowly but surely, our wonderful strappers coaxed Billet to stand on the edge of our dam. One would stand in the water and offer him carrots, which he loved. Eventually, Billet walked into the dam and stood happily munching his carrots. Yeh!

Next test! The swimming channel.

We held Billet near the channel, encouraging him to watch other horses swim. I will explain how it's done. Two people attach a lunging lead to either side of the horses' headstall. They walk down either side of the swimming channel while the horse swims in the middle until the end and then walks out. We then lead the horse back to the other end and start over. This gives the horse time to catch its breath. Plus, swimming in a straight line lessens the pressure on their lungs. Many professional studies have been done on the effects of swimming horses. And swimming in a straight line was the safest way. A horse should not swim for more than three minutes in one session. Our swimming channel took one minute to reach the end. We would usually do two or three laps, with a rest in-between. It was a perfect setup.

To start Billet off, we needed four people, two in front with the accomplished equine swimmer, followed by Billet, who would hopefully copy the horse in front and give Billet the confidence he needed. It worked! Billet was brave beyond belief. He used his brain and possessed a willingness not often found in most horses. Many of our racehorses had refused to swim, to the point of almost drowning themselves. We had to give up for their safety, plus ours.

Billet managed courageously to run a close second after bowing a tendon. He never shirked a task. Unfortunately, the accident happened in a night meeting at Canterbury, over 1900mts. Billet went for a run in the home straight that wasn't quite there. The Jockey needed to fling Billet back to the fence to avoid a collision, and with this, his tendon ripped. However, Billet got a clear run about twenty meters from the post and ran second by a whisker!

When Billet cooled down after the race, his tendon blew up enormously. The prognosis was not good. "He may never race again." Said the Raceclub Vet.

It took twelve months of slow work, in and out, walking Billet, then trotting him. In and out. Again and again. After an arduous twelve months, Billet returned to race well and won another race. We retired him when weakness showed in his tendon. He is now cared for by Kimmy Gibson, one of our most endearing employees and friends.

This story leads to the Goodwin family's second and probably more memorable equine purchase. But first, Billet deserved his due.

Ray was interested in buying a horse at the 'Inglis Classic Yearling Sale.' Sadly, the sale ended without Ray purchasing a horse. That night, Ray dreamt he owned a black horse who kept winning races.

Rhonda then suggested Ray phone Inglis's office to see if any black horses had been passed in – (not sold.) Luckily for Ray, there was a black colt by 'Clang' out of 'All About Love.' The yearling had injured himself before the sale, so he was withdrawn. Rhonda told me the story over the phone and then asked if Wade and I would like to accompany them to Tamworth to see the black horse, who had healed from his injury.

"Of course," I said. "yes."

The horse was most impressive, standing over ground which favoured a long stride. He reminded us of Cheval De Volee, especially when he moved. Then Wade took a closer look and noticed the yearling had only one testicular. This beautiful black horse was a rig!

The young woman Samantha, who'd bred him, tried to tell Wade the other testicle would come down in time.

"No, it won't!" said Wade. "It would have come down by now."

She wasn't happy with Wade's opinion and smartly put the horse back in his stable. We left in silence. Then after driving away, Wade said. "If you want to buy that horse, Ray, go back. Tell Samantha you'll pay her price but not until he's gelded."

The gelding operation would be risky. However, theoretically, the horse was not worth a penny as a rig. Therefore, Samantha had to take the chance of gelding him if she needed to sell. Or train the horse herself.

We spun the car around, amused at what had just taken place. Meaning Samantha had angrily rushed the horse back into his stable, and we'd smartly hopped in the car and left—no goodbyes, no thank yous.

We returned, and Wade did the talking. He assured Samantha the horse was worthless if she didn't risk gelding him. She reluctantly agreed.

With the deal done, we discussed the future of Ray's black horse on the way to a Motel in Scone, where we four stayed. Over dinner, we chatted about what to call the horse and came up with the obvious name, 'Black Pirate.' After all, Ray was the instigator of buying a black horse, plus Ray was called 'Pirate.' We all agreed that it suited the horse to a tee. In retrospect, we should have called him TROUBLE!

Thankfully, all went well with the gelding operation.

However, later, when training Black Pirate, I felt sure part of his hidden testicle remained. Although I found him funny, he was a wild character and knew every trick in the book. Not only was he a rig, but a poddy foal. No wonder the horse thought he was half-human and had little respect for us!

After a difficult start, Black Pirate later showed above-average ability and won 8 races from twelve hundred meters to two thousand meters. He gave Ray the thrill of his life and the opportunity to repeatedly tell his Black Pirate stories, peppered with humorous embellishments. And Grant Buckley was his leading rider. He also found Black Pirate's antics amusing.

Later in his career, Pirate lost form, so we gave him one last chance to redeem his past glory. I was unable to attend on the day Pirate raced at Wyong, and Grant was unable to ride him. So the late and great jockey, Nathan Berry, rode Pirate for the first time, along with my written instructions. And I quote.

*Dear Nathan,*

*Please allow Pirate to jump and be precisely where he chooses to be. Last or first, it doesn't matter. If coming from behind, try to find room for Pirate to stretch out. He has an enormous stride, and we just need to see if his heart is still in racing. Thank you, and good luck.*

I watched the race on TV and never imagined seeing Pirate tailed off ten lengths behind the second last horse, especially in a twelve-hundred-meter race. I threw my hands in the air and declared - to myself.

"That's it. He doesn't want to race anymore!"

I was deflated until I saw Pirate tag onto the field at the home turn.

Then like lightning, Black Pirate flew down the outside of the field to end up in a winning photo! I stood and screamed the walls down. I kid you not; Pirate would have made up twenty lengths within seven hundred meters. The only reason he didn't win was within the final one hundred meters; another horse had shifted out on him, costing Pirate at least a length. He ran second by a nostril.

The Stewards re-played the race over and over, watching in amazement.

"We've never seen anything like that run of Black Pirates. It was truly spectacular!" One Steward said to Wade.

The Vet smartly took Pirates blood for inspection. Not surprising after that performance! Unfortunately, such was the nature of the beast. Pirate could run like a champion one day and decide the next. He was not interested. But still, I loved that horse. So smart. No. Cunning is more apt.

And the point of my story is that sometimes the racing Gods

reward good people who have their hearts in the right place, which Ray has. He has never given up; he keeps trying, as did the horses he owned or had shares in - they all won! Yes, the Goodwin family-owned many shares in other horses that Wade and I trained, and as I've said, they all won. How fortunate is that?

Before Windermere was sold, Pirate lived happily down in the river paddock, but sadly, he had to be moved off the property when the sale came to pass. Ray and Rhonda were fortunate again. They have a friend who owns twenty acres not far from where they now live at Salamander Bay, North Coast, NSW. Pirate is cared for there and enjoys his daily visits from Ray and Rhonda!

Needless to say, I love a challenging horse.

# Chapter 25
# On a Finishing Note

It is now January 3rd 2020, and I am writing in my Michael Street, North Richmond office. Formerly, Wade's parents' home. We purchased it when my AMP superannuation fund became accessible in 2007, and I insisted we put money into brick and mortar. The search began.

Daniel, our son and the expert builder, had just returned from spending five years overseas. He brought home with him in 2004; his wife Teona and three-month-old son Nicholas. The morning they arrived, after a long flight from Amsterdam, I stood at the Airport arrivals, shedding happy tears, when Daniel walked towards me carrying a smiling Nicholas attached to his back in a sling. What joy, as we hadn't heard from Daniel in the first three years he was abroad. Not until one Christmas morning, when he phoned us. "Hello, Mum. I haven't got much money for the public phone. Can I talk to Dad? I need to know how to cook Virginia ham."

I said, " I'll give you bloody Virginia ham, Daniel! If you were here, I'd stick it where the sun doesn't shine!" And with that, Wade grabbed the phone and continued to relay the recipe without saying hello. I couldn't believe it. Maybe it's a man thing. Once they fly the coup, the family doesn't matter. They're okay, and so they assume the family is.

After recovering from jet lag, Wade, Daniel, and I inspected many small-acre properties and countless houses to renovate, as we were planning to go halves with Daniel. But it was proving difficult for Dan to borrow money, so the idea of doing a Pre-Will with Wade's two sisters and buying 9 Michael Street became the best option.

Doreen Joyce Slinkard, Wade's beloved mum, had suddenly died, leaving Herman alone. Herman had been an American Soldier based in Rockhampton, where Doreen Joyce lived. It was there that they fell in love during the Second World War. Herman forever told the story about when he asked General MacArthur permission to marry Doreen

Joyce, and The General said, "NO, it's against Army protocol!"

Herman married her anyway, as it was not against *his* protocol.

After the war, they lived in California for many years before returning to Australia. They settled in Beecroft, NSW, close to 'Nelson Stud Welding,' an American Company where Herman had secured the position of General Manager.

We were entertained many nights watching Grandma Joy being flipped over Grandad Herman's shoulder, then flung through his legs. It was spectacular! Plus, they'd do 'around the world!' That's when the man rotates his partner from one hip to another. They were the best jitterbug dancers I have ever seen live.

The family came first. Yes, they were terrific people. They were great hosts, we had lots of fun together, and my parents got along with Herman and Joy famously.

*Wade's Dad, Herman always smiling and Joy, Wades devoted Mum.*

Herman and Joy's final home in North Richmond was L-shaped. I always thought it had a lot going for it, although, in my opinion, the house needed renovation. One great advantage was that Wade's youngest sister Joetta had a 2-bedroom cottage built in the generous backyard. This came about because her young husband had died of a heart attack, leaving Joetta to raise their six-month-old daughter Jacqueline. Being a Nursing Sister, Joetta worked long hours. It was considered a good idea by all the family that she built the cottage in the backyard, and Herman and Joy, as Doreen preferred, would help care for Jacqueline. It worked well, as Jacqueline has since grown into a beautiful young mother herself. She is also a compassionate nursing sister, living in Geelong, Victoria, with her husband Jamie and daughter Matilda.

We planned to extend the frame of the house from L-shaped to square.

Our friends all said we turned our North Richmond home into a Northern beaches home. We couldn't be happier. Daniel did an outstanding job, plus he added great ideas, like a cathedral ceiling in the extension, giving a feel of grandeur and space.

Dan and Teona lived in the cottage throughout the renovations while Herman moved from room to room in the main house. Poor old dear, though it was funny when he'd say in his heavy American accent. "Oh God damn, what are ya wreckin now?"

Eventually, it was worth it. Even Herman admitted what a wonderful home Dan had created. However, we all worked tirelessly, including our son-in-law, Dominic, Lisa, and many friends who came to lend a hand. Some we paid, and some wouldn't take money. Thank you all. It is a beautiful home.

We'd cook for the entire family every Tuesday night at Micheal Street in respect and love for Herman. These entertaining dinners continued until we needed to place him in a Nursing Home. Herman died at age 98.

Helen Sanderson, formerly Daisley, decided to sell Windermere as she needed the money; I'm not blaming her, but it forced our retirement on 11/11/2019. We then needed to sell Micheal Street to cash up and downsize.

We searched and chose a home in an over 55 retirement village at Saint Georges Basin, South Coast, NSW. One of the best beaches globally, namely Hyams Beach, is next door! Wade can walk 300 meters to fish off a pier where 70cm flatheads are caught. I'll continue to write stories and enjoy long walks on the beach with Peggy, our Border Collie. Perfect!

It is December 2019, and we're spending our final Christmas at Michael Street. The entire country is burning with massive bushfires! The endless drought and the laws preventing backburning during winter have created a monster, feeding fires to the extreme.

And so we all suffer from the poor darlings who have lost their homes, loved ones, and livestock to those who suffer health risks from smoke inhalation.

The visibility from our glass doors at Michael Street, facing Northwest, usually allows magnificent views of the Blue Mountains. However, today it is completely blocked by heavy smoke.

Our dear friend Jenny Churchill, writer and editor of 'Blood Horse' Magazine, is staying with us at this disastrous time. Plus, Jenny was involved with the book 'Stallions.' She is also the author of 'Great Thoroughbred Sires of The World.' Jenny is a well-respected and much-loved member of the Thoroughbred industry. Her home is in Kurrajong Heights and is a high-risk fire area, and her health has deteriorated to the point of her needing an oxygen machine 24/7. But for the moment, she needs our help. Jenny's health is fading, so she is staying in our two-bedroom cottage, 'Dor's Cottage,' which I advertise on 'Home Stayz.' I love meeting new people, and due to our generosity, it has become a premier listing. Although now, Jenny is our priority guest.

If you have ever watched the sitcom 'Mother and Son,' I can tell you the situation between Jenny and her son Richard was similar. We survived the depressive atmosphere of a burning Christmas due to the entertaining antics of Jenny and Richard. EG. After a few days of living in the cottage, Jenny became overanxious about her old skinny cat, Tavy. And so Tavy was delivered in a cage by Richard, who stayed home to protect their belongings in Kurrajong from fire. With the cat?

To make sure Tarvy could not escape into the wild blue yonder, Jenny wrapped her much-needed oxygen cord around Tavy's neck, attached to her oxygen machine. Now and then, we'd hear Jenny yell, "I can't breathe! Help! I Can't Breathe."

And, of course, she couldn't because the cord had collapsed due to being wrapped around the cat's neck. In turn, the cat couldn't breathe, and they both near-chocked on many occasions until we insisted the oxygen cord wrapped around Tavy's throat was not a good idea.

"Just let him roam free, Jenny. Tavy can't get out. All the doors and windows are closed." We assured her.

Closing the door was necessary due to the dense smoke, and of course, the air conditioner was on day and night because it was bloody HOT.

Jenny would scream whenever we entered the cottage through

the sliding glass doors. "Shut the door! Tavy will escape! SHUT THE DOOR!"

Little chance of that happening with the bloody oxygen cord wrapped around its throat! Wade was sick of being yelled at, so he yelled back, "Fuck the cat!"

And Jenny replied seriously, "Don't you dare fuck my cat!"

We laughed till we cried. RIP Jenny.

# Chapter 26
## Moving On

Thankfully, Windermere sold to another lovely family, the Rosiers, who have begun massive renovations to the home and property. We wish them as much happiness as we had while living there for 46 years.

We sold Michael Street and moved to Saint Georges Basin, NSW, on 26/2/2020. We love the area, plus our well-appointed, cozy home.

All of the 'Village People,' I call them, are friendly, accommodating, and highly social! Wade has joined a few village ladies, plus one other man, in a cooking extravaganza. Today they are producing a Mediterranean three-course meal, beginning at 2 pm. Later, partners will join the cooks with a bottle of wine and enjoy the spoils.

Wade goes fishing off the pier, which is within walking distance. Peggy, our Border Collie dog, sits beside him. Occasionally she checks out other anglers and has become a favourite with everyone.

Four days after moving in, I began searching for dog-friendly beaches. At first, I drove to Jervis Bay. Walking down the entrance and turning right onto the beach, I noticed a very chubby hubby and wife, brown as ticks, glowing with good health and sporting huge smiles, seemingly at Peggy. I stopped to chat. Tempted as I was to announce Wade's saying, "brown fat looks better than white fat." I refrained. We talked for a while, and they told me where all the dog-friendly beaches were. They, like everyone else here, were friendly and helpful.

I walked along the shoreline while Peggy, seeing waves for the first time, danced and played with the white foam. I followed the shoreline around a precipice and was stunned by the beauty. A massive headland jutted out to sea, yachts sailed serenely around Jervis Bay, and a large flat rock formation created rock pools of white sand and crystal-clear ocean. Behind me rose a cliff with abundant vegetation that added shade and shelter from the westerly winds. When turning back to where

I had come, I faced North. This, I thought, is the perfect place for me, *the old beach baby*, and Peggy. Also, the smaller grandkids would enjoy spending a day here. I can't wait. Though a bit further south, I see gentle waves rolling onto the shore, soaking the whitest of white sand. This, I learned, is THE Jervis Bay off-leash dog-friendly beach named Nelson's. Stunning!

*

Nothing is perfect, they say.

Corona Virus has just arrived in Australia after spreading its tentacles around the globe. Entire Countries have gone into hibernation, including America, New Zealand, and China, where the virus began. And possibly Australia - soon.

It has not been Since The Second World War that Australian sports were cancelled. Attendance at racetracks and other large spectator gatherings will not be allowed. Say the Government.

The official announcement will be made Monday, 16/3/2020, regarding what Law the Australian Government will carry forward concerning entry and leaving the country. Plus large gatherings in any field of sport, entertainment, education, etc. So far, it has just been discretion and common sense.

The virus is a highly contagious flu-like bug. I don't know the worldwide death rate, but I know we cannot buy toilet paper anywhere. Does dysentery come with Corona? I think the frantic buying is just in case of quarantine.

Today, we sit on our couch, 14/3/2020, watching the Autumn Horse Racing Carnival. The Australian Government, guided by our Chief Medical Officer, has said, 'NO CROWDS admitted to a major sporting event, including the upcoming Royal Easter Show.'

I feel for our country folk, who once a year forget their worries and join in the camaraderie of the Graziers, the Growers, and the talented Rural Arts and Craft Brigade. At least the owners of Racehorses, plus the punters, still enjoy seeing their horses race from the comfort of their lounge room. But what a tragedy for the Royal Show contenders, including our granddaughters, Grace, and Emma, who compete in horse events, particularly 'Pair of Riders.' So sad for us all, especially them.

Australia is now officially in lockdown. Any citizen returning from overseas is, by law, obliged to self-isolate for two weeks, starting from 15/3/2020.

Drastic measures are in place! Although, I have just heard that a one hundred and two-year-old lady has survived, as have the majority. So, if you have no underlying health issues, you have a good chance of recovery. The main concern is how highly contagious it is. So cafes, restaurants, pubs, and the like, have been temporarily shut down—orders from the Government.

We have been forewarned about mutating forms of Corona. Since the virus began in Wuhan, China, three months ago, China has reported a lessening effect. In other words, the bug itself is dying. I don't think so, China.

Woolworths has endeared itself to the elderly by opening its doors to pensioners from 7 am to 8 am. And so it was; we lined up, 17/3/2020 at 6.45 am, at Vincentia shopping mall to join the toilet paper charge! With my sense of humour, I saw the funny side. Standing outside the enormous roller doors at Woolworths, Wade and I waited, ready for the dash. The gates finally opened, and I began rolling the camera while commentating.

"The barriers have opened! And they're away and running! The 'grey-haired man's two lengths in front. The grey-haired woman's sitting second! Oh no, there's interference in the aisle! Shopping trolleys colliding, elbows attacking elbows. Call the stewards!"

Most of the oldies laughed, though some thought I was mad.

I grabbed a trolley while Wade sprinted to the toilet paper aisle, snatched two lots of 6 rolls, then threw them across a mass of grey heads, to which they landed in my trolley! Very funny and very clever, Wadey.

The sun shines bright today, so I'm off to the beach with Peggy. Luckily, the South Coast beaches are not in lockdown, so I have officially given myself two weeks off editing to turn my white fat brown. And ponder the unusual fact that I began writing my memoirs during an Equine Pandemic, and now I'm finishing them during a Human Pandemic. I think it just takes a lot to keep me still.

*

Before I leave the chosen chapters of my life, I need to give a small glimpse into our aging existence. Saint Georges Basin presents beautiful, picturesque walks around the water's edge, so I persuaded Wade to join me.

"Only five minutes, though. My feet hurt." Said Wade. Meaning he'd rather lay on his bed and read a book.

Five minutes into our *slow* walk, Wade said, "I'll just sit here on the tree stump with Peggy and admire the view. You go ahead. My feet are sore."

He wore old thin plastic crocs. Of course, his feet were bloody sore!

I walked briskly for another twenty minutes, then returned to Wade and Peggy, who followed me joyfully towards the car. Wade ambled behind, and Peggy and I hopped in the car. Where was Wade?

A blue sedan had *since* parked on the left-hand side, plus a white SUV, similar to ours. I'll give him that. Wade had made himself comfortable in a stranger's SUV. When I realised this, I waited for him to wake up to the fact. Five minutes passed before I drove around, wound my window down, and yelled, "Wade!" He smiled and waved.

"Wade! What are you doing?"

"Isn't this our car?' He asked - not moving.

"Well, if it is, what am I doing driving this car?"

"How do I know?" said the genius.

Needless to say, we did see the funny side, but not until Wade had made all the excuses in the world why he got into the wrong car.

*After a long marriage filled with love, battles and mayhem we remain in love.*

## Peggy
4th April 2013 - 23rd April 2022

OH how we miss your wagging tail,
your smile and rumbling voice.
Not many places did we go or times we spent without you.
We remember your joy at simple pleasures,
chasing a ball, or grandchildren down the hall,
showing your love and loyalty for all.
Your days on the farm sitting with horses and herding chooks.
"Go swimming", I'd say on hot summer days.
And into the pool you'd go. For whatever I said, you'd know.
You loved our seaside change, fishing with Wally,
saying hello to anglers, putting smiles on faces, so they felt jolly.
Little dogs walked by but you took no heed at their yapping,
while laying on your nature strip napping.
Off to the beach we'd go, umbrella and snacks for Queen Peggy,
those days were many.
I should not cry for there will be no more hair all over the carpet.
No more dogy poo to pick up on escarpments.
No more brushing your beautiful coat.
No more cleaning the shower after shampooing on a weekly note.
But I would not complain if only our days had remained the same.
Now you have left us, a mother of sheep dog champions.
And grandmother of the same to come.
We have shared our life with many dogs,
but none more special than you.
You will live in our hearts forever,
our mate so loyal and true.
Rest in peace our beloved Peggy.

# Peggy

**4/04/2013 - 23/04/2022**

# Authors Notes

I hope you have enjoyed my muddily memoirs.

The easiest way to note my dearest friends and immediate family is to post photos with short captions. I have done so and trust you will take pleasure in the gallery.

My advice, whether you want it or not!

Remember the knockout blow and the dumbbells?

Fill your heart with love and empathy. We have no right to judge anyone, but we never have to accept bad behaviour.

And! Owning a Melbourne Cup winner is possible as long as I'm alive!

'I'm older now. But never too old not to dance with the wind and the waves.

Please appreciate and protect nature.'

PS. Our beloved Peggy died on 23/4/2022. I wrote Peggy's tribute through tears. It will take a long time to mend our hearts.

*Our God daughter Amanda is all set for a polo match.*
*Lisa and me there to cheer her on.*

*Me, Helena, and Toni Mathews inspecting the utes at Hay races.*

*Helena and me with my first winner as a trainer, Misty Tempo.*

*Wades Mum, at the entrance to Boonooke Sheep Station.*

*My brother Wayne, his wife Leslie, and children Marcus and Melissa.*

*Mum is still entertaining the troops, playing her ukulele.*

## Cheval's big swim

There was an interesting response to the incorrect placing of Cheval de Volee in last month's mention of the 1978 AJC Sires' Produce Stakes. It appears Manikato did not finish fourth but fifth, just behind Cheval de Volee. Doreen Slinkard, wife of trainer Wade Slinkard of Wilberforce (NSW) writes: "That year we were flooded in on our property situated on the Hawkesbury River and the only work we could give Cheval de Volee was walking and swimming in the flood waters. On the day of the Sires' we had to swim him out through a neighbouring property and travel him around the mountains to Randwick . . . a journey in a two-horse float which took five hours.

"On our arrival, 'Cheval' was white with foam and obviously didn't enjoy the trip at all. However, we arrived in plenty of time and being a good tempered horse, he settled down and relaxed. During the race, Cheval lead all the way until about the last 80 metres where Jewel Flight, Manikato, Jubilee Walk and Karaman came down the outside and headed him. He was going to run 5th behind Manikato, but came again to officially finish fourth. Please don't leave him out of the race — he was most gallant in defeat!"

Cheval de Volee these days stands at Windemere Stud, Wilberforce.

*Write-up about Cheval in the "Sires Produce".*

*Mum and Mi Mi, her beloved poodle.*

*Sharing a smile with Gai and Charlotte.*

*Me at the entrance to the Deniliquin Ute Muster, which took place after our inaugural Hay Races Ute Competition.*

*Lisa and Dan loved their ponies, and Dan would never use a saddle. He rode bareback even over jumps. Incredible balance!*

*Wade is delivering a foal on the farm. The Stud Seasons were extremely busy.*

*Mark Tolhurst and his mum Frieda at my fortieth birthday.
Looking great dressed as hippies.*

*Lisa's Formal.*

*Our adopted with love, grandson Jed with Daniel's second daughter Izzy smiling in the background and Daniel's second partner, the delightful, bubbly, Emma.*

*Our lifelong friend and Apprentice Jockey, Samantha Ehmann on her wedding day at Windermere Farm where the wedding photos and plenty of champagne was consumed before her wedding reception.*

*Sylvia loved her days with us on the farm, amongst the roses.*

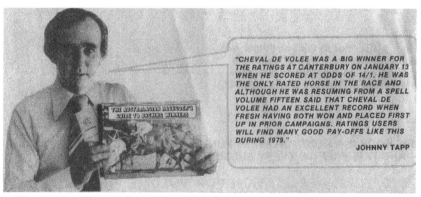

"CHEVAL DE VOLEE WAS A BIG WINNER FOR THE RATINGS AT CANTERBURY ON JANUARY 13 WHEN HE SCORED AT ODDS OF 14/1. HE WAS THE ONLY RATED HORSE IN THE RACE AND ALTHOUGH HE WAS RESUMING FROM A SPELL VOLUME FIFTEEN SAID THAT CHEVAL DE VOLEE HAD AN EXCELLENT RECORD WHEN FRESH HAVING BOTH WON AND PLACED FIRST UP IN PRIOR CAMPAIGNS. RATINGS USERS WILL FIND MANY GOOD PAY-OFFS LIKE THIS DURING 1979."

JOHNNY TAPP

*Cheval was always a favourite with Johnn Tapp, race caller extraordinaire!*

*Having a great hippy party with two of my favourite boyfriends. Tim Walsh, left and Graham Collis right.*

*Playing golf at Kangaroo Valley with Dina Lee, back row, alongside Terry Robinson, Moniques husband.*

*The two Betty's. Mum on her last visit staying with cousin / sister, Betty at her home in Mount Eliza.*

*The late Belinda Miller. Moniques beloved sister who lovingly cared for Sylvia. Belinda was a brilliant horsewoman, and one of the outstanding riders in the popular El Cabello Blanco Horse Show.*

*Lisa and me at the races.*  *My favourite photo of Teona, Daniels first wife and their daughter Arianna.*

*Wades side of the family at Jacqueline, his nieces wedding in Geelong Victoria*

*Jane and I at Surfers Paradise, looking the part.*

*I took Festive Knight to Melbourne to race which*
*my brother Wayne and son Marcus enjoyed.*

*Lisa receiving her Nursing Certificate.*

*My mum Betty.*

*Lisa and Dominic's wedding.*

*Sailing around Sydney Harbour with Mark Tolhurst at the helm
and the late and beautiful Muffi Barbor.*

*A pensive moment, before naughty Cheval D'Clare raced one time.*

*Teona and Arianna, having fun on Melbourne Cup Day at the Farm.*

*Son Daniel loved all the farm animals and they loved him.*

*Our apprentice Jockey, Samantha Ehman, top right, amongst other notable female jockeys. Sammy came to us, as a tiny fourteen-year-old, with a huge passion to become a jockey. I remember the broom was bigger than her.*

*Wade's 60th birthday. 'Cook for the cook' party, Jacqueline and Phillip were there with bells on.*

*At the Villa Delmaney. Jacqueline, our hostess, showed the men how she loved having them come and stay.*

*Reading my Wicky Wacky Farm stories around Primary Schools.*

*Winners are grinners. Hawkesbury Fashions in the field.*

*Cousin Betty picked me up from the Airport and drove me to surprise Mum and Dad in Rye Victoria. I was dressed as Marika, Cons wife from the Comedy Company TV series. They didn't have a clue it was me!*

*Herman.
Wade's dad at age ninety-three.*

257

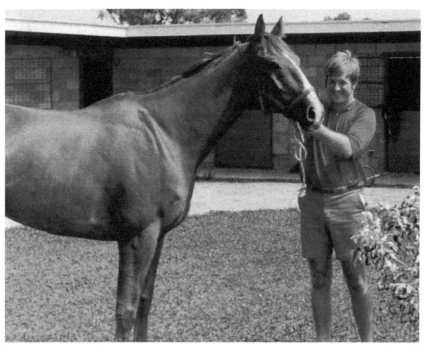

*Wade with Vanglo at Tommy Loy's stables in Deniliquin.*

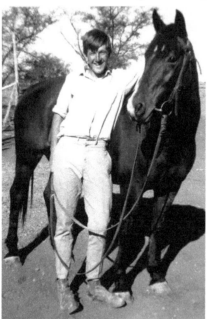

*Wade after a hard day jackarooing with Prince at Booramell, Queensland.*

*Me standing behind Dorothy Forsters dress at Bunburgh Castle.*

258

*Back: Emma, Nicholas. Middle: me, Izzy, Wade. Front: Arianna, Grace.*

*Promoting Patrick in the UK with Helena and the late Brian Mayson.*
*He and his wife Val were so welcoming and helpful.*
*Such a kind and generous gentleman was dear Brian.*

*A young Wade and Dor after their marriage in a registry office.*

*Proud grandfather Wade with Lisa's twins. Emma (left) and Grace (right).*

CPSIA information can be obtained
at www.ICGtesting.com
Printed in the USA
BVHW021432090822
644142BV00013B/748